THE WEDDING

Tiana Helisha

Contents

Rameen is an architect working in a Consulting firm. She is the only child of her parents. She is bold, sassy, and intelligent. Rameen is engaged to her childhood sweetheart Imaad. All is well in Rameen's life until she meets Waleed Kamal.

Waleed Kamaal is an arrogant, aggressive young CEO of Kamaal Constructions and Consultancy Firm. His Grandfather, Yousuf Kamaal, brought up Waleed after the death of his parents in a plane crash. He is a spoilt brat, and if he likes something, he gets it either by love or force.

The first few encounters between Rameen and Waleed are complete disasters. They hate each other and can't withstand one another even for a few minutes. But fate has a different plan for them when they get married accidentally.

Chapter 1

Rameen

I looked into the mirror as my hands were skillfully folding my waist-long black hair into a bun. I finished it by inserting a few Bobby pins, as I applied the new nude lip color on my lips, and just at that moment, my cell phone started ringing.

God this must be Sheema, I thought bitterly. How I hated her for being such a freak, she was insanely punctual and disciplined in everything, and I on the opposite hand was as wild as anyone could be.

Yes, I am the most unorganized person in the world barring my job. Well, I didn't want my ass kicked by my boss for not doing my work properly and on time. Most of the time he would ignore my mistakes just because I was damn creative.

Well like most people know talent doesn't come without flaws, and though I was a very good architect, I was unorganized, undisciplined, rebellious, wild, and fierce. Not a single quality a sane mind would be proud of but I just loved myself.

Well back to my screeching cell phone and Sheema, as I received the call and said"For God's sake, Sheema! stop freaking me out, I am already uncertain whether my mom and aunt would let me put a foot outside the house today".

" Mia, why didn't you woke up early this one day, you know how many people are here in the queue. I have secured our places but I would need back up. Please come soon", Sheema said in a pleading tone. She very well knew how I hated someone bossing me around.

"Okk I am just leaving, don't worry I will be there in half an hour. Bye", I snapped in the cell phone then picked my bag and hurriedly made my way out of my room.

I prayed to Allah that my mom or my aunt didn't bump into me while I was sneaking out. The deal was since the day my wedding date was fixed with my childhood sweetheart, my mom and aunt had made my life a hell.

They wanted me to learn cooking, you heard it right, me freaking cooking. God who really does that in this 21st Century. Not a working woman though, I would just hire a maid to help me with the household chores and a cook who would cook for my in-laws and my hubby. Why the hell was I working my ass off for?

So that I could live my life the way I wanted and spend my money on the things I desired. I didn't like cooking I will hire a fucking cook. I didn't like cleaning I will hire a fucking maid. What was so difficult for my mom to not understand such a simple thing?

But no, they had to make me do everything like I was some fucking 16th-century girl.Well sorry for all the foul language but we freaking live in the 21st Century.

So, I was telling about my mom and my aunt's insanities. Well, I think they are insane, cause I only get a day off from work in a week, and instead of letting me chill out with my friends they would force me into the kitchen and would make me cook all those terrible dishes. Well, they are not terrible if anyone else cooked them but when I use my skills on the recipe they always turned out terrible.

Still, the ladies of my house were not ready to give up on me. They had taken a holy vow to make me accomplish in everything I hated.

I made sure to make as little noise as possible, as I descended the stairs. When I landed on the last stair I heard my mom's furious voice" And where do you think you are going?"

Shit, shit, shit, I cussed. This was the thing I was scared about and it had to happen, my ill fate never ran out.

I turned and looked in the direction from where her voice was coming, Mom was standing in the corridor.

"Uhhhh, mom actually the thing is my favorite author is in town and he is signing off the special edition of his book. And I really have to get one", I said dreading the dressing down I was to receive from my mom.

" By what time you will be back?" Mom asked.

I couldn't believe what just happened, my mom, I mean, my real mom was allowing me to go out on the weekend instead of locking me up in the kitchen?

"Mia I asked you something", mom didn't look delighted with my reaction to her question.

I was starting at her wide-eyed with my mouth open. I came back to my senses and replied " Couple hours".

" Alright fine, but you will cook the dinner today", She said and turned towards the kitchen without even giving me another glance.

I was on cloud nine, mom had just allowed me to go out without even putting a fight, maybe they were fed up with me, I giggled.

I hired a cab and arrived at the desire mall where the book shop was situated where my favorite author was coming for a promotion of his new book.

I was shocked to find the long queue of the people presents there. Like Geez, didn't they had anything else to do in life?

I found Sheema standing a few places before the queue ended. I hurried towards her, she was staring me with a frown on her face.

"Hey baby, thanks so much for securing a place for me", I told her as I slid between Sheema and the girl standing in front of her.

"Excuse me, Miss, you just can't walk into the queue like that we have been standing here for an hour", The boy behind Sheema said to me.

I glared at him with a don't fuck with me look, and said "What will you do? I already did?" I dared him, the poor guy hadn't expected such a harsh reaction.

He just mumbled something in his mouth and backed off, good for him I thought. I would have loved to beat the shit out of him, don't think I am boasting or something. I am perfectly capable of defending myself, I have a black belt in karate. My uncle had made me learn karate so I could defend myself if any situation arises. But I loved to flaunt my karate skills now and then on some asshole who tries to fuck with me.

"Mia, could you at least behave for once?" Sheema said through gritted teeth.

"Sheema, I don't understand why the hell you have to be such a good girl all the time. Don't you get tired and bored of it?" I snapped at Sheema.

She looked at me with resentment, she knew I was the complete opposite of her. People who knew us always wondered how we were best friends in the first place. We didn't have a single habit that was common in us. She was a girl next door kind of person and me, well, I was just me.

"I don't understand how Imaad tolerates you?" Sheema asked annoyed.

"Because if he doesn't, I will beat the shit out of him too", I said shrugging my shoulders.

Imaad was my fiance, yeah he was the only boy, mad enough to fall in love with someone like me. I knew I was pretty and kinda hot also, and the opposite sex was attracted to me. But once they got to know me they would just back off. Wich sane mind would want a wife or a girlfriend who would keep kicking their ass?

Still, Imaad fell in love with me, his parents were our family friends and we knew each other since childhood.I did have a crush on him though, he was hot and handsome, foreign qualified and from a well off family. But it was just a crush and nothing more.

Imaad had proposed me a year ago and I was taken by surprise, well it rarely happens that your crush proposes you out of the blue. I said yes, and he was overjoyed. He then told me that he was in love with me since we were kids, and I just couldn't believe how can anyone fall in love with a girl like me?

Imaad confessed it was my quality of not giving him any attention like the other girls that attracted him towards me. Well, I really didn't think before that a guy could really get attracted to a girl, who didn't give a damn about him. It just happened in movies or love stories but this had really happened with me.

Our families were overjoyed when we told them we wanted to get married. We got engaged in a grand ceremony, with all the A-listers of the town attending our engagement.

Damn, he was looking so hot in that black "Pathani Suit"(a traditional dress for men in southeast Asia). I really wanted to eat him up, sorry I should have kept that thought to myself.

So, where was I? Yeah, we got engaged and now our parents had fixed our wedding date three months from now. Both our families were busy with the preparation for our wedding.

The ladies were buying all those weird clothes which I hated, the lehengas, the gharara's, salwar kameez (traditional ladies clothes from southeast Asia) and I don't know what other shiny glittery clothes. Why was it necessary to make the bride look like a clown?

I hated those traditional clothes, my favorites were joggers and loose big t-shirt or hoodies, which I used to wear every time at home.I liked dressing up but not in that shiny glittery stuff that my mom and aunt called clothes.

Right now I was wearing a peach blouse and a cream-colored knee-length skirt and cream-colored stockings paired with peach stilettos. I knew my outfit complimented my figure by the stares I was getting from the men around.

I ignored those stares and started chatting with Sheema. She was telling me about her fiance, they had got engaged only a month ago. It was arranged by their parents, and Sheema was so insanely happy about it. I never understood how people could get into an arranged marriage?

These days at least the couple would meet and talk after the engagement but a few decades before most of them would meet on their wedding night. And how the hell can you fuck someone in your first meeting? This was the question that had always nagged my mind, but I didn't find the courage to ask this to my parents.

Yeah, you guessed alright, it was a arrange marriage for my parents and they had met each other on the wedding day. Mom had once told me they didn't even have a telephonic conversation before ma rriage.And I wondered how did they get away with it right on the wedding night(blush) cause I was born exactly nine months after their wedding.

Back to Sheema and her fiance what's the guy's name? Yeah, I remember Saad. So Saad was throwing a birthday party for Sheema which was after two weeks and Sheema was insisting me to attend the party. It's not like I didn't want to, it's just that I was not sure my mom would let me. She was on a shopping spree and making me accomplished spree these days. But maybe I could ask dad to convince her.

We stood in the queue for nearly 4 hrs before we got the chance to enter the book store and make our way to the dais where the author Subrato Roy was seated. We had bought our copy of the special edition and approached Roy.

He smiled at us and asked our names and then signed off on the first page of the novel. I wanted to ask him some questions regarding his novel but a staff member of the book store requested us to move ahead because there was still a very long queue.

We came out of the store nearly exhausted and with sore feet. Wearing stilettos was a bad idea, but who would have thought it might take so long, I had thought a couple of hours must be more than enough.

" Mia I think I will faint, let's grab something to eat", Sheema said holding her head with her hands.

I quickly supported her with my arm and we walked to a nearby fast food joint. We ordered a burger with cola each and sat on a corner seat. The joint was crowded because of the weekend.

We looked at the burger greedily, the burgers from this joint were just yumm. A moan escaped from my mouth as I took a bite, the juices of the patty and the melted cheese oooh.

I loved this burger, I looked at Sheema her expressions were the same as mine as she bit into her burger. Then we both looked at each other and laughed.

We had just finished the burger when I got a call from Imaad, I had asked him to pick us from the mall. Imaad told me he was in the parking and asked me to bring a cup of coffee for him.

We walked out of the joint and got into a coffee shop. I ordered Imaad's cappuccino with double cream and waited while the girl started working on it. While she was making the coffee, I pulled out the novel from my handbag and skimmed through the pages.

After a few minutes, the girl handed me the coffee. We walked towards the exit of the coffee shop and just as I set foot outside the coffee shop I collided with something.

Whoever it was who collided with me was in a hurry that he couldn't see my 5'8" self.

I watched in horror as the coffee cup slipped from my hand and landed on the floor, to top it up the novel which was in my other hand fell into the pool of coffee on the floor.

I stood frozen on the spot with my eyes petrified, after few seconds I glared at the person who collided with me. He was dead meat, I was not going to leave him.

Chapter 2

Waleed

I had come to the mall to buy some accessories for my cell phone. After buying and billing the required items I left the Apple Store and started towards the coffee shop.

I was in a little hurry cause I had planned to meet my friends in half an hour at the boxing club. Yeah, boxing, was my favorite sport. It was a good way to take the steam out whenever I was pissed, and it happened often. Sometimes it would be some business client who would become a pain in the ass or some employee of my firm who I don't understand why never get the way I worked and always messed up things.

Geez, was it so difficult to understand my way of working, I was a workaholic. And I had a particular way of working which to my annoyance very few people understood. I had taken over the firm two years ago after my grandfather had retired and went to live in our native village where most of my relatives were settled.

My grandmother had died when my father was just a boy, Dada(grandfather in Urdu) had raised him all by himself. My Dada must be madly in love with Dadi(Grandmother) for he never married after her death.

When I was 14 years old my parents died in a car accident. They had gone out for shopping and I was at home with data.

If not for Dada, I would never have got over the grief of the untimely demise of my parents. But Dada always kept me in check, he became my parents and my best friend. We both had developed a very special relationship with each other.

He sent me for my Graduation to the US. I had done my MBA from the University of Pennsylvania (Wharton), Philadelphia, PA. It was one of the best business schools in the US. And Dada was the proudest grandpa on my Convocation Day.

I could feel his joy when I presented him with my degree. He had come to the US especially for my convocation and was ecstatic when all my teachers were congratulating him for my success and were praising him for raising me into such a good human.

I am a workaholic alright, I am even a control freak I admit, but I always respect my elders and had never ever behaved with them in any improper way.

It's not that I was a dull person, Oh no I use to chill in the company of my friends. When it comes to working I am highly professional and organized. I can't tolerate indiscipline.

So back to my coffee, I hurried towards the coffee shop to grab a cup of coffee but I bumped into a girl just outside the coffee shop. She lost her balance due to the collision and the cup of coffee in her hand had fallen on the ground, the cap opened and there was a pool of coffee on the floor now. She somehow steadied herself, but in the way, the book she was holding, in the other hand, fell into the coffee pool, "Fuck, Bad timing" I thought.

My gaze traveled from the book to her stiletto which now had coffee spilled over them. Then to her toned and shapely long legs in the cream stocking which was now stained with coffee. Her pencil skirt started just above her knees and then I looked upward to the curve of her hips and then to her slim waist and then her bosom, she had a fabulous body.

Unwilling I made my eyes travel above her bosom to her long and slender neck then to her chin and those lips, God she had those sensual full lips then her Greek nose and all the way to her amber eyes which were filled with rage.

Then I focused on her complete face, her hairs were black I couldn't guess the length cause they were tied in a bun. Unknowingly my gaze started sliding down her body again when she snapped her fingers in front of my eyes and said " Eyes up here buddy".

I am sure I blushed and then I saw her bending down and picking up the book from the coffee pool. I checked her out again, she had a great ass, " Woah get a grip Waleed" I scolded myself.

The girl then looked at the book horrified which was almost soaked in coffee then she glared at me. I felt a little guilty for ruining her book and thought of apologizing.

"I am sorry," I said sincerely.

She looked in my eyes for a few minutes, and hissed "You will be very sorry when I am done with you".

"Excuse me,"

"If you want I will pay for your coffee and the book", I said as I withdrew my wallet from my jeans pocket.

She snatched the wallet from my hand and threw it on my face which directly hit my nose, I was blinded by the sudden pain in my nose and as I was rubbing my nose trying to understand what happened she thundered "Take your money and shove it up your ass".

I looked at her in disbelief forgetting about my hurting nose, I was astonished at her words. Never had any girl insulted me in such a way, they always used to drool over me.

But this vicious vixen was insulting me in broad daylight in a crowded public place. People had started gathering around us, and were staring with amusement in their eyes.

" Miss I think you really have some mental issues and need therapy" I just couldn't stand silent and let her insult me.

I decided to pay back, my words acted like fuel in the already burning fire and the flames erupted.

"Listen Mr, I had stood five hours in a queue to get this book signed from my favorite author, and now you have ruined it completely", She snapped.

Then I noticed her friend standing beside her looking at her with desperation. She was holding her hand and pulling her away from me.

" Mia let's go, we are already late", The other girl said.

So this chick was named Mia, though she was hot as hell, right now she looked like a witch to me.

"Sheema wait, let me teach a lesson to this asshole first", She turned her head to look at her friend and said. Then she pulled her hand away from her friend's grip.

I was furious after hearing the word asshole she used for me. I looked at her enraged and damn she was looking right back at me fearless.

We had this stare down for a few minutes when I saw her friend whisper something in her ear. I saw the change of expressions on Mia's face from fury to worry and then I guess it was fear.

" Don't think this is over and I forgave you, it's just I have an urgent business to look after", she said through clenched teeth and walked away from me with her friend.

I looked around at the people who had gathered to enjoy the scene taking place between us and roared "Don't you have any work to do".

The crowd started dispersing, that bitch had humiliated me in front of the whole damn town and I was really very pissed.

I gave up the idea of coffee and pulled out my cell from my pocket and dialed Asjad. He received the call after a few minutes " Hey buddy, where are you? I just reached the club".

I heard Asjad's cheerful voice, I felt like killing him."I will be there in 10 minutes, meet me in the ring".

I reached the club rashly driving my SUV. I changed into my boxing gear and went to the ring where Asjad was already waiting for me.

I didn't give him any time to think and punched him in his face.

Asjad yelled in pain "Man you looked pissed, what happened?"

Asjad might have sensed my rage by my facial expressions. He was my childhood friend and knew me very well.

I didn't reply and kept punching him. He was blocking my punches. After some time when I had calmed down a bit, Asjad grinned and said to me "It's a girl you are pissed at, aren't you?"

I looked at him startled, how the hell did he know I was pissed because of a girl?

"Come on Wal, spit it out", He said annoyed.

I told him what happened back at the mall, and that asshole burst out laughing.

" You got your ass kicked by a girl, Oh my God, I can't believe it. The Waleed Kamaal got his ass kicked by a girl", Asjad was laughing hysterically holding his stomach.

I was mad at the way he was laughing, "What the fuck is so funny about that?" I said as I punched him in his face and got an "Ouch" as a reply.

"You are really pissed," He said laughing.

As I was about to punch him again someone grabbed my arm from behind, I looked at the intruder. It was Saad, he was looking at both of is in confusion.

"What's the matter, guys?" Saad asked surprised.

"Wal, got his ass kicked by a girl," Asjad said pausing from his hysterics and then they both burst into laughter again.

I was now getting irritated by their laughter, I punched them both on their faces, and they raised their hands in surrender.

"Sorry, But it's so unusual cause most of the time it's you who kick other people's ass", Saad said and then he started laughing again.

" Fuck you", I cursed them and turned to leave.

"Ok, sorry we won't laugh again, just tell us, was she hot?" Saad teased.

I was reminded of Mia's hot body by Saad's words. She was damn hot but her mouth was too vicious.

"I don't give a damn if that bitch was hotter than Angeline Jolie", I hissed.

" Oooh, at least it was a hot chick who kicked your ass. That's some consolation for you", Asjad said grinning.

I punched him again and this time he cried out "Damn Wal, find yourself a punching bag".

" Why would I need a punching bag when I have you", I retorted.

"Okk guys stop it, I have something to tell you", Saad said.

We both looked at him at the same exact moment. Saad looked at us and then said raising his hands " It's not what you are thinking, Sheema's birthday is coming up in a couple of weeks and I am throwing a party for her. And I want your help to find a suitable gift for her'.

"Dude we are not your girl friends, we can't help you in this matter. Go get help from a girl", I said dryly.

" Maybe I should ask help from that hot chick", Saad said teasing.

I ignored him and walked out of the ring to the locker room, there I took a long shower till my senses were calmed.

When I came out of the shower the two assholes were sitting on the bench in the locker room waiting for me. They both had already taken a shower.

Asjad and Saad were my classmates since kindergarten. They both belonged to well off respectable families though they were not super-rich like me, we were still best friends. They both were like my family after Dada.

And I know no matter how much we joke and tease each other we will not think twice to sacrifice our life for one another.

Saad had got engaged last month to a girl of his parent's choice, and they had instantly bonded, Saad was already in love with his fiance and I was happy for him.

I was not able to attend their engagement, an urgent business had come up and I had to leave town. Saad was mad at me for nearly a month and had pardoned me after many requests from Asjad and Dada.

Asjad was in a relationship with a girl but their families were against their marriage. I had met the girl many times and she was really very sweet and pretty, like girls ought to be, not like that vicious bitch I had met today.

I cursed myself for remembering her again, but I was helpless I couldn't forget the humiliation and insult I had to face at her hands. I hope I get to pay back to her some time in life.

I agree I had ruined her book and I was sorry for that, I had even apologized to her but the way she behaved with me cannot be justified. She was extremely insolent, arrogant and crazy. Yeah, she was one crazy bitch to have acted in such a way.

I felt my blood boiling again, the more I wanted to forget the incident of today the more I was thinking about her.

"You okay buddy?" Saad asked looking at me.

"Yeah I am fine, was just thinking about that girl. She was literally crazy to act like that", I said rubbing my wet hairs with the towel.

" Do you have her name or address we can figure out a way to pay her back?" Asjad asked.

"Her friend called her Mia", I replied.

Saad shot a look at mc and suddenly turned his gaze to Asjad as if he was trying to avoid eye contact with me and started looking at his cell phone. I was a little surprised at his reaction when he heard the name of the girl but I ignored it.

" Boys I am starving let's grab something to eat", Saad said suddenly rising from the bench in the locker room.

"Yeah, I am starving too, come let's go have some Chinese," I said looking at Saad carefully, he was acting a little weird.

I didn't understand the reason for his weird behavior until the night of his fiance's birthday.

Chapter 3

Rameen

I looked at him, he was staring at the novel lying in the spilled coffee then his eyes started running upwards through my body. As his stare traveled from my stiletto to my legs then upward to my skirt and my waist and to my breast. I felt tingles erupting on my skin, no one had looked at me like this before.

His gaze held an intensity I never had noticed before in anyone else's eyes. He was wearing a white thin tee shirt and blue jeans. He had broad shoulders that tapered into a narrow waist, his biceps were bulging from his half sleeves demonstrating his strength, the 6 pack were visible through his thin t-shirt. And his long toned legs were on display in his skin fit jeans. What it will feel to be wrapped in those arms and legs? "Woah, Woah, Woah Get a grip Mia" I scolded myself.

His eyes stayed at my breast for a little longer than necessary then they traveled upward to my neck, chin, and lips. I saw him tracing his tongue on his upper lip as his eyes were focused on my lips "Son of a bitch" I thought trying hard to keep myselfcalm.

When he had checked me out from toe to head, his eyes started traveling down again but this time my patience was up. I snapped my fingers in front of his eyes and hissed "Eyes up here buddy".

I leaned forward and picked up the book from the floor, it was soaked up in the coffee. I checked the autograph page, the ink had spread and now it just looked like some blue stains.

Fucker, he had ruined everything, I felt like crying. How the hell will I ever get a special edition signed by Subrato Roy ever again?

I looked at him bewildered, he was looking ashamed, then I heard him say" I am sorry".

Asshole what was he thinking, he can get away with a mere sorry?

I looked him in his grey-brown eyes and roared "You will be very sorry by the time I am done with you".

" Excuse Me", he looked stunned.

Guess he was not used to getting insulted by girls. He was handsome like those damn hot models in the fashion magazines. And I am sure he always cashed his looks with girls.

Not me you arrogant hunk, you can't get away with your looks every time.

" If you want I will pay for your coffee and the book", he said as he pulled out his wallet from his jeans pocket.

His words stung me like a poisonous snake. Bastard, that book was priceless for me. And no amount of money could repay the loss.

I snatched his wallet from his hand and threw it at his face with all the strength I could muster. It hit him right in the nose, I am sure he was stunned that's why he didn't dodge it.

I saw the expression of pain on his handsome face, which gave me a little satisfaction. Then I snarled "Take your money and shove it up your ass".

My words stung him and he forgot his aching nose. I sensed how furious he was right now, he never got his ass kicked by a girl before, I guessed. And that was about to change for the good.

" Miss I think you really have some serious mental issues and you need therapy", I heard him say.

Therapy my foot, I thought bitterly and then I snapped at him "Listen, Mister, I stood five hours in a queue to get this book signed from my favorite author and now you have ruined it completely".

He was thinking I had issues just because my book was soaked in coffee. Idiot, it was not just another book but a special edition with the autograph of The Subarato Roy.

Sheema started to pull my arm in desperation to stop me from arguing further and said " Mia let's go, we are already late".

Hell, I didn't care if I had to stay here the whole night to teach this asshole a lesson to not mess with a girl again.

I glared at Sheema and then said: " Sheema wait, let me teach a lesson to this asshole first".

I pulled my arm from her grip and then glared at that asshole standing in front of me. He was looking at me furiously, I was sure he was pissed. We had a staring contest for some minutes then Sheema whispered in my ear.

"Mia if someone sees you here and informs aunty you will be grounded, and you realize that she won't allow you a bachelorette party".

Listening to her words all my rage vanished, I was worried because this was a mall and it was weekend, if anyone from my Mom's acquaintance saw me kicking a guy's ass I am sure they will report it back to my mom.

Suddenly, I felt a feeling of fear engulf me, what if someone saw me? Mom will never allow me to leave my house except for work till my wedding.

I won't have a bachelorette party, nor a bridal shower. Holy shit. I can't risk all this just because of this fucker.

I looked back at him, he was looking at my face with amusement, he had noticed the change of expression on my face. I really wanted to punch him in his face. " Calm down Mia, you can do this". I tried to calm myself.

"Don't think this is over and I forgave you, it's just I have an urgent business to attend", I said through clenched teeth and walked away with Sheema.

" Mia, do you have any idea how you behaved? Girls from respectable families don't act like that", Sheema said to me as we entered the elevator.

"My foot, that fucker ruined my book", I stomped my feet on the floor of the elevator imagining it was he who I have kicked.

" Thank God, Imaad didn't come looking for us. What would he have thought about you", Sheema said.

"It's because of him, if he would not have asked me to grab a coffee for him my book would have been safe with me and I would not have met that asshole", I hissed.

" He was hot though and quite handsome. And he even checked you out before you started spitting venom on him", Sheema said teasing.

"I don't care if he was hotter than Brad Pitt, he will always be an asshole to me",

I was really very mad right now, I knew that guy was really very hot. In other circumstances, I would have drooled over him but now I was really pissed at him.

I was sure if we ever met again I might kill him. How dare he accused me of having mental issues?

We exited the elevator and entered into the parking, Imaad had parked his car near to the exit gate. We hurried towards him as I slid into the passenger seat I heard him say " Hey, you forgot my coffee".

"If you ever again mention coffee in front of me I will kill you", I lashed out at him.

" What's the matter with you?"

Then he looked at Sheema in the rearview mirror who was sitting in the back seat and asked "What's the matter with her?"

"Actually, Imaad her book fell into the coffee which had spilled on the floor after she collided with that hot guy", Sheema blurted out.

" Which hot guy?" Imaad had only heard this part of the sentence.

I glared at him, he didn't care that my book was ruined all he cared about was I collided with a hot guy?

"That guy in the mall, he collided with Mia as we left the coffee shop", Sheema said looking tensed.

" Do you know him? Where did you meet before?" Imaad asked me coldly.

"Shut the fuck up, you don't even care that my book was ruined which I got signed after standing 5 hours in a queue. All you care about is I collided with a guy", I hissed.

Imaad looked ashamed, I knew how possessive he was about me. But still, he should have consoled me for the loss, instead, he started inquiring about that hot guy whose ass I had kicked.

I didn't care how handsome or hot he was, or how fabulous his body was I was mad at that jerk (but still you wanted his arms and legs wrapped around you) my conscience showed me the mirror.

" But that was before I found out how arrogant he was" I argued.

"So if he was not arrogant you will allow him to do things to you?" Conscience is a bitch, I thought bitterly.

It was just a thought. I didn't mean it. I was engaged and can't even think of cheating on Imaad.

"Sorry Mia, I was just a little jealous to hear you bumped, into a hot guy" Imaad's voice brought me back from my thoughts.

"I am done with your jealousy and possessiveness", I snapped.

" Sorry baby, you know how much I love you and I get furious even if I hear a guy's name from your mouth", He said.

"I know, but you should trust me. I will never do anything that will hurt you. You know how much I care about you" I said trying to console him.

"That's why I stay worried Mia, you just care about me. You never say that you love me", He replied.

" We have been through this Imaad", I said uneasily.

I didn't want to have this conversation in front of Sheema. It was not my fault that I didn't love him in the way he loved me.

Imaad just looked at me with resentment and started driving. His lips were pressed in anger and his vein was thumping against his forehead, a sign that he was furious.

I couldn't help it, I was just incapable of love, I don't believe love exists. It's just infatuation, we are attracted to someone and we really like them and care about them. And we are in such a hurry to give a name to our feelings that we give a tag of love to them.

I liked Imaad he was a nice guy, and I really cared about him. But I don't think I love him, because I don't know what love is. Yes, I am attracted to him, but it's not in some spiritual kind of way. I know I want him but I can't term these feelings as love.

We have a good understanding, we like each other may be he even loves me. I was happy and content that I was marrying him because I know he will make me happy and vice versa and I think that is enough.

But Imaad I don't understand why he was hell-bent on making me confess that I loved him, because I do not. Isn't it enough for him that I liked him and that I was looking forward to marrying and settle down with him?

Imaad didn't say anything further, he just kept mum the whole way till he dropped Sheema at her home and then me at my house.

Hell, I didn't want to talk to him either, I was pissed first at that hot jerk for ruining my book and then at Imaad for discussing our personasl in front of Sheema. Though she was my best friend I didn't like the idea of discussing our relationship issues in front of her.

He didn't even say goodbye and raced away from the gate. "As I care", I thought angrily.

There was a different scene inside my house, mom and aunt were furious that I was back after seven hours when I had told them it will just take a couple hours.   I didn't pay any attention to what they were saying and just stormed towards my room in anger. This was one of my worst days of my life.

Chapter 4

R ameen

"Happy Birthday love," I said as I hugged Sheema.

"Thanks, Darling, I am so glad you came. I hope your mom didn't mind you coming here", Sheema teased as she accepted the bouquet and gift from me.

Saad was standing beside her, I gave him a broad grin and shook his hand.

" So what's up lover boy?" I teased him.

He smiled and rolled his eyes at me, then he replied laughing " Nothing my love".

" You don't get to hit on my friend", Sheema said trying to look annoyed.

"I can't resist, she is too hot", He teased Sheema and earned a punch in his arm.

" So where is your fiance?" Saad asked me.

"I don't know, haven't spoken to him in two weeks", I replied rolling my eyes.

We haven't spoken since that incident in the mall took place. He was mad at me and I was in no mood to reconcile, myself, let him rot him in hell who cares.

" Hey baby" At that very instant someone slid his arm across my waist and whispered in my ear.

I didn't need to look at his face to know who it was, I had recognized him by his voice. I turned my head away from him, to show my annoyance.

"Mia, I am sorry. Will you please forgive me", He said as he turned my face towards him placing his finger below my chin.

Damn how can I stay mad at someone so hot, and who was hell-bent on trying to gain my forgiveness.

" I don't want to talk to you, I am still mad", I acted mad, well who doesn't like a little attention from your fiance.

"Baby I am sorry", He said caressing the back of my palm.

I couldn't keep up the act anymore, so I just smiled.

" All well between you too", Saad asked looking at us with amusement.

"Yeah" we both replied in unison.

" Come then join us on the dance floor", Saad said as he held Sheema's hand into his and led her to the dance floor.

Saad had organized the party at the roof of one of the best hotels in the town. The arrangement and decorations were top notch.

I noticed he had invited many people, but their parents were missing. Guess it was just for the young generation.

The music was loud and many couples were enjoying their time in each other's arms. Imaad smiled at me as he led me to the dance floor.

We started moving with the rhythm of the music, Imaad held me at an appropriate distance. He knew I never liked someone getting into my space.

I was enjoying my time dancing, Sheema and Saad were dancing near us. Sheema was looking overjoyed, Saad was handling her like she was some fragile item and would break with excess force.

I smiled at them, maybe arrange marriage was not a bad thing after all. Looking at them I was sure they couldn't have found anyone better.

"Penny for your thought", Imaad asked me.

" I was just thinking how wonderful Saad and Sheema look together", I said keeping my voice loud enough so he could hear it above the music.

Imaad just nodded at me in agreement and we continued dancing.

After a while, I felt tingles erupting on my body as if someone was staring at me with an intensifying gaze.

I scanned the people around me but I didn't find anyone looking at me, maybe my imagination was playing tricks on my mind.

I started feeling thirsty after nearly half an hour and excused myself from Imaad.

Imaad's cell phone started buzzing as we left the dance floor and headed to the sitting area. He spoke on the call for a few minutes.

Imaad told me he would have to leave because of some emergency, I looked at him with a scowl on my face.

He laughed and apologized that he will take me out for lunch the next day. I was not happy about him leaving so early.

We had met after two weeks and didn't even spend an hour together.

He consoled me saying he won't have left if it was not urgent. I just shrugged my shoulders at him, I really didn't want him to leave.

"Sorry baby, see you tomorrow at lunch. I will pick you from your office", He said as he hurried to the exit.

I looked at him till he was out of my sight and then turned and head towards the bar.

I asked for a pina colada and sat on the chair near the counter. The guy gave me my drink and as I was sipping it a couple slid into the chairs beside me.

" Hi, I am Raina", the girl introduced herself.

"Mia", I smiled and replied.

The guy with Rania checked me out from top to bottom after hearing my name, then he looked in the direction of Saad.

I saw Saad give him a nod, and that was enough to make me suspicious. What the hell was going on?

" Excuse me," I said to the guy with Raina.

"Yes?" He replied trying to look indifferent.

"I just noticed you and Saad passing glances at each other", I said trying to control my rising temper.

" Saad is my childhood friend", He replied.

"And why were you checking me out" I snarled, realizing he was fooling me around.

"You were checking her out" Raina exclaimed.

Payback time dude, you don't get to mess with me. I grinned at him.

"No babe, why would I do that", he replied, shooting daggers in my direction.

Rania just stomped her feet and left from there. He followed her immediately but not without giving me a death glare.

I chuckled in my heart, satisfactorily and started sipping my drink.

After some time Saad came towards me taking long strides and said: " Mia, what was that?"

"What? " I asked pretending as if I didn't understand.

"Why did you do that to Asjad?" He asked through clenched teeth.

He was looking furious, pays him well for plotting against my back whatever it was, with his friend.

"Mia you need to apologize to him and Rania," Saad said.

I couldn't believe what I just heard, was he out of his mind. Me, Rameen Shahab will apologize to his pathetic friend?

"Are you out of your mind?" I roared.

"Mia because of your stunt Rania is really very upset. They have been in a relationship for three years now", Saad's tone was softer this time.

" He should have thought that before he checked me out in front of his girlfriend, and you both exchanged glances with each other and you nodded at him. Tell me what's going on here?" I stopped beating around the bush and confronted him directly.

"It's not what you are thinking", Saad said looking tensed.

" Then tell me exactly what was that about?" I insisted.

"Mia please don't ruin this party, please for Sheema", Saad requested.

But I was not in a mood to entertain anyone. I crossed my arms on my chest and shook my head in disagreement.

"Damn Mia, what kind of friend you are? Saad said annoyed.

" A good one, but I want to know what is going on between you and your friend?" I answered.

I was not giving in to the emotional blackmail, Sheema was my best friend but I wanted to find out what exactly was going on.

"Mia please don't spoil the party for us" Saad pleaded.

His pleas softened my heart, and I was about to give in when I heard him behind me.

"Saad if you have wild cats on your guest list, you can only expect the party to be ruined"

I turned towards the person who had just called me Wild Cat, I was fuming in anger. Saad had an expression of desperation on his face.

And when I saw the face of the man, I lost my temper. He was the same hot jerk from the mall.

Waleed

As I reached the roof of the hotel I was greeted by the sound of loud music.

I had arrived late at the party because of an urgent meeting.

I hurried inside, most of the guest had arrived and were having a good time.

I looked around in search of Asjad and Saad but I couldn't find any of them.

Then I saw them both on the dance floor, dancing merrily with their partners, as I watched closely I noticed the girl dancing with Saad looked somewhat familiar as if I had met her before.

I had never met Saad's fiance before but how come she looked familiar, I tried recalling but failed.

Then my gaze shifted to the couple dancing close to Saad and her fiance, the girl in the white gown was exquisite.

Her back was to me, her waist-length black straight hairs were set loose on her back. And they were bouncing with her every move.

Her fishtail white gown was like a second skin on her body, enhancing her curves.

This is just a depiction of the gown Mia was wearing at the party.

The man dancing with her was looking at her with lust-filled eyes, and so were the other men around them.

I felt envious of the man dancing with her, lucky son of a bitch, the girl had the sexiest back and ass I had ever seen.

The man circled her in his arms, while she was giggling at something and at that moment I saw her face.

I felt like lightning struck me, she was the hot bitch from the coffee shop.

"What the fuck" slipped from my mouth.

"Why are you cursing dude?" I heard Asjad from beside me.

I looked at him in surprise I hadn't noticed him leaving the dance floor and coming towards me.

"Was I so busy gawking that bitch?" I wondered.

Asjad was looking at me suspiciously.

"That chick from the coffee shop", I said to him pointing towards the dance floor.

" Where?" Asjad looked in the direction I pointed and asked.

I looked there, but she was nowhere on the dance floor.

I looked at Asjad he was looking at me like I was mentally unstable.

"Dude you are thinking too much about her, and now you are hallucinating" Asjad teased.

"She was right there in a white sleeveless fishtail gown" I gave emphasis on white fishtail gown.

"Woah, Woah, since when are you looking at ladies' clothes so keenly?" He asked.

I glared at him in anger, but he was right I have never noticed such small details about any other girl in my life.

Why was I looking at her in such a way? Was she really getting on my nerves?

I didn't reply to Asjad and just stormed out of there in anger, which was directed at myself.

I went and sat at a corner seat near the bar. Alcohol was not permissible in my religion so only nonalcoholic drinks were being served.

I asked for a Mojito and started checking emails on my cell.

After a few minutes, I saw Mia walking towards the bar. She was alone this time, the guy who was dancing with her was nowhere to be found.

I wanted to approach her to even the score, but she looked so forlorn and lonely that I restrained myself from going to her.

She ordered a drink and was sipping it when Asjad and Raina slid on the chairs beside her.

I watched the encounter between them with amusement. She was a ticking bomb ready to explode at any moment.

I was glad Asjad had a taste of her medicine, now he will know what I have been through.

Then I saw Saad approaching her, he had asked her to apologize to Asjad and Raina but she stood her ground. I realized she was stubborn as a pig.

I couldn't resist anymore, so I rose from my seat and walked towards them.

"Mia please don't spoil the party for us" Asjad was literally pleading her.

"Saad if you have Wild Cat on your guest list, you can only expect the party to be ruined", I blurted out.

I noticed her body getting tensed at my words, she slowly turned around towards me.

A hint of recognition flashed in her Amber eyes as they met my grey orbs.

Third Person POV

They both were looking at each other with rage-filled eyes.

Waleed noticed how her Amber eyes were burning with rage.

" Wal now is not a good time", Saad pleaded to Waleed in desperation.

Waleed glared at Saad in fury and that proved to be his biggest mistake.

Taking advantage of his diverted attention Mia took her drink from the counter and threw it on Waleed. His tux was soaked with the pina colada within seconds.

She looked at him with triumph in her Amber eyes. Waleed didn't even flinch he was just looking at her coldly.

And before Mia could realize he picked a drink from the passing waiter and threw it on her face.

Every moment on the rooftop came to a standstill, there was complete pin drop silence. Even the music had halted.

Mia was taken by surprise, her eyes started burning, the drink squirted from her face to her dress and started soaking in it.

It was a raspberry cocktail, dark in color, her white gown was completely ruined from the drink.

Mia threw herself at Waleed, she wanted to kill him but was stopped by Rania and Sheema who had come to their side nearly running.

Mia started struggling to get out of their grip, Sheema and Raina were barely able to hold her.

Saad was holding Waleed's arm making sure he didn't do anything stupid.

Mia and Waleed were looking at each other with a death glare.

Raina and Sheema led her to the bathroom holding her firmly in their grip, making sure she did slide from their arms.And as soon as they entered the restroom Sheema lashed out.

"What the fuck was that Mia? Do you have any idea what scene you have created?"

Mia stomped her feet on the floor in fury. And then she glared at Sheema as if wanted to kill her with her bare hands.

"If you would have not restrained me, I would have kicked his ass" She hissed.

"Shut up, just shut the fuck up", Sheema swore.

Mia looked at her in shock, Sheema never used to swore no matter what the circumstances.

She looked ashamed, "Had she really crossed the line?"

"I am going home", Mia said taking a deep breath.

She had seen her reflection in the mirror, her hairs were all messy and sticky due to the drink. Her beautiful white gown had stained from her neck to the abdomen by the drink.

She was a complete mess, what will she say to her family, why had she returned from the party in such condition?

Chapter 5

R ameen

I was nervous waiting at the backdoor, hoping my cousin Umair would open the damn door without arising any suspicion.

After a few moments, I heard a click and the door was opened carefully to not make any sound.

"Mia what on Earth, did you got yourself into this time?" Umair glared at me.

I rolled my eyes at him, he was four years younger than me and always acted like he was the elder one.

"Will you just shut up and let me get to my room", I scolded him in a low voice.

I was afraid either my aunt or my mom could walk upon us and I didn't want them to see the mess I was right now.

Though Saad had given me his jacket and his driver has dropped me, my hairs were still sticky from the cocktail.

" What the fuck?" Umair exclaimed as I got inside and he saw me in the light.

"Shhh, can you just not talk till I make it to my room", I said annoyed.

He followed me silently to my room, we both making sure no one saw us till we reached the door.

Ours was a joint family, my father, and his brother my uncle living in the same house along with our grandfather.

" What have you done this time Mia?" Umair grabbed my arm as we entered my room and closed the door.

"Relax dude, no big deal. I threw a drink at the party on a guy and he retaliated", I replied trying to make it sound as insignificant as possible.

I wish Ali was here instead of Umair, he would have given me hi-fi. Though Ali was 2 years older than Umair he was the cool guy.

Umair was the spoilsport from the three of us. Ali and Umair were siblings, and they were the complete opposite of each other.

Ali was currently in the US doing his MBA, so he could come back and look after our family business of leather export.

" You did what", Umair asked trying to digest what I just said.

"Do you think I have all the time in the world to keep repeating the same thing again and again?" I said annoyed.

" Can you imagine what will happen if our mom's found out?" He said looking at me in disbelief.

Well, I can't help him if he was such a nerd. The most exciting thing in life he would have done would have been if he bunked a class if he ever bunked one.

"They won't if you don't tell them", I said taking out my clothes from the closet.

I was desperately in need of a shower to calm my senses. Now that I was back in the safety of my room without any of the elders of my family finding out I was reminded of that bastard again.

Umair just stared at me with distress and left my room.

I went straight to the shower, after an hour-long shower when I was back to my senses I was thinking about how I was going to repay that cocky bastard.

The following week I was busy with my office work, I was working as an architect in a newly established firm.

A distant cousin of mine had established this firm a few years back and was doing well. After I completed my graduation in architecture he had offered me a job in his firm.

I didn't want to join his firm in the first place, because I knew my mother will always keep an eye on me through him.

But I did not have any choice it was his firm or sit home and wait for my wedding.

And here I was working my ass off, though Daniyal was paying me well and I was learning a lot under him, still I didn't like the idea of him spying on me for my mother.

Sheema had called me to meet on Saturday, at a calligraphy exhibition in a hotel. Some Arab artist was holding an exhibition here in our town and Sheema was a great fan.

I didn't have any plans for Saturday as Imaad was busy with his business dealings and staying at home meant cooking dinner.

I had told my mom I was going to be late as I left my home, changing into something casual from my office attire.

Gladly she didn't protest because my Dada (grandfather) was sitting in the living room with them and I was his favorite grandchild.

When I arrived at the exhibition I was surprised to see Rania along with Sheema, those two were getting along very well.

I felt a little embarrassed after remembering our last encounter. I needed to apologize to Rania for what I did to her and her boyfriend.

Thankfully, they both didn't bring up the subject of the party all the while we roam the exhibition hall.

The artist was a master, we all marveled at his art. The calligraphy was so perfect. Mostly, it was the verses from the Quran.

I bought one for Dada, he was very fond of calligraphy. I planned to visit the exhibition along with him again the next day, he would surely love to see these.

We decided to have dinner at the restaurant in the five-star hotel, where the exhibition was held.

"So Mia, tell me about you?" Rania asked after we sat at a table and ordered our food.

"Nothing much to tell about, you have already seen what I am like at Sheema's birthday", I tried to sound as indifferent as possible.

" Well that was one great feat you pulled that day, never have seen a girl to stand up to Waleed my entire life", She said as if she was really in awe of me.

"Until he got the better of her", Sheema teased.

" You both have a thing for beverages you know, whenever you both meet they are spilled", Sheema added laughing.

I gave her a death glare, but she didn't seem to care. I had to do something about this Waleed guy.

"Did they meet before that day?" Rania asked surprised, to which Sheema narrated the incident of the mall to her.

"Ohhh my god, I can't believe it. Did you really say that to him? He would have been really pissed", Rania said laughing.

" Well you have just met her, the whole night won't be enough to narrate her feats to you. Mia had been kicking guy's asses since school", Sheema replied.

I was just sitting there like an idiot listening to their conversation, trying to figure out how I was going to apologize to Rania.

" I am shocked why Asjad didn't tell me about the coffee shop incident, I am sure he knows about it. There is no way Waleed hasn't told him and Saad" Rania said thinking.

"Actually they didn't know Mia was my friend until the night of my birthday. Saad had a doubt that it was Mia but he didn't tell Asjad and Waleed", Sheema replied.

They were still discussing that incident and I was trying to get myself to apologize to Rania.

The thing was I never apologized to anyone in my life before, it never came to that once I had a few with someone.

But Rania was different she was a nice person, she was trying to get along with me, though I had tried to take a jab at her boyfriend.

" Rania, actually I wanted to apologize to you for the way I behaved with you and your boyfriend", Finally, I was able to say the words, it didn't feel that bad.

She looked at me and smiled "It's okk Mia if I had been in your place, I would have done the same thing".

" So it means we are good", I asked her shocked.

"Of course we are good, I won't have been here right now having dinner with you if we weren't", She replied.

We were having our dinner when I noticed a couple sitting on a table across ours.

It was the hottie which Sheema and Rania were calling Waleed. He was engrossed in a conversation with his date, who was a very pretty girl.

I smiled as I got a devilish idea in my mind, by the look of them it looked they had arrived not long.

As we finished our dinner and paid the bill, I asked Rania and Sheema to wait for me near the entrance of the restaurant.

I walked at their table, strolling like I didn't have anything better to do.

Waleed

I was enjoying my time with Maram, she was the girl I was pursuing for the last six months and finally, she had agreed to have dinner with me.

She was very different from the girls I had dated before, she hadn't thrown herself at me like the other girls used to do.

Instead, she had made me chase her, it had taken me nearly three months to get her phone number and another three to get her to agree to dine with me.

We had just ordered our food and were busy in our conversation when I noticed a girl walking towards us in my peripheral vision.

"Hey hottie", She whispered in my ear.

I was completely dumbfounded, I know girls are attracted to me but never in my life had any girl done something like this.

I turned and my eyes were immediately locked with the Amber of hers, I knew exactly who she was.

Her intoxicating scent filling my nostrils, this was the closest we got since our first encounter I couldn't help but take a deep breath to fill my lungs with her scent.

She was extremely close to me just a gap of a few inches between our faces.

Then she wrapped my tie around her forefinger and pulled me a little closer to her and said in a seductive tone.

"No matter how much I try, I couldn't get that night out of my mind honey".

"I wish we could do it again"

I was looking at her shocked, trying to understand what she was saying, she then leaned back up and unwrapped my tie from her finger.

I looked at her from top to toe, she was wearing a red crop top and a black Capri, with red pumps.

Damn this girl knew how to take away the breath of the opposite sex.

She then turned around and walked towards the entrance, her hips swaying in a seductive way.

I couldn't help but stare at her till she reached the door, I notice two other girls were standing there waiting for her but I didn't care to look at them, my mind was too occupied with that vixen.

She turned and gave me a bright smile and winked as she flipped her middle finger at me, mouthing the words "SCREW YOU".

And I realized what that bitch has done to me, as I turned and looked at Maram who was shooting daggers at me.

"Maram I can explain," I said.

"Hell you can", She hissed and stood from her chair.

She collected her clutch and cellphone from the table as I tried to stop her from going.

"Don't you dare call me again", she snapped and was out of the restaurant before I could realize and I stood there fuming.

This was the second time that bitch had gotten the better of me. I wanted to kill someone at that instant, I knew I had blown away all my chances with Maram.

No girl in her sane mind would ever talk to a guy again if she had witnessed what just had happened. That bitch was getting on my nerves now.

Chapter 6

We came out of the restaurant laughing, Rania and Sheema were literally crying with laughter.

"Ohhh my God Mia, you totally blew his date", Rania said trying to control her laughter.

"No one messes with me," I said with a proud wink.

The expression on Waleed's face was priceless when I left from there. And his date looked furious as if smoke was coming out of her body.

Well, any girl would react in the same way if some random girl comes and tells her date how she missed their night together.

Poor Waleed, I felt a little guilty for what I did to him, but I couldn't help he had ruined one of my favorite dresses and novel.

It was the least I could do to gain some satisfaction, I hope we never meet in the future God knows what he will do to me.

Sheema and Raina were still laughing as we entered the parking and got into Rania's car.

Rania was the only one who could drive from the three of us. Sheema never learned and I have vehophobia(driving phobia).

My dad and uncle had tried many times to make me overcome my fear, but the moment I turned the key in the ignition I would totally freak out and start panicking.

I had also tried hard to learn driving but it was no use, I was never able to overcome my fear.

At least everyone had given up on me and mostly our driver would drop me or I would use a cab.

Our firm had a pick and drop service for all females employees so conveyance was not a problem for me to go to work.

"I can't wait to tell Asjad what happened today, he will die of laughter," Rania said driving.

I was sitting on the passenger seat while Sheema was lying on the back seat, still laughing.

"Mia, I think you should give the guy a break", Sheema said lifting her head a little to look at me.

" Don't worry sweety, I got my revenge. I don't think I want to see him ever again", I said smiling.

It felt really nice like a heavyweight was lifted from my heart. Nothing is sweeter than revenge.

Now I can die in peace, that guy had really given me a hard time.

We dropped off Sheema first and then Rania dropped me, she told me she lived just two lanes from my place.

I was glad it was a convenient distance, I could just walk to her place if I wanted to visit.

As I entered the living room, I was shocked to see Ali sitting along with everyone.

"Ohhh my God Lee!!!!!!", I cried in disbelief.

Ali nearly ran to me and gave me a bear hug, at that moment I realized how much I missed him.

" I missed you so much lee", I said as a tear rolled down from my eye.

"I missed you too Mia, and guess what I am here for two weeks, and we can hang out together", He said messing up my hair.

In other circumstances, I would have retaliated, but now when he was back nearly after a year I just wanted to enjoy every minute of his company.

Ali was two years younger than me, and we were inseparable from the day Ali had started walking. He was my partner in crime, our mothers would just go crazy trying to control our mischiefs.

" I thought you were coming for my wedding", I said as I remembered suddenly.

"Sorry Mia I don't think I can make up for the wedding, my sem is scheduled in those dates", He said as he leads me to the couch he was sitting on.   " That's not fair Lee, I won't get married if you don't show up", I said disheartened.

I couldn't imagine going through such an important event in my life without my bestie.

"Mia please, I am already sulking over missing your wedding, don't make it hard for me", Ali said in grief.

" Yes Ali, you can at least try", My aunt said to Ali.

Ali just looked at her in disbelief, it was his semester exam he was talking about, and my aunt was telling him to miss it.

I was upset that Ali would not be able to attend my wedding, still, I would never tell him to miss his semesters.

The thing with the ladies of our house was, they were still stuck in the 20th century, where all these rituals, traditions and customs were important.

"Don't worry Mia, I will send you a nice present", Ali tried to cheer me up.

Everyone started talking again about Ali's studies then the discussion shifted to my wedding and finally it came back to how pathetic I was in the kitchen.

" Mia doesn't need to learn cooking, her in-laws have a wonderful cook", Ali said trying to take my side when both our Mom's tried to get on my nerves.

"Having a cook doesn't mean the lady of the house should not know cooking, how will she impress her in-laws and husband if she doesn't know how to cook", My mom said in a heated voice.

" Oh, come on mama, I am a good architect. I am really good at my job and that's important. I don't need to be master of all" I said to my mother, Ali's support had given me the strength to stand up to the torture I was been put through in the last few months.

" Yeah you will feed blueprints and elevation designed to your family when they are hungry", My mom retorted.

"Aany, please, this is the 21st century, not 15th. Why don't you ladies let Mia enjoy this time before her wedding", Ali said?

" It's the support of the men in this house which has rotten this girl to the core, not a single habit of her is good enough to get married", My mother said in bitterly.

It was true, I was the only girl child in the family, hence my Dada who didn't have a daughter loved me, Uncle loved me cause he didn't have a sister and a daughter Ali and Umair loved me because I was like a sister they never had and Dad he just loved me cause he was my dad.

Though my mom and aunt were female, they were the only ones who made my life miserable.

But all the male members in my family had spoilt me beyond repair.

"Aany, Imaad loves her and that is what is important and I am sure he will take good care of her. Please don't worry about these useless things. I can assure you, no man in this century want a miserable wife", Ali said enthusiastically.

" It's useless, talking sense into the men of this house", Mom said and walked out of the living room in protest.

I looked at Ali and gave him a wink, I was proud of him. He was the only one who stood up for me.

Dada, dad, and uncle had given up under the pressure from the ladies. I knew this freedom will only last till Ali was here, and that was enough for me. I just wanted to chill with my buddy.

Waleed

I had cone to watch a movie with my date Hiba when I saw Mia standing near the entrance of the multiplex with a guy.

I figured out that guy must be her fiance, Saad had told me in our last meeting she was engaged and was going to get married in a couple of months.   It happened that Rania and Sheema were along with her when she had come and ruined my date completely.

Rania had told Asjad about what had happened, and again Saad and Asjad were pulling my leg over that incident.

I was already furious because that bitch had blown my chances with Maram completely, whom I really liked and had a feeling that she would have been a good life partner.

Maram was so mad at me that she didn't answer any of my calls and didn't reply to any of the text messages I sent her.   She was justified in what she was doing and I had given up on her realizing she was not going to forgive me ever.

I had lashed out on Saad and Asjad and they both were very regretful regarding what happened between Maram and me.

And Saad had told me that she was engaged and if I was thinking about some revenge it could destroy her life if I did something wrong. Like I cared if her engagement broke or her wedding was called off. I wanted revenge and I was not going to be soothed until I got that.

Now as I saw her standing there with that guy, engaged in some kind of banter a wicked idea clicked in my mind.

I told Hiba to go and wait at our seats and I will get some popcorn for us. When I was sure Hiba was safely inside the hall I turned and walked towers them.

I went close to them and held her hands acting desperate.

"Mia, did you tell our parents about us? You promised you were going to talk to them", I said trying hard to control my laughter.

Mia was completely shocked at what I said to her. She was just looking at me stunned.

" Please Mia, I know you love me, and we can't live without each other. Only a couple of months are left for your wedding, please talk to them and tell them about me, about us", I said trying to keep my act.

"Excuse me, do we know you", the guy standing with Mia asked.

" No you don't, but I know you and I request you to please help us. We love each other and her parents are making her marry someone else", I said looking at him.

He was a handsome guy with an athletic build and bright brown eyes and a boyishness in his personality.

"Are you out of your mind?" Mia said as she pulled her hands from me.

"Please Mia don't do this, don't marry him, Mia. I know you love me", I said pleading.

Mia was looking at me as if she would kill me right now with her bare hand, I was glad I had taken her unawares. The bitch deserves this after what she had done to me last time.   " I think you should leave", the brown-eyed guy said to me as he pushed me backward.

"Hey bro, just chill it's not like I am stealing your girlfriend, she is in love with me", I said taking backward steps.

I didn't want to start a physical fight in a public place when the guy really looked pissed at me.

" How dare you?" He was about to plunge at me when Mia grabbed his arm and started pulling him in the opposite direction.

"Ali not now, Imaad and Umair can get here at any moment", She was saying to him at the same time shooting daggers at me.

Hell yeah, I was enjoying her helplessness, you just can't mess with Waleed Kamal twice and getaway.

I looked around many people had gathered to witness the scene unfolding, I gave her a smirk.

Now all the people around will think she was a bitch fooling two guys at the same time.

And maybe this Ali guy, if he was her fiance will give her a tough time after what I had said to her.

I pointed a middle finger at her, smirk on my face like she had done at the restaurant and turned and walked away to the entrance of the hall, where Hiba was waiting for me.

Chapter 7

Rameen

"Care to explain", Ali was looking at me with his brown eyes filled with fury, his lips were pressed tightly and a frown on his face.

I found out at that moment, I didn't like a pissed off Ali, yet I have to answer him.

That arrogant bastard had got me unaware this time and thank god Imaad was in the queue for popcorn and hadn't seen the drama that unfolded.

If he had witnessed the scene I was sure my wedding would have been called off at that very moment, I know how possessive he was of me.

" It's a long story Lee, I don't think you would like to hear", I answered him swallowing the lump that had formed in my throat.

His brows furrowed as he leaned towards me and said " I have all the time in the world unless what that guy said was true".

"Hell no, you think I would be involved with that cocky bastard", I replied with a scowl.

I didn't expect this from Ali, at least I thought he was the one who really understood me.

" Then what was that all about", He asked, clearly he still didn't believe what I was saying.

"Well that asshole and I have been in a feud lately, and he just got back to me", I said sighing.

I was really very pissed, what if Imaad was with me instead of Ali? He might have killed me, just hearing I bumped into a hot guy he was so mad what would have happened if he saw a guy confessing he loved me.

I was really sweating at that moment, I felt a knot in my stomach when the realization struck me that I had just escaped a disaster.

" You mean he was just fucking lying, why didn't you let me beat him then?" Ali asked he looked more furious than before.

"Imaad is here with us, if we would have been alone then I would have kicked his ass myself", I snapped at him.

" Hey guys, what are you doing here? We looked for you everywhere", Imaad said as he approached Ali and me, we have been standing near the restrooms.

I have dragged Ali here so I could calm him down before he did anything stupid, I knew he had a volatile temper like me.

"Nothing, I saw a friend here and so I came here to talk to her", I replied to Imaad.

" Where is she then?" Imaad asked looking around.

Shit.

"She just left", I replied hoping he would believe my lie.

Imaad didn't ask any further questions, we just entered the hall and took our seats.

Ali was in an awful mood the whole time, he didn't speak much at the dinner, Umair and Imaad had noticed his silence.

He just excused himself that he was having a headache.

The other week of Ali's stay passed peacefully without any major incident.

I was very sad after he left, he was really my bestie and I missed hanging out with him.

All was well in my life at home as well in my office, until Daniyal decided to do a joint venture with a consulting firm for a five-star resort.

It was a huge project and naturally, everyone was excited about working on it.

Daniyal had selected a team of three architects from our office, which he was leading himself.

Currently, our firm had a staff of 40 people and was growing with time as we got new projects.

Daniyal had said we would need to hire more employees for this particular project.

He had been having meetings with the CEO of this firm for quite some time now.

It was Thursday when he asked me to accompany him to one of these meetings, he trusted me with everything regarding business.

We were family and he knew no matter how difficult my attitude can be sometimes I was really good at my job.

" Mia just stay calm throughout the meeting, I don't want any fallout. We have signed this deal last week and today he wants to introduce me to his staff" Daniyal said as we drove to the office of Kamal construction.

"Don't worry Daani, I got your back", I said smiling.

" That's what I am worried about, it takes only seconds for you to lose your temper", He said with a frown.

"Then why are you even taking me with you? You should have asked one of your well-behaved pups to come along", I replied annoyed.

" See, just a sentence and you lose it", Daniyal retorted.

I didn't reply, didn't want to have any argument with him.

Though he was my cousin he was very professional when it came to working. He had a no none sense attitude that was the reason he had gained such success at the start of his career.

I couldn't help but admire the office building of Kamaal Constructions, it was a 15 story building with a staff of hundreds.

They had a long list of projects under their belt, flyovers, highways, hotels, stadiums, hospitals, malls residential and commercial complexes you name it and they had constructed it.

A man was waiting for us at the reception for us, he smiled as we approached him and said: " Good afternoon, Mr.Kamaal is waiting for you, if you will please follow me".

He lead us to the elevator and to the top floor of the building, I couldn't help but admire the interior of the building.

I was sure Mr.Kamaal really had a very good taste, there was another receptionist on the top floor. She was hot as hell.

She smiled and lead us to the office of the CEO, I was wondering how did Daniyal convince this man for a joint venture?

This firm was more then capable of doing this project all by themselves, and if they were allowing Daniyal to work with them there should have to be a good reason for it.

"Don't tell me you are sleeping with this guy, how on Earth you convinced him for a joint venture?" I whispered in Daniyal's ear.

Daniyal didn't reply to my obscene remark he just gave me a sharp look, which was enough to shut me up from saying anything further.

"It's Mr. Daniyal, Sir", The receptionist said as we entered his office.

His office was marvelous, with wooden flooring and paneling. A mahogany desk was placed in front of a large glass window looking out the view of the whole city. Paintings and other artworks hung on the wall, there were two couches with a coffee table in the middle on the right side of the desk.

And when my eyes landed on the person sitting behind the mahogany desk, I was shocked beyond description.

His grey eyes were locked on me, he looked completely different from what he looked in our last meetings.

He was wearing a grey two-piece suit with a white and grey checkered tie on a white shirt, his eyes were cold and face was completely blank without any expression.

The way he was looking at me, I truly felt intimidated. I swallowed a lump in my throat, today was turning out into one of the worst days of my life.

" Daniyal, you are late by 10 mins", He said shifting his eyes to Daniyal.

"Waleed, you know how traffic is in our city", Daniyal said as he walked towards his desk.

They both shook hands and Waleed directed Daniyal towards the couches.

" Hey Mia, why are you still standing there", Daniyal called out to me.

I was still standing near the door, unsure of what to do next. To he honest, I was planning to flee his office never to return, but my boss was looking at me with a threat in his eyes.

"Mmh nothing Daani, I think I just don't feel very well" I mumbled in my mouth.

I was literally freaking out, like of all people in this world, Daniyal had decided to do a joint venture with this asshole.

The way Daniyal was looking at me like he would strangulate me right at that moment left me with no choice but to walk towards the men who were seated on the couches opposite to each other.

"Waleed, this is Mia. She is the best architect in my firm" Daniyal introduced me to Waleed.

Not that we need any introduction we knew each other really well. Barring the fact that he was the fucking CEO of KCC.

"Hello", I greeted as I sat beside Daniyal.

Waleed just replied with a nod, 0he didn't even spare me a glance.

He was completely in his CEO form right now, and I was glad he pretended as if he didn't know me.

They started discussing the details regarding the project, Waleed's secretary had joined us in the meeting she was busy taking notes while I was busy examining her.

She was breathtakingly beautiful, with her soft hazel eyes and golden brown layer cut hairs. She was wearing a pencil skirt and blouse her hourglass-like figure quite on display.

The glances she was giving Waleed every now and then was enough for me to understand she was infatuated to him, while Waleed was behaving with her in a strictly professional way.

It was difficult to deduce if he had any feelings for her if there were any he was hiding it really well.

After the formal discussion his secretary left us, another girl brought in refreshments she was nearly as pretty as his secretary.

This guy really liked to surround himself with pretty girls I thought amused.

There were sandwiches, lemon cake, cheesecake, puffs, and other mouth-watering items, still, I hardly felt like eating.

I just wanted to leave the place, it was difficult to imagine working on this project along with this cocky bastard.

I was just thinking of an excuse for how to tell Daniyal I didn't want to work on this project, but by the looks of Daniyal, he was really very enthusiastic about this project.

And if he had brought me along with him on this project meant he wanted me by his side.

I was just sitting with a croissant in my plate and sipping coffee when Daniyal got a call and excused from there, he left the room and went outside talking on the call before I could react.

I was left with Waleed alone in his office, and Waleed who had ignored me all the time since I was here speaking only with Daniyal now was staring at me with a piercing gaze.

His eyes always made me uncomfortable, the intensity of those grey eyes with which he watched me felt like they were stripping me.

He didn't speak a word with his mouth but the things his gaze was making me feel were completely different from what I have felt my whole life.

I was just sitting there with my head bowed, trying to ignore his cold stare. I was getting mad at myself, I shouldn't be intimidated by him. I should retaliate, my mind was motivating me.

I took a deep breath and looked him in his eyes, fuck off, you asshole. You might be some CEO but I won't be ever intimidated by you.

I didn't know how long our staring contest lasted, but as Daniyal entered the room Waleed shifted his attention towards him.

I was sure Waleed will never mention our last encounters to Daniyal, cause his reputation was at stake more than mine.

"So what do you think?" Daniyal asked me as we drove back to our office.

"Are you sure it's a good idea to do a joint venture?" I asked him.

I was not sure how I was going to tell Daniyal I didn't want to work on this project. We couldn't stand each other for a few minutes and this project might take months to complete.   I couldn't say him directly that I didn't want to be a part of this project. Daniyal knew how career-oriented I was and I won't miss a chance to work on this prestigious project with an A-list firm in the country. And if I would straightaway say no he will get suspicious and if he found out what happened between me and Waleed I would be dead meat.

"Why are you being skeptical? I thought you would be overjoyed to work on such a big project and that too with such a good firm" Daniyal looked at me with suspicion.

Oh no, here we go again. Why does Daniyal have to know me so well?

"No, I mean I was just thinking why he is willing to work with us when his firm can probably do that project by themselves", I had to say something and this looked the best reason.

" The man who owns the land is my friend and the hotel chain group who are building the resort are Waleed's acquaintance. So I helped Waleed and his clients to convince my friend for selling the land in return for working on this project together", Daniyal explained.

"Ohh, I see", I replied.

Now I understood the reason why Waleed Kamaal had decided for a joint venture with a new firm like ours.

But my problem was still there, how was I going to convince Daniyal. Damn why it had to be Waleed with whom I collided that day outside the coffee shop.

I was getting mad at Imad again, I was in this mess because of his coffee. I knew Waleed hated me, and I don't think we can work together without ripping apart each other.

"We are doing the sight survey on Saturday, and I want you to come with me. Kabir will be with us and I think Waleed and a few employees from his firm", Daniyal informed.

Wtf, now was I going to spent hours with that man on the site. This was getting scarier than I had expected.

I need to think of something, should I just resign? Or should I just commit suicide? Which one was the better option?

"Mia don't worry, there are still two months for your wedding and you can take one month off for your wedding and if you want you can work from home. There won't be any pressure on you, but just think this project, will be a start point of your career", Daniyal said looking at me.

Maybe he had read my expressions and was thinking I was worried because of my wedding.

Shit, Mia, you are an ass I cursed myself, I could have thought about my wedding as an excuse but now Daani had already cleared that point.

" Waleed is a great guy, I am really looking forward to working with him, and you can also learn a lot from him Mia", Daniyal added.

"Yeah he seemed okk, I think it's his grandfather's hard work. I know his grandfather he is a good friend of Dada", I said to Daniyal, honestly saying I don't find anything remarkable in Waleed.

He had just taken over the farm from his grandfather, the firm was well established even before Waleed was born. That I had known from Dada, I had never met Waleed though his grandpa used to come to our house a lot.

Waleed was mostly out of the country for his education, but I had heard a lot about him from Dada. It was almost like Dada really admired Waleed, yeah maybe he was really nice, but my experience, with him, was awful.

He was an insensitive, arrogant asshole and I really despised him.

Chapter 8

Rameen

"Hey, What's up baby?" Imaad said as soon as I picked his call.

"Nothing," I replied as I channel surf on the television for something interesting to watch.

"You free for dinner tomorrow? It's been nearly a week since we met," Imaad asked me.

Boy, he was missing me, I felt really good. Imaad was what a fiance ought to be loving and caring just subtract his possessiveness.

" Yes, I think so I can spare some time for you," I said teasing.

"It would be a great kindness, your Royal Highness," He replied with his tone full of sarcasm.

"I'm really kind towards my loyal subjects," I replied laughing.

"I am just bidding my time until you are mine, and then I will repay you for your kindness", His voice held a promise, I won't lie, I was a little excited by his threat.

" Imaad."

"Mia."

"I will call you tomorrow," I said as I disconnected the call.

I looked at the wall clock it was 11 in the night, I thought what Ali might be doing and decided to give him a call. He received my call after few rings his voice sounded little sleepy.

" Hey Mia."

"Hey, love, where you sleeping?" I asked him embarrassed, I didn't mean to wake him up.

"No, just woke up. You tell me what's up?" He asked.

"Remember, that guy at the multiplex?" I asked wondering if I was doing a mistake telling him about Waleed.

"Yeah, that asshole? Why is he bothering you again? If he is I will come and kick him in his balls" As expected Ali was mad.

"Ohh God, why do you have to be so hyper?" I said rolling my eyes.

"Actually Daniyal is doing a joint venture with his firm, and guess what he is the grandson of Kamal uncle," I told him.

" Wtf Mia, you really messed up with the wrong person this time. He is the Waleed Kamal?" Ali asked cursing.

Yeah, I also knew that I have really messed up with the wrong person. What if Kamal uncle ever found out about what happened between us? He was really fond of me, and I was worried he won't like me much after this.

"Do you think I don't know this," I asked annoyed.

" What are you gonna do now?" Ali asked me.

I really didn't know, how was I going to handle this. How could I work with him, when we had such terrible encounters in the past with each other.

"I don't know, tomorrow we have to go for sight study," This was what was bugging me, I really can't stand that guy for such a long time.

" What if tell Daniyal or Kamal uncle about what you did to him? I am sure Daniyal will tell Aani and mom."

I had called him so that he might give me some moral support, instead, he was scaring me to shit. I can't afford my mom to know about that.

"Shut the fuck up, I didn't call you so you can only heighten my fear," I said annoyed and disconnected the call.

Well calling Ali turned out to be a mistake, I thought he might give me some good advice but that asshole had only added to my anxiety.

I turned off the television and went to bed, turning and tossing in bed thinking of a way to avoid going tomorrow to the site.But I couldn't think of anything good, I fell asleep dreading what was to come tomorrow.

I even had nightmares that night and in it, Waleed turned out to be a Vampire who was thirsty for my blood, blame it on the fantasy movies or novels I was fond of but I was really sweating when I woke up from that nightmare.

It took almost an hour for me to fall asleep again and I was woken up by a shrieking sound.

I tried to figure out where the sound was coming from with a heavy head, first I thought it was Waleed in the form of a vampire shrieking with joy after he found me.   I quickly sat up and looked around terrified but it was just my cell phone ringing. I cursed myself for keeping that horrific ringtone just to annoy Daniyal and my mum.

I reached out to the side table and picked my phone, it was Daniyal calling. What the hell did he want so early in the morning? It was just six in the morning.

" What the hell Daani, can't I even sleep peacefully?" I hissed.

Honestly, speaking I was not a morning person, and my head was pounding due to lack of sleep and stress.

"Mia, I told you I would pick you up at 7, I knew you will forget. That's why I called you, get ready I will be there in an hour," He said as he disconnected the call.

"Ohh no!!!!!!" I exclaimed in horror as I slammed my face into the pillow.

Daniyal hadn't left me any choice other than to oblige with what he ordered. I got up from bed went along with my morning routine, took a shower and got ready.

It was nearly 6:45 by the time I had dried my hairs and dressed, I left my room with my iPad and my backpack with all the essential required for the site study.

My mom and aunt looked at me shocked when I went to the kitchen for breakfast. I never used to go down before 8 in the morning.

"I am going with Daani for a site study, it might get late by the time we return," I said ignoring their reactions.

I knew my mom would send me to hell if Daniyal accompanied me, I never understood the reason my mom trusted him more than me.

I was sipping my tea along with a toast when I heard Daniyal's car, I got up frustrated from the small dining in our kitchen. Why does everyone around me have to be so punctual? It was really a joke on me by my fate.

I said my goodbyes to Dada and mom who were sitting in the living room and went outside.

Daniyal was on the driving seat while Kabir was on the passenger seat, I slid into the backseat and slammed the door.

" Ouch," Kabir said.

"Someone is grumpy," He added.

"If you want to walk on your legs don't mess with me right now," Kabir chuckled while I saw Daniyal trying to suppress his laughter.

" Sorry Mia, I know you are not a morning person, but it is 2 hours drive from here and plus the traffic. Give and take it will nearly take three hours to reach our destination," Daniyal said, he was looking in a good mood today, otherwise, he would have scolded me.

The drive was fun, Kabir had put songs on full volume and was narrating his childhood escapades to us. Kabir was an architect working in our firm and we both bonded really well with each other.

Daniyal was enjoying himself, shedding his boss's image and mingling with us like colleagues.

We took a few stops on the way, it was really turning out to be a fun trip. Daniyal even sang for us at one point out of boredom of the long drive. He had a really awful voice, Kabir and I barely controlled our laughter. Kabir even recorded it, without Daniyal knowing he sent me the audio clip on WhatsApp.

I forwarded it to Ali and Daniyal's wife Reema, I was sure Daniyal was gonna have a gala time when he went back home.

Finally, after two and a half hours, we reached our destination. The place was serene, the seawater extended beyond the horizon, the sound of the waves crashing on the beach, there were hills around the open ground where we had parked our car and they were planning to build a resort.

Whoever had chosen this spot really had a great taste, I could notice Kabir had the same feelings as mine regarding the place.

"This place is heaven," I exclaimed as we got out of the car.

" Agreed," Kabir added.

"I am glad you both like the place, and I would be merrier if you both get your asses to work now," Daniyal said as he walked towards the group of people standing a little away from us.

" Hey Daniyal," A man in his late fifties greeted as Daniyal approached the group.

I noticed most of the people we're Waleed's employees I had met them at his office when I had accompanied Daniyal to the meeting and Waleed had introduced us to the people who were working on this project.

"Hello Mr.Shah," Daniyal greeted back as they did handshake.

" Let me introduce my team to you, this is Kabir and Mia they both are architects in my firm, " Daniyal introduced us.

"Guys, this is Mr.Shah our client, whose resort we are going to construct," Daniyal said with a formal smile.

We both greeted Shah and then he introduced us to his secretary and the two of his partners.

After the formal greetings with everyone, we started with our work, I noticed Waleed was silent today unlike in the last meeting with Daniyal and me. He had avoided looking at me as he had done in our previous meeting apart from the formal greetings.

When we had covered all the points required for the site study like the geography, topography, climate, site placement and the road facing side, etc.

We went to the cabin which looked like, it was recently constructed. Waleed, Daniyal and Shah were sitting in the cabin along with his partners.

They were discussing the requirements of the project, Waleed's secretary was busy taking notes. There were a total of five employees from Waleed's firm. Two engineers and three architects.

They were all men and were really good, except the senior engineer who was in his fifties and looked really mean.

The four of them warmed to me and Kabir really fast and we had fun exploring the place and conducting the study.

As we joined the meeting, the discussion shifted to the site study we all have our observations, and then Shah and his partners started discussing their demands and what they wanted in their resorts.

The meeting was going smoothly until my cell started shrieking again the horrible ringtone I had set.

I hated when all the eyes landed on me, shit I was screwed. Daniyal was going to kill me. I had completely forgotten to turn my phone silent before the meeting.

I looked at Daniyal but my gaze shifted to Waleed who was sitting beside him, he was looking at me in the same as in my nightmare last night and I began to panic that anytime now he would flash his fangs before he pounced on me and drank my blood.

" Mia, you can go out and take the call," Daniyal said through clenched teeth. I could see how pissed off he was.

I nearly ran out of the cabin and checked the caller it was Imaad, shit I had told him I would have dinner with him and it was almost 4 in the evening now. And by the looks of the men inside it didn't look liked they would leave anytime soon.

"Hi," I said as I picked the call.

" Hey, I just called to tell you I will pick you at 7," Imaad said as he heard my voice.

I was a little distressed, I was sure there was no way we could get back to the city by 7. I will have to hold off the dinner for tomorrow night.

"Immi I don't think I can dine with you today, I am still at the site and it will take nearly three hours for the drive back. And still, the meeting is going on," I knew he would be really mad.

" What the hell Mia, you told me last night you will have dinner with me," From the tone of his voice he really looked mad.

Fuck, I was really having the worst day, my boss was mad at me for the disruption caused by my ringtone in the meeting and Waleed was ready to drink my blood any moment and to top it all now my fiance was mad at me.

"I will give you a call after the meeting Immi, take care. I will see you tomorrow," I disconnected the call and entered the cabin not forgetting to put my phone on silent.

After a discussion for one more hour, Shah and his partners left. I sneaked out of the cabin with Ben an architect from Waleed's firm. We had planned we would go to the beach to enjoy a little in the seawater.

The beach was deserted unlike the beaches in our city, the water was crystal clear and we could hear the sound of the waves, the surrounding hills were green and the sun was nearly setting.

Ben and I walked into the water till the water reached just above our ankles, I had folded my jeans so as to avoid them getting wet.

Ben was really charming and sweet. He and I were of the same batch though we belonged to different architecture schools, he had been working for KKC for over a year now.

He teased me regarding my ringtone and that how he loved it and I proved a savior from that boring discussion.

I told him about the look Waleed gave me with the reference of the vampire. Ben roared with laughter and agreed on how similar Waleed was to a vampire they both feasted on the blood of the humans around them.   At least I was convinced I was not the only one that hated Waleed, there were people who shared my dislikes in this world. Ben reminded me of Ali, he had the same carefree attitude as

Ali and I was sure we were going to bond well together, as we worked on this project.

Waleed

We were having a discussion with Shah and his partners after our team gave their observations regarding the case study, I was glad, the way the discussion was going it felt like this was going to be an interesting project and lucrative too for my firm.

All of a sudden I heard a horrible shrieking sound, all the people in the room were startled by the sound. And when I looked at the source of the sound it was coming from the cell phone of none other than Mia.

I felt like killing that girl and drinking her blood, she was really a pain in the ass. I wondered how Daniyal tolerated her.

" Mia you can go out and take the call," Daniyal said through clenched teeth from beside me, he really looked pissed.

My mood was destroyed, I couldn't concentrate to the discussion anymore. I was thinking about Mia, I don't think I have enough patience to tolerate her for the time we work together.

I needed to talk to Daniyal, I had to tell him to pull her out of this project. If she keeps acting in such an irresponsible way it's not going to be good for the image of my firm.

The discussion finished after an hour and Shah along with his partners bid adieu. I and Daniyal started discussing how the meeting went and planning for the upcoming procedures.

I saw Mia sneak out from the cabin with Ben, I was curious to know what she was up to this time. I dismissed my staff and Kabir, who had accompanied Daniyal went out along with them.

"Daniyal, do you think Mia is good enough to work on this project? I mean I don't think she is mature and responsible for this job. Don't take me in any other way but the way she behaved today is not good for the image of our firms," I said to Daniyal as soon as we were alone in the cabin.

"Yes, I know she can be a pain in the ass sometimes, but trust me she is very talented and she is one of the best. I am sure if she keeps up the hard work she will be one of the best architects in the country," Daniyal replied.

I was a little surprised by his revelation, I never thought someone like Mia who was so reckless, can be good at their job. I knew Daniyal was intelligent and hard-working and he had done really well in the few years since he established his own firm. And if he was saying she was good at her job meant she must have something.

" If you say so, but how do you tolerate her, I mean if I would have been in your place I would have fired her," I said with amusement.

I didn't want Daniyal to think I had some personal agenda against her, I couldn't tell him about our feud, it will only damage my reputation.

"She is family, and no matter how much you despise them and they embarrass you, you just can't abandon them," He replied smiling.

" Ohh, sorry man. I didn't know she was your sister," I apologized.

"She is my cousin, our parents are really close and I really feel she is a sibling I never had," Daniyal said as he rose from the couch.

" It's getting late, I don't think my wife would like if I stay here for a little while more," He said picking his stuff.

"Ohh, yes. I don't think there is any need to delay our departure, " I collected my stuff and we exited the cabin locking it behind us.

" The labor camp will be set up near the closest village and we can start working on the plan from Monday, " I said as we walked towards the car. I put my stuff in the trunk and then noticed I had forgotten my cell in the cabin.

I asked Daniyal to wait till I get back my cell phone, as I went inside the cabin retrieved my cell and walked out I heard someone shouting.

I turned around and looked, it was Mia she was running towards me. Her face was turned backward and Ben was running behind her. Mia was holding a cell in her hand and was laughing.

I don't know what happened but I didn't move from the spot I was standing. Ben probably saw me because he was looking in front and Mia was looking at him. He called Mia to the lookout but it was late.

She stumbled into me and was about to fall on the ground on her back. My arms shot up and I held her waist, I was pulled towards the ground with her but I managed to balance on time.

She was leaning in my arms holding my shoulders while one of my arms was around her waist holding her tightly and the other had moved up and was holding her neck from behind.

I breathed in her scent, it was so damn good and intoxicating, I found she smelled better than when she met me in that restaurant and pulled that stunt.

Her amber eyes were locked with mine, there was disbelief in them like she didn't expected me to have caught her before she fell on the ground.

She was so close to me her face inches apart from me, my eyes slid down to her lips. They were so luscious and full, I really wanted to dip my head and taste her. I was sure she would slap me if I acted on my wishes.

I felt her breath hitch and realized it was not just me who was affected by our proximity. She bit her upper lip and traced her tongue on it, I was glad to find that she was nervous from being close to me.

Her sass and fire had vanished and she looked anxious as she saw me staring at her with an unknown hunger building inside me.

She was looking in my eyes, waiting, anticipating. She was so damn close to me that I noticed the green-colored streaks around her iris for the first time. Her eyes were beautiful, everything about her was beautiful.

Her hands traveled from my shoulders to my neck and I waited for her to pull me towards her.

"Hey Mia you okay?" Ben asked as he approached us.

Never had I hated anyone so much like I hated Ben at this moment, I wanted to see what she would have done next if Ben had not interrupted us. I pulled her up till she was standing on her feet, then

I loosened my grip on her waist, I ran down my other hand on her back and then pulled away.

I saw her blushing as she pulled her arms from around my neck and turned towards Ben to avoid looking at me. I knew she was affected as I was, she looked embarrassed.

" I am fine Ben, I think Daani is waiting for me, thanks for walking with me on the beach. Here is your cell, " she said to Ben handing him his cell phone as she tried to compose herself.

"Thanks, " She turned and said to me, I looked at her she was still breathing fast and her cheeks were still tainted red, she left before I could reply.

Damn, this girl was driving me crazy, I didn't like the way I was affected by her, and the way I felt when she was in my arms.

" She is so hot, " I heard Ben mutter under his breath, but I heard it.

"She is engaged, and she is Daniyal's cousin. Better not mess around him, " I said to Ben, but I felt I reminded it to myself more than him.

Chapter 9

I was sitting in the car fuming at myself, what the hell was I thinking? How could I let myself get carried away?

I still couldn't forget the way my body burned by his touch, the tingles that erupted all over my body and the shivers that his intense gaze sent through my body.

I have never been so close to any man in my life, not even Imaad. I hated the way my body reacted to his touch, it was not anybody but Waleed Kamal the person I despised most in my life. I felt disgusted by the way I reacted to him, the way he made me feel.

The way his eyes lingered on my lips, and the way my arms traveled from his shoulder to neck like they had a mind of their own. Fuck, what the hell was I thinking? I cursed myself, for acting like that. And I was sure he noticed the way he was affecting me.

If Ben wouldn't have come at that moment I might have done something stupid. I still could feel his touch on my waist, the back of my neck. The way his hand traveled from my neck to my back, it had sent sparks throughout my body.

I thanked God that Daniyal and Kabir had not seen that, they were already waiting for me in the car. The embarrassment would have been doubled.

I still couldn't forget the mischievous smile that Ben gave me when I turned towards him. I was sure he was going to tease me the next time we meet.

Kabir tried many times to engage me in conversation with him and Daniyal, but I didn't feel like talking with anyone right now. I just sat in the back seat listening to them, they dropped me and declined my invitation for dinner politely.

Dad and chachu (father's brother) inquired me about how the case study went and was very enthusiastic that I was getting a chance to work on such a prestigious project.

Dada was more interested in inquiring about Waleed, his friend's grandson. The more I tried to avoid that man the more I had to see him, fate really played funny jokes at us.

The next day was Sunday, mom kept me engaged in the kitchen for preparing lunch. I really admired her determination to make me a master in cooking. Well, at least I was able to fry an omelet without burning it, apart from that I didn't think I made much progress in this department.

I had called Imaad and apologized to him for yesterday, he was upset with me but with a little persuasion, he was normal again and had told me he would pick me up in the evening.

I took a shower and dried my hair, I selected a traditional dress to wear. It had been a long time since Imaad and I went on a date and I really wanted to dress up for him.

The traditional dress Rameen was
wearing on her date with Imaad.

Imaad arrived at 7 O' clock in the evening, he met with my family chatted with them a few minutes before we left for dinner.

He told me he was taking me to a new Italian restaurant while driving. He was looking at me after every few minutes during the drive and I was glad my hard work didn't get wasted. I was sure he liked my dress, he was very fond of the traditional dresses.

The food was great, and most of all I was enjoying his company. He had complimented me nearly a hundred times how good I was looking in my outfit. His eyes barely left me during dinner.

We discussed my new project, he was glad I got a chance to work with such a prestigious firm. Imaad had always supported me in my career, I really admired this quality in him. He had always motivated me to take up challenges.

I asked him about his business and was a bit surprised when he avoided my question and started inquiring about Ali and his studies. I was a bit confused about why he looked a bit uneasy when I inquired about the business.

We discussed our upcoming wedding and the fuss our moms were making regarding everything. He looked as much wearied as I was by the constant nagging of our mothers.

We discussed destinations for our honeymoon, he wanted to go to Australia while I insisted on going to Europe. I think the alpine mountains were the most romantic of all places in the world.

He gave in after a little persuasion from my side, I knew he loved me too much and he would do anything that would make me happy. Sometimes I couldn't believe how lucky I was to have him.

And I was sure my married life was going to be bliss with this wonderful man. I skipped dessert after dinner and ordered coffee, I was dieting these days to fit into my bridal dress, I knew my figure was good but I wanted it to be perfect on my wedding day.

We went for a long drive after dinner listening to our favorite songs. And when we were on the porch of my house I thanked him for the wonderful evening.

"Thanks, Immi. I really had a great time after so many weeks", I said as I turned to pull the handle and was shocked when Imaad held my hand.

I turned and looked at him in surprise when he suddenly leaned and tried to kiss me but instead his lips brushed against my cheek as I had leaned back and turned my face.

He pulled me towards him and turned my face by holding my chin with his fingers.

" What the hell Imaad? Are you out of your mind?" I growled.

"We are getting married in two months", He snapped.

He didn't look please by my rejection of his advances, I was confused, why he was trying to kiss me? He had never tried getting physical with me before even though we had been engaged for more than a year.

" I think we can wait till we get married, it's only a matter of a few weeks", I brushed his hand aside from my chin.

I really didn't understand why I felt repulsed by his touch, he was my fiance and we were getting married in less than two months. I knew these days couples would engage in more than kissing after their engagement.

But I was not ready to for this, I had always thought all this would be after we got married, and I was in no mood to change my mind.

"Mia please, just one kiss, I have been wanting you for so long now, I don't think I can wait more", He said in a husky voice.

I was suddenly panicked by his changed behavior, I noticed he looked a little stressed. He had never made any sexual advances to me until now. I was worried about what had changed now all of sudden.

I was not wearing any sexy outfit today, that he was turned on by it, no matter how bold I was I had no experience in this field.

" I am sorry Immi, but I don't think I am ready for it now, I am sorry if I hurt you but I think we should wait until our wedding", I said and slid out of the car, I noticed he was really upset at my rejection but I couldn't help it.

I went into my room and changed into my nightdress, still thinking of what had passed between us in his car. I was literally puzzled if I had wanted I could have kissed him, it was not such a big deal.

I video called Sheema and added Rania in the conference, me and Sheema had welcomed her in our group, she was a fun-loving girl.

I was desperately in need of talking to someone who could give me some good advice.

I told them what had happened and they started at their screens in shock.

"What the fuck Mia, how could you leave him high and dry?", Rania looked like she would faint due to shock.

" He is so handsome and poor guy is head over heels in love with you", Sheema sympathized with Imaad.

"It was just a kiss, he didn't ask you to make love." Rania was still not able to overcome the shock.

"So did any of you kissed your men?" I asked looking at them with suspicion.

"Of course", Rania replied.

Sheema ignored the question completely, what was she hiding?

" Didn't you wanted to kiss him?" Rania asked.

"I don't know, I mean I thought we had a silent agreement that we would wait till our wedding", I replied.

" So old fashioned", Rania rolled her eyes.

Sheema was just listening to our conversation staring at the screen.

"Babes not everyone snogs their fiancee before their wedding. And it's not accepted in our religion", I said with a frown on my face.

" Meeting the fiance alone at night is also not acceptable in our religion", Rania retorted.

I didn't say anything just rolled my eyes, actually, she was right. This is where our problem lies, we only follow those teachings, which are convenient for us.

"Okay leave it, now tell me what should I do if he tries something like that again?" I asked.

"I don't know", Sheema was of no use, she was too good for her own good.

" Did you feel anything when he touched you? Like butterflies in your stomach or current running through your body or tingles erupting on your skin?" Rania asked.

I didn't feel any of these things which Rania mentioned instead I felt repulsed and don't know, why did I feel like that?

"No, I didn't feel any of these things", I replied honestly.

" Then you are not attracted to him", Rania replied.

"Wtf, I really like him and I am marrying him, how am I not suppose to be attracted to him?" I asked in alarm.

" I mean he doesn't excite you sexually, you like him but maybe in a platonic way", She replied.

Now I was really confused, I like a guy to the extent that I accept his proposal to marry him and I am not attracted to him sexually? What the hell?

"Rania I don't understand what you are saying, will you elaborate", I said.

" Look did it ever happened to you that when a guy touched you or you touched him you felt a wave of excitement through your body? Or some shivers from his touch?" Rania asked.

I went into a state of shock, all these things I had felt when Waleed had saved me from falling. So was I attracted to Waleed Kamal sexually?

Dammit, I hate that guy and I really despise him, how the fuck was I attracted to him. Rania doesn't know anything she is just bull shitting.

"So did you?" Sheema asked.

"Did I what?" I asked, my mind was still trying to figure out what was that I wanted?

"Did you feel those things with any guy?" Sheema said gritting her teeth.

"No" I lied.

"Then it's simple, you are asexual", Rania replied laughing.

" Very funny", I said rolling my eyes.

These girls were as lame as I was in this department, we just talked about how our weekend went and just the usual stuff and discon-nected.

My confusion had only increased after the call, I was literally clue-less about how I was feeling. But one thing was for sure I didn't like it when Imaad tried to kiss me. And I think the reason is I am just following my religious teachings.

Waleed

I had come to the Italian restaurant for a meeting, don't panic guys I am workaholic and it doesn't matter if it's weekend. My firm is my first priority.

My client was going abroad for two months on Monday and want-ed to finalize the last details, so here I was discussing while having dinner.

We were in the middle of our dinner when I noticed a couple entering the restaurant. I recognized her immediately, though she looked completely different today. She was wearing a traditional dress and I couldn't help but admire that whatever she wore she always carried it with grace.

She had curled her hairs today and had braided them, I think like that girl in the Disney movie, who freezes everything. Why can't I remember her name, Rania had made us watch that movie and I had hated every bit of it. Girls and their obsession with Disney princesses, I could never understand that.

She was with the same guy I had seen her dancing at Sheema's birthday, the way they were looking at each other and smiling, anyone could have figured out he was her fiance.

The guy was okk, I mean he was good looking, but there was nothing remarkable in him other than his looks, no I am not jealous.

I mean she was beautiful, and today she was looking gorgeous, all eyes in the restaurant were fixed at her. I was ogling her and so was my client, and I was not really pleased with it.

If she had been with me I would have killed every guy in the restaurant who was looking at her, but fortunately, she wasn't. She only had eyes for her fiance, whom I noticed was barely keeping his arms off her.

They were busy in conversation with each other, and I was finding it extremely difficult to focus my mind on what my client was saying. This never happened to me before that I was not able to concentrate in a meeting because of a girl.

I had my share of girls, I liked hanging out with them. Going on dates once in a while but never had a girl occupied my mind to this extent as Mia.

I think I was overthinking about her, I was not able to concentrate because that girl was the only girl who didn't give a damn who I was.

She was absolutely not my type, I always liked girls who were easy going well behaved, whom you can take home to meet your family. Mia was the exact opposite, she was wild, insolent and defiant.

But today she was looking like a complete girl next door, the warm smiles and nods she gave her fiance were so different from the glares I usually received from her.

No matter how much I tried, I couldn't take my mind off her, especially when I had held her in my arms.

The way she got nervous from my touch and stares, the way she traced her tongue on her lip. Dammit Waleed get a grip on yourself, she is just a girl and there are millions like her in this world or even better.

The next week went busy with meetings with Shah and the team working on this project.

Mia had been sensible this whole time, and I thought it was a miracle. A week went by and that girl hadn't exploded, it was a feat in itself.

The month passed smoothly, with the labor camp being constructed on the outskirts of the nearby village of our construction site. To decrease the cost we had just built cabins which were cost and energy-efficient for the laborers.

We had drafted a rough plan of the resort in the month and it had been approved by the partners.

The administration building, restaurant, and spa was assigned to the architects from my firm while the rooms and villas, the common swimming pool was assigned to architects from Daniyal's firm.

We had a deadline of nine months to complete this project and I always tried to complete the projects before them.

We have been working our asses off this project, my architects had come up with really good plans for the buildings and I was looking forward to our next meeting with Daniyal and his employees where we were going to discuss the designs our architects have come up with.

One month into the project the meeting was arranged with the architects of both our firms and we had to select the plans we were going to show to our clients.

The presentation was going well, I have to admit the architects from both our firms had really done a good job.

After a few discussions and little changes, we had finalized the design for the administrative building, which was designed by the senior-most architect of my firm.

The same was the procedure with the restaurant, spa swimming pool, and the rooms.

Mia was assigned the task to design the villas, and I had to admit her plan was really good, she had made use of the allotted space really well.

She had designed two types of villas one was a single story and one was a duplex. The single-story was as per the requirements of the client's but the duplex villa was a little variant and I had the opinion that it was good on paper but, it won't be good enough after construction.

I raised my points and I found out it didn't go down well with her, she looked quite annoyed by my criticism. And I was surprised by her reaction, I had criticized other architects as well but everyone had taken it in good spirit.

Daniyal had shared my views and we had advised her to come up with a revised plan within two days, I know it was not possible but we had a meeting with our client and have to present the plan to them.

After the meeting, everyone had left and I came back to my office, Daniyal had told me he was going to meet an engineer of my firm and he would join me later.

My Secretary came in after a few minutes, informing me that Ms. Shahab has requested an immediate audience with me. I took a deep breath and asked my secretary to send her in, I know what was coming, she must have taken my criticism personally.

I never mixed personals with business, I was highly professional in every dealing and that was the reason I never had engaged with Mia in any personal discussion while working on this project.

Whatever happened between us was past and now we were working on a project together and needed to act in a truly professional way. But with Mia, I think it was not a possibility.

Chapter 10

Rameen

I stormed into his office, he was sitting on his office chair, behind his desk, his laptop in front of him.

"How could you? I thought you were a professional, I never imagined you could bring our feud into this", I thundered.

He was looking at me extremely calmly his grey eyes fixed on me as if he was expecting this, it made me angrier than I was.

" I am talking to you", I said as I furrowed my brow in anger.

"Take a seat Ms. Shahab", He said in a cold tone, his deep voice making it more intimidating.

I felt like someone poured a bucket of ice water on me, my anger vanished and I felt puzzled, I had expected him to yell back at me, but right now he was playing the cold sexy CEO.

I pursed my lips into a tight line and sat across him. I wanted to listen to what he had to say in his defense. He had criticized me in front of the whole team and had just given two days to come up with a new design for the villa, which was not impossible but extremely difficult.

We stared at each other for a few minutes, and I was determined to not be the one to break the stare down. He took a deep breath and diverted his gaze to the laptop.

" Ms.Shahab, I am sorry, if I gave you the impression that my criticism was based on the personal feud between us. But I can assure you it was just a professional remark", Waleed said looking into my eyes again.

I gave out the breath I was holding for long, I didn't want to believe but he sounded sincere and honest.

"Ms. Shahab, I believe in breaking the stereotype. I don't want to be the rule I want to be an exception.

You can disagree with my views, but as long as this project is concerned you will have to synchronize yourself with my way of working.

I know it's not easy, and I might be making an already challenging project much harder than it is. I can't describe to you, the feeling of contentment and satisfaction when your hard work pays off", He was saying and I was concentrating on the warmth in his voice.

It was like he was opening up himself to me, he could have just ordered me out without any explanation because he had the power to do it, instead, he shared with me a part of himself.

I agree he was making the project more difficult than it already was by setting his standard so high that an average person can never think of it.

But I was not an average individual, I was Rameen Shahab, and I loved challenges. I can prove to Waleed Kamal no matter how awry I can be sometimes, I was one of the best architects in the city.

And I will make him admit it, I will change the misconceptions he had regarding me, Daani had told me that Waleed thought I was not good enough for the project, because of the one mistake of mine of not turning my cell silent.

I admit, it was carelessness on my part, but that doesn't mean I was not good enough at my job.

" Ms. Shahab, are you listening?" He asked me, I had zoned out on him.

Shit.

"Yes, I am, Mr. Kamal", I lied.

In truth, I had missed the last sentence he had said to me.

" Okay, I will call Mr. Khan to help you out", He continued.

"Ohh no, please. I think I will manage by myself", I replied in hurry afraid he might call his head architect.

I wanted to surprise him, by doing it all by myself and was not ready to share the credit with anyone.

I might need to spend two sleepless nights, but I was ready for the challenge.

" Are you sure Ms. Shahab, you just have two days, it will be a lot easier for you if you let Khan help you", He looked uncertain, maybe he didn't think I was up to the challenge?

And I was going to prove him wrong, you might have just witnessed the wild side of me, Waleed Kamal. Trust me the professional side of me is going to blow away your mind.

"I have never been more sure of anything else, in my life before", I replied with a broad smile.

I have heard in my professional circles how Waleed Kamal was different from others, but I have never believed it.

But now, I do.

I had spent the next two days on the plan of the duplex villa, sleeping merely for two hours each night. I had never pushed myself, to this extent to prove myself to anyone before, but I wanted to prove Waleed wrong. I wanted to show him I have it in me to be the best.

Mom and aunt were not very pleased with my efforts to please the arrogant CEO, they were concerned I was ruining my beauty by skipping meals and sleep.

Aunt went to the extent to drag me in front of the mirror and pointing out my dark circles in the morning the meeting was scheduled to be held when I was getting ready for office.

They were worried about the fact my wedding was in two weeks and if I kept overworking myself I would be the most awful bride. Umair went to the extent to tease me that I might look like a zombie bride.

I ignored their remarks as I gulped down toast with tea, and left when I heard the horn of my office Van.

Daani had told me to come directly to the office of KKC so that he and Waleed could go through my design before they presented it to the clients.

Waleed's secretary ushered me to his office directly where Waleed and Daniyal were waiting for me. Daniyal gave me a curious smile as I turned on my laptop, while Waleed was sitting with a blank expression.

I won't lie but I was feeling nervous, I know my design is very good, but Waleed had a very different way of doing things and I was worried if he would reject it.

They looked at my laptop screen with anticipation as I turned and showed them my work, Daniyal's eyes lit up instantly as I started demonstrating each detail. I could feel how proud he was of me, and I was glad I didn't disappoint him.

Waleed was looking at the screen with a serious expression and when I paused after completing my presentation he sighed as if he gave out a breath he had been holding for long.

" Excellent, Ms. Shahab. Honestly, I was not expecting you might pull this off, in two days without any help", Finally, he said.

And I felt a way of excitement travel through my body, I never expected him to praise me with such honesty. He looked impressed with my work, never had I felt this way before when anyone had complimented my work.

But coming from the mouth of this arrogant and control freak CEO, it was really special. It was as if I had gained recognition for my work in the eyes of the whole world.

"I am so proud of you Mia, I knew you would never disappoint me", Daani said tapping my shoulder.

I was sure I was grinning like an idiot, Waleed was looking at me with an amused expression.

" Thanks, I am really glad you both approve of my work", I replied gratefully.

" I am trying to wrap my head around it, great job", Waleed said smiling.

"I am sure you will come out of the shock soon", I said teasingly.

" Believe me, I am trying hard", He replied.

Daniyal passed both of us a glance, I sensed he was surprised with the ease in which we were speaking to each other.

And I was surprised too, I had never thought we could ever warm up to each other. I still believe he is an arrogant asshole but at least he was trying to be civil and I appreciated his effort.

Waleed

I congratulated our team for their hard work, Shah and his partners had just left the conference, room and they looked impressed with our plan for the resort.

The hard work of all the architects had paid off, and everyone looked relax as if a great burden had been lifted from their bodies.

"But let's not forget, we still have a lot of things to work on, I would like you guys to start working on the elevations of the buildings", I couldn't help it, I was a control freak and perfectionist and I wanted everything to be of the highest standards.

" Yes, boss", My firm employees replied in unison, while Daniyal and his team nodded in agreement.

"I did like to make an announcement", Mia said as she stood up.

" Yes", I looked at her in surprise.

"I am getting married, a fortnight from today and I would like you all to bless my wedding with your presence", She said with enthusiasm.

She was overflowing with joy and emotions, and I don't know why I felt a little distressed. I knew she was engaged and was getting married, really soon from Saad still I didn't expect it to be so soon.

We had started to warm up to each other and there was a chance we could get along well in the future, but I didn't like the idea of seeing her with any other man.

She had surprised me earlier today with her work, honestly, I was not expecting that she might complete it within such a limited time. I had asked Khan to design the villa in case she was not able to complete it, which I thought was quite obvious due to her reckless attitude.

But she had blown away my mind, she just not had completed it, but it was better than what Khan had designed and shown me before Daniyal arrived.

Khan was considered to be one of the top three architects in the city and with an experience of nearly two decades, I was sure Mia would be no match for his expertise and here she proved me wrong.

I had felt a sudden urge in my heart to get to know her better, and I had planned to do that but now listening to her announcing her wedding I was grim.

" And this is going to be my last week with you all before I officially take the title of Mrs. Imaad Hassan", She added mischievously.

She pulled out her wedding invitations from her bag and started handing out to each of the team members personally.

Everyone had surrounded her and started congratulating her for the upcoming event. I felt like storming out of the conference room. But I had to put a facade of joy in front of everyone.

Everyone started leaving the room one by one until just Daniyal and Mia were left along with me. She approached me, where I was standing near the Screen and handed me out an invitation card, and said.

"I would be glad if you would come",

I took the card from her with a polite thank you and was about to leave when Daniyal got a call and excused himself.

I was dying to say something to her to make her feel miserable and scratch away the smile playing on her lips from the inner joy.

" Ms. Shahab, you should have not taken up this project, if you were planning to get married. It's highly unprofessional to take a long leave of absence for more than a month when we are expected to complete this project on the given deadline", I saw the change of expression on her face.

She was looking at me in shock like she couldn't register the words I had just spoken.

She opened her mouth to say something, I wanted to hear what she had to say. The joy had vanished from her eyes and had been replaced by hurt and resentment. She kept looking at me with contempt and then turned and walked out of the room.

I hated myself for hurting her, but I couldn't help it. I was completely oblivious to why I was feeling like this and what made me act in such a way.

Shah had arranged lunch on the site in celebration of keeping the foundation stone of the resort on Friday. He had invited all the employees from our firm who were part of this project.

It was a grand event, the decorations and catering were the best, what else can you expect from a Five Star Hotels and Resorts chain owner.

I reached the gathering late than the mentioned time because of the last moment meeting with another client. All guest have already arrived before me, I greeted Shah who had come along with his wife. His partners were also accompanied by their spouses.

I looked around and to my astonishment, everyone was present in pairs, I cursed myself for forgetting to bring a date along with me.

Daniyal approached me with his wife Reema, she was an elegant, lady. They greeted me and Daniyal asked me why I didn't have a date with me.

"I totally forgot, it had been a busy week as you know", I told him and he nodded in agreement.

" Mia is also alone, her fiance couldn't make it due to some business. I am sure you both can give each other company", Reema said pointing to her right side.

My eyes followed the direction in which she pointed and I found Mia, standing there with Ben and a girl, who most probably was Ben's date.

My breath caught up in my lungs, she was wearing a dark pink lace dress and beige colored shoes. She had set her hairs in a French roll, with natural makeup and pink lipstick she was enough to tempt a saint, and I was just a hot-blooded male.

I was ogling her when I heard someone clearing their throat beside me, it was Daniyal. Fuck, he had caught me staring at Mia, I felt embarrassed to have got carried away like that.

"I wonder who is Ben's date, doesn't look like from my firm", I said looking in their direction.

Daniyal just shrugged his shoulders and walked away. Dammit, he must be mad at me, I followed Daniyal and pulled his arm and stopped him.

" I am sorry, I didn't mean to. I don't know what happened to me", I apologized.

Daniyal kept looking at me for some moments and then said.

"She is about to get married, and I would advise you to stay away from her".

I just nodded in agreement, I wanted to go to Mia, sort her out and speak to her and apologize for being such a dick in our last meeting, but I realized it won't go down well with Daniyal.   Mia was avoiding me, probably because of the way I behaved the last time. I kept myself engaged with Shah and his partners.

Food was arranged in a buffet, I noticed Mia sitting lonely, at a table in the last row near the beach. I looked around for Daniyal, he was busy chatting with his wife, I planned to approach her and then turned and went to the table where Daniyal and his wife were sitting.

Daniyal was back to normal again, we started discussing a project when his wife got a call, and her expression change to panic.

" Daani, dad had had a heart attack. He is been taken to the hospital", She said panicked.

And before I could realize they both left apologizing to Shah and his wife. I finished lunch and just strolled to the spot where the columns were finished digging and the first column had been filled with concrete by Shah.

I stood there for nearly half an hour without any reason and went back when one of my employees told me the partners were looking for me.

People had started getting dispersed, everyone was going towards their vehicles, I bid them goodbye and went to the cabin. It was empty, I sat there sulking about what happened earlier and all of a sudden, I remembered Mia was still here, she hadn't left with Daniyal.

I came out of the cabin and looked around for her, mostly everyone had left barring the employees of the company that arranged the lunch.

There was an engineer from my firm, walking towards the parking. I strolled towards him and asked if he had seen Mia leave with anyone. He replied he didn't know if she had left or not. I looked around but there were no women around, maybe she left with some of her colleagues.

I went back to the cabin and just laid on the couch, I was upset with myself, for the last five days for mistreating Mia. She looked so happy when she invited me and I being an asshole, had killed her happiness.

I heard some voices from outside the cabin, it was a female voice and I could recognize it from a million other voices, I rushed outside and there she was standing completely panicked speaking with a man who was rounding up the chairs.

"Mia", I called out.

She turned and looked towards me, and I saw the instant relief that spread on her face, I noticed she was barefoot and was holding her shoes in one hand and her clutch in the other.

" What are you doing here?" I asked as she walked towards me.

I was afraid to think about what she would have done if I had left along with everyone.

"I went to the beach for a walk and lost the count of time and when I returned everyone was gone. I just can't believe Daani left me behind", She replied.

No matter how mad I was at her for being so reckless, I kept a calm composure, I didn't want to start an argument with her, when this could turn out to be our last meeting before I see her again after her wedding.

"Reema's father had a heart attack, they left in a hurry", I informed her.

" Ohh, I see"   "My other colleagues have also left, I don't know how I will go back", She looked worried.

" I will drop you", I replied.

She looked at me with gratification, there was no need for it. I would have done this no matter who the girl was. I couldn't leave her there in the middle of nowhere.

"Thanks", She replied.

" I need to use the restroom if you don't mind", She said.

I went back inside the cabin and she followed me, I gave her direction for the restroom and sat on the couch waiting for her.

Chapter 11

Rameen

I washed my feet to remove the sand grains stuck on them, I loved walking on beaches barefoot, just listening to the sound of waves splashing. It works as a stress buster for me, and today I have been feeling awful.

Imaad had been acting weird in the past few weeks, always trying to getting close to me. Caressing my hands or my face, made me feel sick to my stomach. I don't know why I felt like that but his touch made me uncomfortable in a bad way.

I even googled for signs of being in love and how I should feel when my partner touches me, they also showed the same symptoms which Rania had told me earlier. I was freaking out, was something wrong with me? Was I abused sexually in my childhood that I was feeling like this? But as far as I can remember nothing of such sort ever happened, instead, I was blessed with the perfect childhood.

Today when he picked me up for the lunch he looked normal, but when we were a little far from my home he tried to kiss me again after he had parked the car to get a call.

And I had snapped, I rushed out of the car and hired a cab to go to Daniyal's house, I couldn't go back to my home because then everyone would ask questions, hence I went to Daani. And luckily enough those two were just leaving for lunch. I told them Imaad had to go for some emergency meeting and he had dropped me here so I could go with them.

My mind was occupied by Imaad's changed behavior, we have been engaged for more than a year and why did he start acting like this out of the blue when our wedding was in just one week.

Something was wrong, and I couldn't figure out what it was. There was a reason why Imaad was behaving like this and I was not able to understand what, unless he was taking some drugs and was horny.

I washed my hands, splashed some water on my face, dried myself with tissue, and walked out of the bathroom.

Waleed was waiting for me, as soon as he saw me he stood up from the couch. I had met him for the first time after he insulted me after the meeting. I couldn't understand this guy either, he looked so impressed with me before the meeting and was really warming up to me and suddenly he started behaving like a dickhead.

Daniyal knew about my wedding and still, he insisted me to work on this project. I was not ready to take this in the first place because of my history with Waleed. But Daniyal had forced me and here I was working my butt off on this project when I should have been busy with my wedding preparations.

And this guy had the audacity to call me unprofessional and insult me, I so hated him.

We walked out of the cabin and Waleed locked it after him, he guided me to his car and opened the door for me, he was being a perfect gentleman today.

I was feeling hungry, I had barely eaten lunch and had wandered off to the beach, and sat there in an isolated place hidden from the view from the spot where the luncheon was arranged.

I knew Daani would look for me before they leave, and I didn't care about how much time I sat there thinking about my upcoming wedding.

I wanted to talk to Imaad about his changed behavior, or maybe he was trying to make me comfortable before our wedding, for the deed. I blushed even thinking about it, I like Imaad. I like him very much, it's just that I couldn't figure out my feelings, and why I didn't feel any excitement from his touch.

"You okay?" Waleed asked me after some time while driving.

"Yeah, I am fine", I replied.

I didn't have anything to say further, so I just kept quiet and stared out of the window looking at the passing scenery.

" So, is yours a love marriage?" Waleed asked I didn't expect him to ask me any personal question.

"Imaad and I had known each other for as long as I remember", I replied.

" Childhood Sweethearts then", He muttered under his breath but I heard him.

"Not exactly, we were just friends, actually I always considered him as a friend. But I didn't know he had other plans", I said remembering the day he had proposed to me, I had never expected anything like that.

" You didn't love him?" He asked.

I don't know why he was suddenly interested in me and Imaad.

"I don't believe in love, but I believe in commitment and relationship. I think trust is more important in a relationship than love ever can be" I replied.

"So you mean, you don't love your fiance", He said looking at me astonished.

" I don't know, I like him and I have feelings about him but how can I know it's love", I said looking at him annoyed.

I didn't like to discuss personals with anyone, yet here I was discussing with Waleed Kamal from all the people in the world, about my love life and relationship.

"Have you ever loved someone?" I asked him, as I was done with answering his questions about my life.

" No, I have liked many girls but it was never close to love", He replied honestly.

"How many girlfriends did you have till now?" I asked him after his comment about liking many girls.

"I don't do girlfriends, I just go on dates with girls, once in a while, never have been in a relationship", He said looking at me curiously.

" You don't think you should have waited to fall in love with someone before getting married, I mean love can happen at any time", He turned the tables towards me.

"I don't think I am ever gonna fall in love, liking is the most anyone gonna get from me", I replied joking.

" Not even your husband?" He asked.

"I can't predict the future", I replied rolling my eyes.

He became silent again like he was thinking about something, I was grateful he didn't ask me any personal questions again.

We discussed the lunch and our project, and thankfully he asked me if I would like to eat something. I was nearly starving, I just shook my head in agreement.

He took a diversion from the highway to a nearby village, then he stopped in front of a small roadside eatery. I looked at him in surprise this didn't look like a place where a billionaire would go.

" What"? He asked rolling his eyes.

I just looked at him questioningly.

"You will love the food", He said as he slid out of the car and walked towards my side, and opened the door for me.

A teenage boy came running out of the shed and greeted Waleed, I was shocked to find he was chatting with the boy like he had known him for ages.

" How is your school going Abdul? I hope you are going regularly", He asked the boy as he sat comfortably on the traditional woven cot.

" I have topped my class in the last exam", The boy replied grinning.

"Fantastic, keep up the good work", He said to the boy and started ordering the food.

I was looking at him with curiosity, he had taken off his jacket and folded his shirt-sleeves above his elbows, and removed his tie. This was a completely different side of Waleed that I was witnessing.

" This is my native place, my grandfather lives here in our ancestral home. He has started a school for the village children. I would have taken you to meet him, but it's getting late and your family would be worried about you", He said sensing my curiosity.

"Ohh" I replied.

" I use to come to this Dhaba (roadside eatery or restaurant) with Dada, we still come here often on the weekends. I love desi food, honestly, I don't enjoy eating in fancy restaurants, as much as I love eating here" He continued.

I was looking at him with interest in my eyes, never have I thought, I could be sitting in a remote village in a Dhaba and enjoying a conversation with Waleed. If someone would have told me this a month ago, I would have advised them to get a life.

He shared with me some of the incidents of his childhood when he used to come here with his grandfather, I didn't realize but I was enjoying my time with him.

The food was really good better than I had ever eaten in those fancy and expensive restaurants. He had ordered butter chicken and Daal Makhani (a dish made from lentils) with naan (a type of bread).

"I only ate a few rolls in the lunch, I had planned to stop here on my way back", He said to me.

I looked and smiled at him, this was one new thing I discovered about him that he was a foodie.

" How do you manage to keep a fit body?" I asked teasing.

" I work out", He replied smiling.

We finished the food pretty quickly, first it was mouth-watering, and second, we both were starving. He ordered two cups of tea, I was not in a mood but he insisted that it was really good.

I agreed with him about the tea it was amazing, I asked him how come it's so good, he replied it was because of the fresh milk from the buffaloes, the owner of the Dhaba kept.

The drive back to the city was silent, I was so full that I was feeling sleepy and Waleed seemed like he was in deep thoughts.

I directed him to my house, and when he parked in front of the gate, I thanked him.

He was looking at me with his same intense gaze which made tingles erupt on my body then he lifted his arm and traced his finger from my cheek to my lips. My whole body was on fire, with just a trace of his finger making butterflies flutter in my stomach.

I was stunned, I could not even think properly, my heart was beating as if it would break out of my rib cage. I was looking at him dumbfounded, his finger halted for a second near the edge of my lips, and I leaned in his touch involuntarily. He then traced his thumb on my bottom lip slowly, real, the tip of his thumb just touching the edge of my upper lip as it traveled on my lip, tugging it at the corner.

"Thanks, Mia, for the wonderful evening", He said as he retracted his hand from my face.

I was breathing heavily, my heart, breaking all records in beating and when I was able to gather my senses, I opened the door and nearly ran out of his car.

Waleed

Mia had just left my car, I was still looking at my hand. My fingers were twitching from her touch, I wanted more. She was driving me crazy, I had never lost control in my life. But she made me do things I had never imagined in my life.

She was fire and I wanted to burn myself in her heat. From the moment she entered my car I wanted to touch her, to experience how her skin felt below my fingers. And I couldn't fathom the sparks that traveled through my body when I touched her.

I wanted to crush my lips on hers, but I knew she would never allow it. I knew it wasn't just me who was affected, Mia felt the same. The way she leaned in my touch the way her eyes were fixed on me.

I knew I was treading dangerous waters, but I didn't care. She was different, from all the girls I have dated, she was never intimidated by me. She didn't care about my status or my money, she was wild and untamed. And I knew she was not mine, she could never be mine.

The more the truth dawned on me that I can never have her the more I wanted her. The more I got to know about her the more I fell for her.

She told me she didn't believe in love, and I wanted to accept her challenge and show her what she was missing in life.

I sat there in my car outside her house for a long time, expecting to get a glimpse of her from any window or balcony. Yes, I was officially a stalker now.

I told myself, I was feeling like this, just because I couldn't have her. I turned the key in the ignition and the engine roared to life. I reversed my car and left after giving up hope that I might see her again.

The next week was hell for me, I couldn't take my mind off her, as the day of her wedding approached my restlessness increased. I had never wanted anyone in my life as I wanted her. She had raised havoc in my life since the day she came into it.

I had ordered a gift for her, but I planned not to go to her wedding, I can't bear watching her with any other man.

Asjad and Saad were busy with Mia's wedding functions, I was invited too. But I made excuses that I was busy with work as usual when they both insisted me to go with them.

I tried boxing, playing video games on my Xbox, and watching documentaries to keep my mind busy and not to think about her, but I was failing miserably. No matter how much I tried not to think about her I was thinking more and more about her.

Dada arrived a day before her wedding to my utter disbelief, I had been insisting him for months to come and say stay with me for some time but he always made some excuses.

And when I asked him, how come he decided to come now, he replied he had to attend a wedding. I was upset because he came for attending a wedding and not for me. But still, I was grateful he came, at least my mind would get diverted from her thoughts.

I spent Saturday night talking to Dada till midnight until I was sure I will fall asleep the moment, I hit my head on the pillow.

At least sleep was kinder to me than my fate, I slept peacefully through the night and woke up to a beautiful morning.

Dada was waiting for me for breakfast, he started asking about work while having breakfast then all of a sudden he said.

" Be ready by 4 in the evening we will be attending the Nikah (Marriage vows) Ceremony of my friend's granddaughter".

I was surprised why Dada wanted me to accompany him to the marriage of someone I didn't even know.

"Dada, what will I do there? It's better if you would go alone", I said.

Dada looked at me annoyed, I was not expecting this reaction from him, he usually listened to whatever I say and never insist me on anything.

" You are going with me, and I don't want any excuse", He said and walked out of the dining room.

This was a sign that he wanted no more tantrums from me and I have to abide by what he says. I took a deep breath and growled, a wedding was the last thing I wanted to attend.

I called the jeweler whom I had ordered Mia's gift after breakfast. He told me it was ready, I called the florist and told him to arrange a bouquet, exactly like the picture I sent him.

I called my driver to pick the bouquet and gift and then deliver it to Mia's home. I insisted him to make sure he handed it to Mia.

As ordered Dada knocked at my door at 4 p.m., I was already dressed as instructed by him. We got into the car and Dada gave the driver the name of the person whose house we were going to.

My heart stopped beating when our car halted in front of Mia's house.

Shit.

I never thought Dada could be friends with Rameen's grandfather, how idiot I was I knew she was getting married today, and I should have at least asked Dada whose wedding he was attending.

But now it was too late, I was here standing outside her house with my Dada. I wanted to run away, I tried to recall all my sins for which God was publishing me like this.

Chapter 12

R ameen

"Mia, wake up", Sheema was shaking me, trying to wake me up.

I was so exhausted and sleepy I couldn't even open my eyes.

" Let me sleep", I said as I pulled a cushion beside me and covered my face with it.

"Mia it's your wedding day", Rania slapped on my arms.

" Ouch!!" I exclaimed.

"Even dogs are more loyal than you", I cried in pain.

" Fuck these functions, I never thought a wedding can be so exhausting", I said as I rolled my blankets over and sat up rubbing my face.

"Wait till you find out what happens next", Rania said giggling.

I pulled the cushion and threw it at her, she ducked it easily and it hit Umair who entered my room.

"A man is here for you, Waleed Kamal sent him", Umair said.

" What does he want now?", I asked surprised.

I remembered the incident from a few days back when the bastard touched me. I was surprised by this guy, he knew I was engaged and was getting married in a week and still, he had the nerve to touch me like that.

I was mad at him and I was mad at myself for not slapping him at that moment. I had never expected he might do something like that. I thought he despised me, his eyes had kept me disturbed for nights. The intensity of his grey eyes, the unknown emotion they held, and the touch that lit up my whole body.

I was not supposed to think about him in this way, I was engaged and soon I would be someone else wife, but his touch affected me. It made me crave for him, and that was not an option for me. I hated him for making me feel like that, he should have controlled himself.

"Come fast, he has got flowers and said he was instructed to deliver them to you in person", Umair said with a bored expression.on his face.

I looked at Sheema and Rania, they both were looking at me curiously. I ignored their gazes and followed Umair to the drawing-room where the man was waiting.

I recognized the man immediately, he was Waleed's driver, I have seen him on a few occasions with Waleed.

" Mam, Waleed Sir has sent this for you, and he had instructed me to hand it to you personally", The driver said as he gave me the bouquet and a gift box.

I took it from him and thanked him, the driver left immediately. I removed the card from the bouquet and started reading it.

"Congratulations on your Wedding,

Waleed Kamal".

I kept the bouquet on the center table and held the gift box in my hand, it was a slender long rectangular box.

I opened it and looked at the item inside with astonishment, it was a charms bracelet with miniatures of a coffee cup, a girl in a white gown, a book, a duplex villa, a car, and a teacup.

I knew what it meant, it was all our meetings assembled on a bracelet. I retrieved it from the box and marveled at its beauty. It was set in platinum and each charm was studded with diamonds and gemstones. I was sure this was worth a King's ransom.

" Oooh Pretty", Rania said as she slid the bracelet from my hand.

"What the hell Rania", I shrieked.

" Sheema have a look, Waleed Kamal has got the hots for our darling Mia", She teased me.

I glared at her, Sheema snatched the bracelet from Rania and looked at it with wide eyes.

"Do you realize, it's worth a fortune", Sheema said astonished.

I didn't reply to her, I didn't know what to say, I could never understand this man and what he wanted.

" Liar", My subconscious said.

"He wants you"

"No he don't, you are just imagining things", I snapped at my subconscious.

I didn't want to think about him, it was my wedding day and I felt he had already ruined it for me. Why for God's sake, this man can't see me happy?

" What's going on between you too", Sheema asked with suspicion.

"What the fuck, this is what you think about me?" I hissed at her.

"I mean had he ever said that he likes you?" She said embarrassed.

"I don't know, what he wants", I replied.

" It's quite simple Mia, he wants you", Rania interfered in the conversation for the first time.

"Why did he gift something like this to me?" I said disturbed.

"Because he wants you to remember him whenever you see this, I don't understand what this car signifies though", Rania said examining the bracelet carefully.

I knew exactly what it signified, but I couldn't tell it to any of them. It would be too weird, they would ask me why I didn't kick him in his balls for doing something like that.

"He drove me home from the site, last week", I said censoring the significant detail.

"Okay", They both replied in unison.

"What are you gonna do about this?" Sheema asked.

"I will return it to him of course", I replied.

I shoved the bracelet in the box and hid it under my shirt when I heard voices outside the drawing-room.

We came back to my room, I hid the bracelet between my clothes in my wardrobe. There was chaos around the house, everyone was busy with the arrangements.

I barely ate anything during breakfast, my hunger famished after seeing Waleed's gift. I never thought he could ever want me, The Waleed Kamal, CEO of KKC the most eligible bachelor in town wanted a girl like me.

" Mia you need to eat properly, you have a long day ahead. And stop thinking about that dickhead, he is an asshole for gifting something like that on your wedding" Rania snapped as she gulped down the paratha (a type of bread) with halwa (a type of dessert)

"I don't know I am still in shock, I never thought that he would ever think about me in this way", I said rotating the spoon in my hand.

" Mia do you like him?" Sheema asked.

"Of course, no, you both know I like Imaad", I replied.

" Then just stop thinking about that asshole, and think about your beautiful future with Imaad", Rania said and stuffed my mouth with the Paratha.

I took a shower and dried my hair waiting for the beautician to arrive. The jewelry and the bridal dress had arrived a day before from the designer.

Sheema had laid them on my bed, it was a chili red colored lehenga with an intricate flower pattern. I had selected this myself, I loved the red color and it was a must on my wedding day. I was looking out of the window when I saw Imaad's father and his uncle coming out of their car, I was surprised why they had come at this time it was only 1 O'clock, and the nikah was scheduled at 5 in the evening.

Sheema came into my room after half an hour, she looked pale and disturbed, I started panicking I knew something was wrong.

"What happened"? I asked her.

" I don't know what to say Mia", She replied, her voice being hoarse as if she would break down any moment.

"Sheema stop panicking me", I cried.

" Imaad's father wants that fifty percent of your company to be transferred to Imaad's name", Sheema said.

I looked at her in shock, I was doubting her mental health, How could Hassan uncle ask something like that?

"You are kidding right?" I asked with suspicion.

"No Mia, it's true", She said.

" They have given time to think till the nikah and if your family agrees they will proceed with the wedding or they will call it off", Sheema said further.

I felt like someone has pulled the ground from below my feet, I fell on the floor, holding my head in both hands.

No, this can't be happening, Imaad can't do this with me. I have to speak to Imaad he will tell me it's all a joke, he loves me right he can't ditch me like this.

I looked for my cell hysterically and dialed his number when I found it. He received the call after a few rings.

" Imaad this isn't true right?" I said, as soon as I heard his voice.

"It's true Mia, tell your family to do as my father tells them and everything will be alright," He said calmly.

I couldn't believe what I was hearing, Imaad can't do this, he loved me and he doesn't want anything else than me.

Sheema hugged me, and we both started crying in each other's arms. No one told me what was happening after that, the beautician came and my mom instructed me to get ready.

I asked Sheema and Rania if my family had agreed to their demands they said that they were discussing it and I should do as my beautician asked me, the elders were trying to sort the matter and I should trust them.

I didn't feel like doing anything, I just wanted to punch Imaad till death for causing this misery to my family.

It was nearly 4:30 in the evening, the beautician had finished setting my hair into a beautiful and fancy style and was now started prepping my face for the makeup.

I looked for Sheema and Rania and they were not in my room, my Nikah was scheduled at 5, it was normal if I got delayed by an hour or two and I was hoping everything was sorted out before it was too late.

Waleed

As we entered her house I felt something different in the air, it was nothing like the usual house looked on a wedding day.

We were greeted by a young boy, and he directed us to the drawing-room, Mia's grandfather and father entered the drawing-room, they both were looking distressed.

I looked at Dada, he also glanced at me. We greeted them with the usual greetings and her grandfather started inquiring about Dada and me.

I was going through an emotional turmoil, this was the last place I had wanted to be right now and here I was sitting, smiling and answering her grandfather's inquiries.

I felt a sudden urge to see her, it was so intense that I was barely able to hold myself from running inside the house to her and carrying her away with me to somewhere remote, where no one could find us.

I was so engrossed in my thoughts I didn't even notice Mia's father rising from the sofa and asking me to accompany him inside. I felt a wave of excitement travel through my body, maybe I could get to see a glimpse of her.

The living room was deserted, only two three people were sitting on the sofa and discussing something serious, my sixth sense was giving me signals something was wrong, but I was not able to figure out what it was.

He directed me to a sofa and offered me coffee, which I politely declined. I was dying of curiosity to ask him what was going on. The house didn't look like there was a wedding, there were no noises nor any charge and celebration in the air. No songs and no young boys and girls running around teasing and enjoying.

What the hell was going on here? My patience was running out, as I was thinking about asking her father, the boy who had greeted us told me Dada was calling me in the drawing-room. As I entered the drawing-room I saw that Dada was sitting there alone, Mia's grandfather was not with him.

"What the hell is going on Dada? This house looks like someone has died here, there is nothing like a wedding celebration in here" I said as I sat beside Dada.

Then Dada started explaining to me what had happened, how Mia's fiance and his family were asking fifty percent if Mia's family business, in turn, to go on with the wedding.

I felt my blood boil, I wanted to kill that son of a bitch for hurting her like that, that bastard didn't deserve her.

"I want you to marry Rameen", Dada said.

" What?" I looked at Dada stunned.

My heart was breaking all records in beating today, I like her there is no doubt in that and I wanted her as I had never wanted anything, but marriage is a great responsibility.

"Think about it, she would be yours forever, do you want anything else?" My conscience asked me.

" Hell no, I want Mia, and I will do anything for her", I replied to my conscience.

"Waleed, you have to hurry. We don't have much time, Rehman is waiting for your answer", Dada said.

" What about Rameen?" I asked him.

"She is a sensible girl, she won't like to get married into such a greedy family", Dada replied.

" But they have been engaged for more than a year?" I argued.

"Yes or No?" Dada gave an ultimatum.

"Yes," I replied.

I knew fortune only knocks once at your door, and if you don't open it, it goes and never returns. I know I decided in haste, the biggest decision of my life, if someone has told me I would be marrying Rameen Shahab an hour ago, I would have told that person to go find a hobby, it was so absurd. But still, it was happening, I don't know how Dada convinced her grandfather and how in turn her grandfather convinced her other family members?

But I was sitting surrounded by ten men which included Daniyal, after exactly half an hour later and the Qazi (Islamic judge) was asking me if I accept this Nikah (marriage contract) with Rameen Shahab with a Haq Mehr (Dower) of 10 million in gold for the value of the current currency?

"I accept"

He repeated his words, I repeated my answer with greater enthusiasm this time.

"I accept"

The Qazi repeated the words thrice and this time I was truly ecstatic when it dawned on me she was going to be mine.

"I accept".

The Qazi then took my signatures on the marriage contract, which Dada and Rameen's grandfather signed as the witnesses.

Everyone started congratulating me, they all hugged me and congratulated me one by one. Rameen's father was the last to hug me and congratulate me

" Thanks, son. I won't be able to ever repay you, for what you have done for us. I just have a request for you, please take care of my daughter, I know she can be difficult but you will be able to mold her with love" His eyes were filled with tears of gratification for me.

I felt someone squeeze my heart, I hugged him again and reassured him,

"Rameen is my responsibility from today, please don't worry I will take care of her to the best of my abilities, and thank you for trusting me with your daughter's life".

He didn't reply, I sensed he was overwhelmed with emotion and gratitude, one person that looked happier than me was Dada as if he had found a hidden treasure.

" Dada stop grinning, you are embarrassing me", I whispered in his ear.

"I would smile all I want, my year's old wish of seeing Rameen as my granddaughter-in-law has been fulfilled, you will be very happy with her, she is a great girl and only she can tame you", Dada replied.

I just rolled my eyes at his last comment, if only Dada had witnessed her side which I had seen in our first few meetings then Dada will realize what he has gotten himself into.

I was impatient for a glimpse of her, I wanted to see how she looked in her bridal dress, I hope it's red. Whenever Dada used to mention my wedding, I always used to imagine a bride in a red lehenga.

I looked around if I could get hold of someone who could at least send me her picture, but there was no one around who could help me, all men in the drawing-room were elderly.

I looked at Daniyal, he was busy in a conversation between Dada and Rameen's grandfather.

Asjad and Saad arrived they were looking like they have seen some ghost, I was sure they must have been informed by Sheema and Rania, they hugged me both looking afraid to congratulate me, I know they thought I must be grim right now after marrying Mia, they still thought I hated her, I have never told them how my feelings for her have transformed within a matter of few weeks.

" Guys, at least you can congratulate me, I just got married", I teased them.

They both looked at me in utter disbelief, and then Asjad punched me on my arm.

"You asshole, what have you been hiding from us," Asjad said in a whisper which only the three of us could hear.

"Long story", I said as I scanned the drawing-room, I can't tell them here anything.

" Come we have to get you clothes to wear at the gathering in the evening", They both dragged me with them informing Dada we were going shopping.

They nagged me with their questions to the designer store, where we got a Sherwani (traditional dress for the groom) altered to my size, the designer still couldn't believe that Waleed Kamal would come to his store for a Sherwani to wear at his wedding celebration that too on such short notice.

Now, how can I explain to the world that mine was an " Accidental Wedding". I have gone to attend someone else's wedding and had got married instead. I was the luckiest man in this whole universe.

Chapter 13

Listen to the song it's one of my favorites. And press the star button on your screen.

Rameen

My makeup still required some finishing touches when mom entered my room along with Rania and Sheema, she asked the beautician to wait outside and then turned and said to me.

"Do you trust us, Mia?"

"What kind of question is that?" I asked.   "Just answer me", She said.

" Yes, of course. I trust you", I replied.

"Will you accept the decision of your elders?" She asked again.

Now I was freaking out, what was happening, are they planning to give half of the company to Imaad.

"Mom, you don't have to do this, I don't want to marry some greedy filthy piece of shit", I said, in other circumstances, my mom would have given me a dressing down for the use of my language but right now she ignored it.

" No, we don't want you near to that family again", She replied.

"Then why are you asking these weird questions?" I asked puzzled.

"Mia if we make a decision for your life, will you trust us and accept it?" She asked.

"Yes, I will", I replied immediately.

I know my family will always want the best for me, I know they loved me and they will do anything to see me happy.

" Good", She said and nodded to Sheema.

Sheema picked up the Dupatta (long scarf accompanied with traditional south Asian dresses) of my lehenga and covered my head with it, my mom asked me to follow her, there were so many questions in my mind that I was dying to ask Sheema and Rania, but I couldn't in the presence of my mom.

They took me to the living room where already a group of men were sitting, they made me sit beside Dada and my mom sat beside me on the couch.   A man started reciting some verses and spoke some words about the nikah, my heart sank "Who were they getting me married too?" I thought bewildered.

I didn't have to wait for long as Qazi asked me if I accept my nikah to Waleed Kamal in turn of Haq Mehr of 10 million in gold of the value of the current currency.

I couldn't believe I was getting married to Waleed Kamal, of all the people in the world, God chose Waleed Kamal for me? I was feeling it difficult to breathe, how can I marry Waleed, I hated that guy, he was an arrogant asshole, and I can't stand him.

"Say yes Mia", Mom whispered in my ear, I wanted to cry no, but I couldn't I can't do this to my parents to my family, they will become a laughing stock.

" Yes," I murmured with a broken heart.

The Qazi repeated his words twice and I replied with a yes, my voice lower than the last time.

"Yes".

The Qazi repeated the words thrice, and I could hardly make out what he was saying as my head started to spin, I replied with a yes and passed out.

I don't know for how long I had been out, but when I woke up I was in my room surrounded by worried faces of the female members of our family.

" She woke up," Someone said and the chain started.

Mom hurried to me and gave me coconut water to drink and blew her breath on me after reciting some verses.   I gulped down the whole glass in a single breath as my throat was dry, I noticed everyone was looking at me with curious faces.

Then I remembered the scene before I had passed out, I was now officially Mrs. Waleed Kamal. I begged God that please may it be a nightmare, but I knew it was true, all of it was true. Fate has played the biggest joke on me, I was married to a man that I despised the most, no not most first was Imaad now, because of the mess that he and his family created I was married to a control freak.

Everyone started congratulating me, telling me how lucky I was to get married to the most eligible bachelor in town. I wanted to cry loudly and tell everyone how much I despised him, but I couldn't, I had to keep this facade for my parents for my family.

Rania and Sheema were silently reading my expressions, they knew how much I disliked Waleed, they are the only ones who understand what I was feeling right now, I wanted to be alone with them, to cry my heart out to them but I didn't get the chance, mom called the beautician inside my room and she started working on my face again.

I don't know how I managed to stay quiet and kept smiling, till she got me dressed, and Sheema and Rania helped me with the jewelry. The beautician set my dupatta on my head and fixed it with some pins, and before I got a chance to speak with any of my friends I was shoved into a car and was being driven to the hotel where the ceremony was arranged.

I kept my head bowed all through the ceremony unless the photographer asked me to raise my head for a photograph, I followed his instructions like a robot, Umair's words that I would be a zombie bride had come true. I was really like a zombie dead from inside but I kept on doing as I was being instructed.

The ladies and gents' gatherings were separate, Waleed joined me at the end of the gathering. I heard the gasps and sensed the envious stares I was receiving from the unmarried female population because I had stolen the crush of half the girls of this town. If I could only tell them how eager I was to trade places with them.

I avoided looking at him, but I could sense his eyes on me, his intense gaze piercing through me, tingles erupted all over my body, and the sparks that traveled through my arm, when he held my hand in his, I heard the hootings of everyone around us when he took my hand, I won't lie but I skipped a heartbeat.

No matter how much I despised him I can't deny the fact how my body responds to his touch, it was a very foreign feeling for me, while Imaad's touch had repulsed me in the last few weeks, Waleed's, on the other hand, made me crave for more and this thought terrified me.

I don't know much about Waleed, I don't know anything about Waleed I panicked.

"Get a grip Mia, you have your whole life to get to know each other", My subconscious told me.

" Was I going to spend the rest of my life with Waleed Kamal?", I asked.

"Drama Queen", It retorted.

" Okay let's ask Mia", I heard someone say, I had zoned out and now I was wondering what they were discussing?

Waleed was still holding my hand his fingers tracing patterns on the back of my palm, I tried to pull my hand from him but his grip only got tighter, asshole I thought bitterly.

"Come on tell us, Mia", One of my cousins asked.

I didn't have a clue what they were talking about I looked at her puzzled, she understood by my expressions that I hadn't heard a word they had said.

" Who is hotter Waleed or Brad Pitt?" She asked.

I looked at her astonished there was no way I was answering this question, in front of Waleed. I just stayed quiet and ignored them.

"Silence means you think Waleed is hot", My other cousin teased me.

"What the fuck", I thought annoyed.

If I stayed silent they will keep teasing me, and if I replied with a no they will start teasing Waleed, and I was in no mood to tease him, knowing the consequences, the power he held over me now made me keep my mouth shut.

" Okay, so it's decided Mia thinks Waleed is hotter than Brad", My cousin said enthusiastically.

"So Waleed now tell us who is hot Mia or Megan Fox?" She asked.

"Mia, she is the hottest, prettiest, and sexiest woman in the whole world for me", He replied boldly, shamelessly ogling me.

Then he lifted my hand to his mouth and kissed the back of my hand. The whistles and the shooting were enough to bring down the roofs on our heads caused because of his words and actions.

" Kiss the bride", I heard a voice say.

I wanted to break the head of that person whoever it was, my whole body was on fire by just a peck of his lips on my hand. My heart was racing and I was sure I was blushing bright red.

"So I have permission?" I heard Waleed's mischievous voice.

I was going to kick him in his balls if he even thought of kissing me.

"Yes" Everyone screamed.

I looked at him terrified, afraid he would act on his wishes, but he just winked at me, his lips were curled up in a wolfish grin. I was going to kill this asshole with my bare hands, he just wanted me to look at him, he knew I was avoiding looking at him and he had done this to make me look at him, cocky bastard I cursed.

But I couldn't ignore the fact that he was looking yummilicious, in that cream Sherwani with a black scarf on his shoulders. My God, he was so hot I can't believe it, and he was all mine. For the first time, I felt it was something to be Mrs.Waleed Kamal.

Our eyes were locked for I don't remember how long, his grey eyes were darker than usual filled with an unknown and unreadable emotion. I couldn't look into them any longer as his gaze was awakening some unknown emotions in my heart. I blinked and turned and looked away from him, he pressed his hand on mine in a reassuring way, making it further difficult for me to divert my mind from the intensity of gaze.

The teasing and the hooting subsided as the elders approached us, there was the usual exchange of words from both sides, photographs were taken, the videographer was recording everything.

And finally, the time came when my family said their goodbyes to me and wished me for my bright future as I accompanied Waleed and his grandfather to the car waiting outside. Waleed had not left my hand all through these rituals no matter how much I tried to resist and pull it from his grip.

To my disappointment, his grandfather didn't join us in the car, Asjad was sitting on the driving seat, and Saad was beside him, Rania had joined us in the backseat. I was thankful she was coming with me, I needed someone for moral support.

Asjad kept teasing us the whole time till we arrived at Waleed's house, it was just not any house it was a splendid mansion on a really large estate. I was stunned by its splendor, and of this house, I would be the Mistress. Elizabeth Bennet's words echoed in my mind from The Pride and Prejudice.

We were greeted in the house by Saad and Asjad's families, they have arrived earlier for the preparation. Most of Waleed's relatives were abroad or lived in their native place. They didn't have any close relatives in the city and due to our sudden wedding, no one could come.

Rania directed me to Waleed's living room, we sat in the living room of his mansion for some time, I couldn't help but admire the beauty of the house it was grand, I felt like I was sitting in some palace. It was a dome on the roof of the living room, a staircase from the middle of the hall, going to the first floor, with galleries all around on the first floor. The dome was painted beautifully in the style of Ottoman architecture, the whole house was a living example of Ottoman architecture, I could not help but be impressed. A huge chandelier hung from the middle of the roof, the walls were decorated with expensive paintings, and the chest and tables were covered with expensive articrafts and vases.

I was looking at everything stunned when a lady approached us and told me that the arrangements in the room were completed.

Asjad's mom asked Rania and Asjad's sister to direct me to Waleed's bedroom, I was nervous even thinking about what was to come. I still could feel the warmth of his touch on my hand.

I followed them quietly to his room which was on the first floor, the staircase was as grand as the rest of the house. I held my breath as I entered his room, it was in contrast to the house, with a modern interior. The scent of flowers welcomed me as I stepped inside.

Every surface in the room was covered with flowers or rose petals. There were lighted candles everywhere, the floor was covered with rose petals, and the walls were decorated with flowers to an extent I couldn't make out the color on the walls.

I loved everything about the decorations, and that it was roses, made my heart leap in pleasure.

A large glass wall was to the opposite of the bed, which I assumed opened onto the terrace, I could make out only that much through the curtains.

Rania guided me to the bed, and helped me to sit on it, this lehenga was making each damn movement difficult for me.   "You know what happens right? Or do you want me to give you a prep talk?" Rania asked teasing.

I just glared at her, I wanted to break the vase on her head which was on the side table, but I knew by the time I reached that in this lehenga, Rania will be out of the room.

" I will just tell you to stay calm and not break that vase on his head" Rania pointed to the vase I was looking at a few seconds ago and teased me.

"I am going to kill you", I said through clenched teeth.

She smiled at me and looked into her handbag for something, when she pulled out her hand I saw the bracelet Waleed gifted me in her hand.

She smiled and clasped it around my wrist, I had told her and Sheema I was going to return it to Waleed. Who had thought I would be sitting in his bedroom with the bracelet clasped on my wrist not more than twelve hours later, fate is unpredictable.

She pulled back to turn and leave when I grabbed her hand and said.

" Please Rania, don't leave",

"Shhhhhh, you idiot. You are going to be alright, just don't freak out", She said patting my cheek.

But I was already freaking out, I didn't want to face Waleed not after how he had teased me and the mischievous smile that played on his lips, I was not ready for this, I was not ready for any of this.

Rania and Asjad's sister left me in the room, I sat there dreading what was to come, and then I felt like I was an idiot this was Waleed I was thinking about, I had handled him in the past and I could handle him now, it was no big deal I was panicking unnecessarily.

I walked to the closet, Asjad's sister had told me she had arranged my stuff there, it was a walk-in closet as large as my room in my parent's house, Waleeds clothes and other stuff was arranged at one side of the closet, while Sania has arranged my stuff on the opposite side, I walked towards the shelves was my clothes were arranged and started looking for a nightdress and to my horror, I couldn't find a single decent one.

Rania and Sheema had accompanied me shopping for buying lingerie and nightwear, and Rania had made me buy all these latest sexy kinds of night dresses. I was cursing her as I went through them horrified and this was how my husband found me on our wedding night.

Waleed

As I entered our bedroom, which was just mine till the last time I was in there, I was greeted by the scent of air freshener and fresh flowers. I looked at the bed but it was empty, I turned and looked at the couch she was not there, I looked at the glass door of the terrace they were locked, so where was my bride?

I had expected her to be waiting for me on the bed as it was the tradition, her face covered with a veil. But I was not married to any girl I was married to a wild and untamed lioness. I looked at the closet the sliding door was ajar, I took a deep breath and walked towards it. I halted in the door and looked inside.

She was looking for something on the shelves where her clothes were arranged, I cleared my throat to get her attention. She turned to me immediately hearing my voice, my heart skipped a heartbeat.

" Hi" She squealed looking at me.

"Hi" I greeted back.

I was shamelessly staring at her, that was what I was doing for the last few hours since the moment I walked into the hall and saw her in that red lehenga.

Her cousins and friends were teasing me for ogling her, but I didn't care. I would stare at her as much as I want since she was officially mine and no one can do anything about it, not even Daniyal.

I had grabbed her hand as soon as I got the chance and hadn't left it no matter how much she resisted, I deserve to hold her hand at least whenever I want.

I loved the way she blushed when I had placed a kiss on the back of her hand, and the terrified look she gave me when I teased her regarding the kiss. I was on cloud nine since I had married her, the only thing that was nagging me was how she was feeling about our marriage?

I had asked Rania, about her before coming to the bedroom if she was regretting the marriage or if she wanted to marry that asshole of a fiance.

And when Rania told me that Mia didn't want to marry her fiance after he had asked for her share in their family business, a burden was lifted from my heart. This means that she was not in love with him and was sensible enough to understand that the bastard didn't deserve her.

"I think I will have to borrow your clothes", she said after a few minutes turning towards me.

" But I think, Sania has arranged all your stuff", I replied puzzled.

"I know but I can't wear them", She replied, I felt she was a little embarrassed.

" Why," I asked arching my eyebrows.

"Are you giving me your clothes or should I sleep in these clothes?", She asked annoyed pointing at her lehenga.

" I would prefer if you didn't wear any", I replied with a wolfish grin.

She blushed but gave me a death glare, this was turning out to be more fun than I had imagined.

"Now come, I haven't even looked at you properly", I said as I walked towards her and grabbed her arm.

" Liar, you have been ogling me since the moment you set your foot in the hall of the hotel," She said as she tried to free her arm from me.

"Do you want to walk, or I rather carry you" My threat worked as she took a step towards the bedroom.

I suppressed my smile and led her to the bed, she sat on the edge of the bed and I sat beside her.

"We aren't doing this are we," She asked after some time, anxiously intertwining her fingers.

"You don't want to stay married to me," I asked in shock.

"No, I didn't mean that" She replied immediately.

"Then what?" I asked confused.

She didn't reply, just kept looking at me.

"Then what Mia?" I asked her.

She swallowed the lump in her throat, I looked at her fascinated as it traveled down her long neck. I felt the urge to touch her, to kiss her neck on the path that the lump had followed.

"The stuff that couples do on their wedding night", She replied blushing.

I roared with laughter, she was the best thing that ever happened to me, we have been married just for a few hours and I felt I was falling for her hard, I was completely whipped.

She stared at me in anger, I controlled my laughter with great difficulty and replied.

" We won't if you are not comfortable", I replied.

I understood it was difficult for her, she was going to get married to someone else but had got married to me at the last moment, she needed time to wrap her head around it. And I was ready to wait for her as long as it took her to accept our relation. It was enough for me that she was in my house right now and she was mine forever.

"I will need time", She said bowing down her head and looking at her hennaed hands.

I took both her hands in mine and leaned in and smelled them, I loved the smell of henna. I remember when my mother used to apply henna to her hands, in my childhood I used to take her hands in mine and use to smell the scent of it for hours.

The scent of henna brought back the memories of my parents to my mind, I was sure they would have adored Mia.

" I can wait for you till eternity", I replied to her with my voice filled with emotions.

" Charmer", She retorted.

I laughed at her comment, I loved this quality of her, she was sassy and her mouth was vicious, and I was crazy about her.

She tried to pull her hands from me, I looked at her annoyed, I haven't even smelled them enough.

"I am tired Waleed", She said but I ignored her remark, my eyes were fixed on the bracelet I had gifted her and which she was wearing now.

I touched it and turned her hand and looked over it, the jeweler had done a great job, it had turned out prettier than I had imagined, I had gifted her this so she could remember all our meetings even after she got married, at that time I only wished she never forget she had met a Waleed Kamal at some point in her life.

" It's beautiful, thanks," She said as she noticed me looking at it.

"I am glad you liked it, I just wanted that you never forget me after you got married, so I had this made so that it will remind you of me whenever you look at it, and all our meeting", I said honestly.

" I know", She said smiling.

"Now can I have your clothes", She said angrily.

I smiled at her, my Mia was back, I thought as I walked into the closet and pulled out a tee-shirt and sweats and passed it to her, which she accepted with a thank you.

Do check out my other books as well.

I love writing Mafia Romance and my other three books are in that genre.

1. Venom - An age-gap, arranged marriage trope.

2. Diablo - An enemies to lovers trope.

3. Cian's Ruinous Love - A forbidden love trope.

Chapter 14

R ameen

I woke up from the ring of the phone, it took me some time to understand where I was, my mind was in a haze for some seconds, then it started clearing up as I drank in my surroundings. I glanced on my side, Waleed was sound asleep, I looked at him curiously, this was the first time I was looking at him while he was asleep. He was sleeping on his stomach facing me, his muscular arm stretched upwards, around his head.

Don't even get me started about his face, it was truly carved by the god. His chiseled jaw, his strong chin with a dimple on it, his greek nose and his dark and broad brows, his long lashes, that covered his intense grey eyes.

Even while sleeping, he was able to take away my breath, how can a man be so beautiful, I wondered.

His brown hairs were scattered on his forehead, I suppressed the urge to push them back from his forehead. If I would do anything like that I would be breaking the bargain we had last night. He had kept his part of the bargain and had stuck to his side of the bed.

We had a long argument last night before sleep when I had told him to either sleep on the couch or the floor because I was in no way letting him sleep on the bed beside me. Call me a bitch for all you want but I couldn't trust him after his machoism in front of my cousins and friends.

I know we are married but that doesn't mean I will sleep with him, I don't even know him well, I don't even know what's his favorite color, so blame all you want but I am not having sex with him right away. He might be hot, of course, he is hot, he makes my heart stop every time he looks at me with his sexy smoldering gaze.

Sex was a big deal for me, I was not going to give my virginity to anyone unless I trusted that person and was sure he will not hurt me ever. If Waleed wanted to claim me, he would have to earn it, because I am not giving it to him just because he was my husband.

Would I have done the same with Imaad? Frankly, I don't know, I was glad I didn't give in to his advances before our wedding, that son of a bitch was trying to lure me because he knew that there was a chance our wedding could not go through because of their plan.

They had come up with a perfect plan, I wanted to give them applause. They had hit where it hurt the most, I was the weakness of my family and they could do anything for me, Imaad and his family knew this and they have waited till the wedding day thinking my family would give in, on the last moment to save me from heartbreak and embarrassment and to not ruin the reputation of the family.

But they won't have expected someone can ruin their plan at the last moment, if not for Waleed's grandfather me and my family would have faced humiliation in the society. I would have never married that greedy shit, no matter what but my family would have to face the consequences that my wedding was called of at the last moment and that my groom had ditched me on the altar.

It was clear from Waleed's behavior that he likes me, and I couldn't understand how and when he had started liking me, I mean there was not a single thing that had gone well between us since the day we met. We both had never left any stone unturned to hurt the other or get back to the other, and still, all through this, he had developed feelings for me.

The cell started ringing again and from the ringtone, I recognized it was mine and looked around and found my clutch on the side table, thankfully on my side. I extended my arm and picked the clutch and opened it as I sat up, I remove the cell from inside it and looked at the screen, I smiled reading Ali's name on the screen. I have forgotten to call him in all the chaos yesterday and I was sure he would be really mad at me.

"Hey", I whispered slowly as I got up and walked towards the couch afraid that I would disturb Waleed's sleep.

" Mia you dumbass, you didn't even call me", He cursed as soon as he heard my voice.

"I think you were supposed to call me for congratulating me on my wedding", I said holding my cell in place with my shoulder and playing with the bracelet in my hand.

Waleed had not allowed it to remove me last night as I was taking out all the jewelry, he even had slipped a diamond ring in my finger, saying that it was a wedding gift. He couldn't propose to me, before our wedding so to consider it as an engagement ring.

It was not a diamond the size of a rock. I had asked him when he had got the time to buy it?

He had replied, that he went shopping for his clothes to wear at the function last night and had bought the ring while on the way to the hotel. He said he couldn't imagine not giving me a wedding gift.

"I am not talking about your wedding, why didn't you call me and told about what Imaad and his family did the moment you found out. I thought I was your best friend", He complained.

" You are Lee, I was just so stressed out yesterday and you know the fuss that everyone makes around the bride I just didn't get the time", I replied.

"Well, how is your hottie?" He teased me. "You are a billionaire now Mia, super-rich huh, with all those fancy dresses and jewelry", He continued his teasing.

" Shut up Lee", I said laughing.

"Finally, he was successful in convincing your parents, aye", Ali reminded me of the incident in the multiplex when Waleed had caught us both of guard.

" Lee."

"Mia."

"Okay, will I be allowed in your palace?" He was not going to give up easily.

"If you kept teasing me like this, I will make sure the guards beat the shit out of you", I said making my voice angrier.

" Are you happy Mia?" He asked me, getting serious.

"Honestly, Lee I don't know", I replied.

" Come on girl, he is the most eligible bachelor and he is kind of super-hot too", Ali was back at teasing again, "You don't like him?" He asked.

"I don't know Lee, it all happened too fast I mean, I was married before I could understand what was going on. It's kind of complicated, I for sure do not dislike him as much as I thought as I do, but I have never thought about him in this way, I think I need time and he said he was ok waiting, till I made up my mind.

He has been nice to me, truly a gentleman but I don't know Ali if I am ready to take our relationship to the next level, not at least now, maybe sometime in the future when I trust him better. You know, I don't believe in love and trust is the most important thing for me in a relationship.

If he earns my trust, and I am sure he won't hurt me, then maybe I will, you know", I poured my heart out to Ali.

I could discuss anything with him and had trust that it would not go anywhere, I was so glad he had called me, I was desperately in need of a friend.

" Hey, sweety everything will be fine, just relax I know you will be ok, remember you are my iron butterfly", He said.

I smiled, Ali used to call me iron butterfly since we were kids because I was tough and beat the shit out of guys with him whenever there was a fight.

We talked for some more time, mostly useless stuff, Ali trying to cheer me up. He hung up when someone called him, I turned and looked at Waleed he had woken up and now was looking at me with hooded eyes.

"Good Morning", I wished him.

" My morning will be good if you come here and kiss me", His voice was deep and husky due to sleep.

"If you want to get your ass kicked you can try", I replied grinning.

" What a killjoy Mia", He said as he sat up, rolling the sheets aside.

"Who were you speaking to?", He asked.

" Ali, remember the guy at multiplex who nearly beat the shit out of you", I teased.

"You wish", He replied with a smirk.

" If not for me, they would have had to carry you on a stretcher", I retorted.

He looked at me for some time silently and got up from the bed, and walked towards me not breaking eye contact, my heart leaped into my throat as I watched him walk towards me like a lion closing upon its prey.

He bent and stopped when his face was a few inches away from me, my breath stopped. This is what I got by provoking the devil.

He kept looking in my eyes and then his gaze slid down to my lips, I saw him lick his lips with his tongue and then he leaned forward, I closed my eyes anticipating what was to come but instead I heard him whisper in my ear.

"I said you wish."

Then he was gone like that, I opened my eyes and looked at him who was standing at the door of the en suite bathroom he winked at me and then strolled inside and shut the door.

" Arrogant asshole", I cursed as I fisted my hands, I wanted to punch his beautiful face until it was bruised.

I walked into the closet to select clothes which to wear today, I looked around in confusion, all the dresses were fancy and traditional, I need to bring my clothes from my house which I used to wear before my wedding I thought.

I selected a green color dress with golden thread embroidery on it and pulled out matching shoes and jewelry. I was going through the lingerie in the lowermost drawer when I heard the bathroom door open and Waleed walked into the closest to my horror naked, only a towel wrapped around his waist.

I suddenly felt that the closet was too small, his presence was making it look like it was a cramped place and the fact that he was only a towel made it even worse.

I was shamelessly looking at his broad shoulders and chest which was glistening with water droplets dripping from his hair. Don't even get me started about his hair, they were wet and sticking to his forehead, making me fist my hands from the urge of pushing them off from his forehead. I slid down my gaze and it didn't help, as now it was fixed on his naked torso, it was a sight to behold, it looked so hard and firm, I studied every toned muscle of his arms and torso.

I licked my upper lip with my tongue, as I gaped at his abs, they made butterflies flutter in my stomach, as his chest tapered to his waist and then to his hips, covered with the towel, Damn, I wanted to pull that towel away.

"Like what you see", He asked with a smirk when he found me staring at him.

" You can't just walk around here naked", I hissed in embarrassment, from being caught staring at him.

"You mean you are not enjoying the show", He said as he turned and started looking through his clothes giving me a view of his broad back and a very sexy butt.

I tried not to stare at his back and look anywhere else but my eyes were acting like they had developed a mind of their own, drinking every detail of his gorgeous body.

My hand started twitching, by the sudden urge to touch him, I fisted my hands in anger and walked out of the closet with my clothes. I hated my traitorous body which I was unable to control when around him, I realized he was too dangerous and my body could betray me as soon as he makes an advance.

I went into the bathroom and took a cold shower, to calm my betraying body, I carefully got dressed in the bathroom and came out drying my hair with a towel.

Waleed was not in the room, and I saw Rania waiting for me on the couch, I guessed she had stayed for the night.

" Good morning", She greeted me cheerfully.

"Though I am more interested in what happened during the night", She teased me.

I just glared at her, she was not the one who would let any chance go to embarrass me. I walked to the dresser and started untangling my hair.

Rania took the brush from me and started helping me with my hair, looking at me through the mirror with a suspicious smile.

" So are you going to tell me?" She asked.

"Nope", I replied.

" You know you are a bitch, Mia", She said pulling my hair with force.

"Ouch", I cried from the pain.

" At least tell me the si", Her sentence was incomplete as I screamed and put my hands on my ears.

Rania looked at me with a frown on her face and continued untangling my hair. I removed my hands from my ears when I thought it was safe.

"This is what I get for being nice", She said mumbling angrily.

" Nothing happened", I felt bad and the truth slipped from my mouth in pity.

I looked at her in the mirror as her jaw dropped to the floor and her eyes were wide as saucers.

"You are telling me nothing happened, when he was eye-fucking you the whole time yesterday," She asked in disbelief.

I just nodded in reply, I didn't know what to say to her that it could make her believe me, that I was not lying.

" Ohh, Mia. What should I do with you", She said in irritation.

"I need time to get to know him better", I was sick of explaining to everyone the same thing again and again.

" Did you guys kiss?", I replied in no with just nodding.

"Cuddle?", I shook my head again in a no.

" Held hands while sleeping?" I again nodded at her question.

She hit me with the brush on my arm, with so much force that I cried in pain.

"Why are you abusing me", I said rubbing my arm.

" You are asexual, it is confirmed now", She said ignoring my protest.

She pulled out the hairdryer and blow-dried my hair and then help me with the makeup. I wore the emerald necklace and matching earrings and paired them with golden and green bangles in one hand and the bracelet in the other.

"Come they are waiting for us for breakfast", She dragged me to the dining room on the ground floor.

The dining room was large with a long table that could fit at least fifty people easily, it had a glass wall through which the lawn was visible, fresh flowers bloomed on the shrubs in the shrubbery and the most significant part was the small lake in which swans were floating.

I looked at the scenery dumbstruck, I was sure my jaw had hit the floor. Rania elbowed me in my ribs to remind my people were waiting on the dining for us.

I closed my mouth and greeted as I looked around the table, Waleed's grandfather was seated on the head of the table Waleed was sitting to his right while Saad's father was seated on his left then Saad's mother then Saad, and so on.

The chair beside Waleed was empty and Asjad was seated beside the empty chair, Rania walked ahead and sat beside Asjad, I had no choice but to pull the chair and sit beside Waleed. Asjad's family was not present at the table, which meant that they might have left at night. I had sensed the tension between Asjad's mother and Rania last night while we were sitting in the living room.

I just took a toast and poured myself a cup of tea, this had been my breakfast for as long as I can remember. I was annoyed when Waleed scooped some scrambled eggs from the bowl and placed it on my plate.

" You need to look after your health", He whispered.

I glared at him and stomped his feet below the table with my heel and grinned with satisfaction as I saw his face contort with pain.

"You are going to pay for this", He whispered as he grabbed my hand in his and held it tightly.

I looked around the table to see if anyone had noticed his actions, but all were busy eating. Saad's father was busy in conversation with Waleed's grandfather and his mother was talking to Rania, while Asjad and Saad were busy in a banter.

I looked at Waleed with pleading eyes and that cocky bastard ignored me and kept eating his breakfast as if nothing had happened.

It was difficult for me to eat the toast with one hand and then keep it aside and take a sip of tea, I was hoping he would leave my hand but that asshole didn't look in a forgiving mood.

" Mia clear your plate", He said aloud.

And I felt like turning the teapot on his head upside down. Now everyone was looking at me, Saad's mom and Dada started lecturing me that I was too thin and I should eat well to stay healthy, I clear my plate cursing Waleed in my mind.

This was only the first day of our marriage and the bastard had gotten the better of me thrice since morning.

I sat in the living room sulking and thinking about how I was going to pay him back, till my Mom, aunt and Umair arrived to meet me and brought lunch with them as was the tradition.

I temporarily forgot about Waleed as I sat there talking to them with Rania. Saad and his family had left after breakfast so had, Asjad. Waleed had gone to our room to make some calls and Dada had retired to the library.

Chapter 15

Waleed

I finished making calls to my second in command, too many projects were going on right now. If my wedding would I have been planned I would have waited for at least a year to wrap up the projects.

I was thinking about going on a honeymoon so that I could get some alone time with Mia and we could get to know each other well. I don't think there is anything left about her that I don't know but she wants to get to know me and I was thinking maybe a honeymoon would be a good option.

"Yes a honeymoon without sex", My mind taunted.

I know it was right, Mia said she would need time and I don't think she would give in just because I take her on a honeymoon. She is stubborn as a swine, I was wondering what she was doing now?

It's not even 24 hours since we got married but I think I can't live without looking at her at least once every hour. I walked out of my bedroom and strolled to the living room, I was surprised to find Mia's mom and aunt along with her cousin sitting and having a conversation with Dada, Mia, and Rania.

I greeted them and started speaking to Umair, he was a decent boy, he was studying Medicine and I instantly liked him. After nearly an hour the maid came and told us the lunch was being served. We walked to the dining hall together.

I remembered the incident from the morning when I had gotten the better of Mia, I was smiling to myself remembering that, Mia had avoided sitting beside me and had sat across me between her mom and aunt, Umair sat beside me and Rania followed him.

I was disappointed, I wanted to tease Mia a bit more while having lunch, but it looked like my darling wife was not in the mood. She was shooting daggers, which meant she was still mad at me because of the incidents of morning.

Dada and Mia's mom were planning about when to arrange the wedding reception, I had told them I was busy for at least a month and I won't be able to make time for that. Dada looked annoyed at my declaration, he looked impatient to show off his daughter-in-law to the world, especially to our relatives.

But unfortunately, he will have to wait for some time, Two of my projects were in the middle while one was starting, three were almost near to completion and these were only the major ones. Multiple medium-scale projects were going on.

I will have to go back to work tomorrow, I couldn't ignore my responsibility anymore, at least I will have to be there for half a day.

I wanted to give time to Mia but the problem was right now I didn't have much time.

Mia's mom asked Dada if she could take Mia to their home as was the ritual that the bride goes to their parent's place on the second day of their marriage, I looked at everyone puzzled. What was this fucking ritual and why had I not heard about it before? I had taken the day off so I could spend it with Mia and if she will go to her parent's place what's the fucking sense of me staying home?

Dada said he was okay with it, and it all depends on what Mia wished, I looked at Dada. Does he even care what I think, or is everything about Mia?

I looked at Mia, she had a wicked smile on her face, I tried warning her with my eyes not to even think about going but she ignored me completely and looked at Dada with an innocent face and said batting her long lashes.

" I would love to go, I am missing Dada, dad, and chachu so much. I have never been away from home for even a single day".

I wanted to carry her off to the bedroom and tie her up, but I just looked at Dada helpless that maybe he would tell her that Waleed is home today maybe you should go some other time, you both just got married and should spend your time together.

But nothing of that sort happened, Dada gladly gave her permission and told her if she wants she could stay for a day or two, what the fuck.

I pinched myself, to make sure that this was all part of my imagination and was not happening in reality, but I knew that was not the case. My wife of one day was leaving me to have a sleepover at her parent's home, what can be more ironic than this?

I was literally brooding the whole time while having lunch, after lunch, we went back to the living room where the maids served coffee. Mia excused herself to get her stuff from the bedroom.

This was my chance to make her change her plan of going, I texted my second in command Tariq to call me and he immediately called back. I excused myself, to take the call and came to the bedroom.

Mia was in the closet she had a small handbag in her hand and she was stuffing her stuff into it, I glared at her which she ignored completely. I walked to her and snatched and threw the handbag on the floor and grabbed her by her shoulders.

"What do you think you are doing?" I asked her.

"Giving you space to walk around naked", She retorted.

I was not able to suppress the smile that came on my lips.

" I won't walk around naked, I promise", I said in a pleading tone.

"If not that, you will force-feed me", She said annoyed, she looked so cute at that moment I wanted to bend her over and take her at that moment.

" I promise I won't", I barely controlled my urge.

"I am going", She said like a stubborn child.

" Mia please", I requested.

"No, not happening", She replied crossing her arms on her chest.

She was punishing me just for having a little fun with her, by her absence.

" You are stubborn as a swine", I said disappointed.

"I know" she replied and picked up the handbag and started stuffing the remaining things.

I looked at her with hope in my eyes, that maybe she would not go and tell me she was just joking, but nothing of that sort happened.

"I will pick you up tonight", I said, I was in no mood to let her stay there for the night.

" No you won't", She replied, in the same tone as mine.

"Yes, I will", I said stubbornly.

" You can come, all you want but I am not coming back with you tonight, maybe tomorrow, maybe the day after tomorrow", She replied, pulling the zipper of the handbag and closing it.

She walked past me but I pulled her back, her back collided with my chest and I snaked my arms around her and held her close to me, inhaling her scent.

"I am picking you up tonight", I whispered in her ear, gently biting her earlobe.

Her skin was so smooth like silk, her waist so tiny, enclosed within my arms, she was so close to me, that I was able to hear her racing heartbeat.

" Waleed", My name came out of her mouth as a whisper, this was the first time she was calling my name, and I can't describe how fuckingly sexy it felt in her voice.

"Mine" I whispered

I rubbed my face on the side of her neck just behind her ear, her scent was driving me crazy. She smelled like fresh apricots. Mia bent her neck on the opposite side and gave me more access, I knew the way her body reacted to my touch against her will. I knew she didn't have control over her body around me and it was turning me on.

I wanted the time to stop, and for her to stay in my arms forever, I brushed her hairs aside from her neck and gently slid them on the other side, as I started kissing her slowly behind her ear, moving down to her crook.

I pressed my lips at the crook of her neck as I bit her gently and felt her shudder in my arms, yes baby, only I can make you feel like this.

"You are mine, Mrs. Waleed Kamal and I don't part with what is mine", I said sucking on her neck and biting it.

A gentle moan escaped from her mouth, and I barely controlled myself, from ripping apart her clothes. I placed a kiss on her cheek and let her go, she was breathing heavily and so was I.

This girl is going to be the death of me, I thought as I looked at her who was chewing on her bottom lip.

" If you don't want me to bend you over, and take you right here and now stop doing that to your lip", I said running my fingers through my hair in frustration.

She looked at me stunned and ran from there, as I was going to eat her. I smiled at her reaction, I think we both needed a break from each other after what happened just now because if she stayed in front of my eyes I might lose control and claim her.

I could at least leave her alone for some hours, but I was not letting her stay at her parent's place for the night. It doesn't matter if we don't do anything but at least I can watch her while she sleeps.

I did the same last night, I stayed awake last night watching her sleep, sounds creepy but I couldn't help it. She was driving me crazy, and to be honest I stole a couple of kisses while she slept, I don't think she will mind if she didn't know about it.

It was just a few minutes she left the room and I was already missing her, I was turning into a lovesick puppy.

Rameen

I had texted Sheema I was coming over to my parent's house funny how till yesterday it was my home and it was just my parent's house now, how easily just a few words can change your life, by the time we reached my parents place she was already waiting for us.

I met and greeted Dada and Dad who were sitting in the living room with Sheema and then we went straight to my room.

The first thing I did was get rid of my clothes and change into a loose tee shirt and sweats, it felt like heaven again. I gave both of them a travel bag to start helping me pack my stuff.

I knew Waleed was going to pick me up tonight, his decisive and commanding tone had told me he was not going to listen to any of my excuses.

My body got heated remembering what happened in the closet, I never thought he could be so possessive and territorial. The way he told me that I was his and he doesn't part with what was his.

The way his lips traveled on my skin, the way he kissed me, Ohh my God, what was happening to me? Was I falling for Waleed Kamal? We haven't even been married for 24 hours and that man-made butterflies fly in my stomach.

I was stuffing my clothes in a bag myself, Sheema was packing my accessories, while I asked Rania to pack my books. I twisted my hair which was hanging loose into a bun and put a clutcher to keep them in place.

I saw Sheema stare at my neck with wide eyes, I looked at her in confusion, Rania who was arranging the books in my bag past us a glanced and came to us, she looked in the direction where Sheema was starting at my neck and burst out laughing.

"Ohh my God, I didn't know you can lie so well, you nearly fooled me", Rania said laughing.

" Wait, what? When did I lie to you?" I asked in surprise.

She dragged me to the dresser and turned me to my side and pointed at my neck, I looked in the mirror horrified.

A hickey, that bastard gave me a hickey.

"He sure sucks like a vacuum", Rania said teasing.

I just wanted to kill Waleed, that asshole has the nerve to give me a hockey, that to on my neck, where it was visible for everyone to look.

" How the hell am I going to cover this?" I asked nearly about to cry.

What if someone from my family saw it, the thought made me want to die of embarrassment. What if mom or aunt have noticed it. What they might have thought, Ohh God, why am I even alive.

"But you told us nothing happened and I didn't notice it in the morning when I was helping you get ready", Rania said thinking hard.

" Because that bastard did this before we came here", I replied through gritted teeth.

Rania and Sheema looked at me with amused expressions on their faces.

"What else did he do?" Sheema asked smiling.

I glared at them, but they ignored my glare and kept looking at me in askance. I rolled my eyes at them and turned and walked towards my wardrobe.

They both pulled me back and pushed me on the bed, Rania sat opposite to me on the bed while Sheema grabbed the stool from the dresser and sat on it.

"We will need details", Rania said in a serious tone as if I was a bloody criminal, and they both were investigating officers.

" There is nothing to tell", I replied in a bored tone.

"Stop bitching okay, and just spill your guts", Rania replied.

I realized I didn't have any choice but to tell them, they were not gonna let me go without listening to everything. I told them everything that happened from night till I came back here.

" Ooooh", They both said in unison as I finished.

"So you left him with blue balls", Rania said.

I wanted to bury myself, somewhere that no can ever find me again especially Rania.

" Poor Waleed", Sheema sympathized with him.

"What more do you want? He gifted you a bracelet worth a King's ransom on your wedding, he saved you and your family from humiliation, you are flaunting that rock on your finger because he gave that to you. And he even agreed to wait for you because you are a dumbass. What more do you want from him?" Rania asked looking at me with contempt.

"I didn't ask him to be the hero and save the day okay, it was his decision", I said annoyed.

" It means he loves you idiot", Sheema said irritated.

"He doesn't love me, oh my god, does he?" I looked at them both startled.

They didn't reply just looked at me with accusation in their eyes. Does Waleed love me? How is that possible? We don't even know each other.

"He didn't say he loves me", I said to them.

" Something is for feeling, maybe he didn't even realize it himself, that he is in love with you. But think about it Mia, who marries a girl who was engaged to someone else for more than a year. And he never asked or mentioned a thing to you about your ex-fiance instead he is being nice to you", Sheema tried to explain it to me she was our "Miss know it all" Hermione Granger.

" He is not nice to me, he walks around in just a towel, he force-feeds me, holds my hand forcefully while I eat and he gave me a hickey", I knew I was acting like a spoilt child, but I didn't want to admit I felt something for him.

"Tell me you didn't feel the urge to touch him when he was standing there in a towel", Rania asked.

Why the hell Rania has to ask, all these awkward questions which I have to lie in answer.

" No, I didn't", I lied, but I know I was blushing thinking about his gorgeous body just in a towel.

"Liar", Rania accused.

" Okay, what if I felt like touching him, what's the big deal. He has this gorgeous hot body one would die for, with all those muscles any girl would kill to touch him and to be with him, and to want those chiseled arms to wrap around her body", I got carried away, imagining the way his arms muscles flexed with every movement and the way his back got tightened when he took a step and by the time I realized they both were looking at me with amusement.

"You want him", Rania said smiling wickedly.

" No I don't", I replied.

"Now you are lying", She argued.

" No I am not", I insisted.

"You are a stubborn bitch", Rania said taking a deep breath.

" I pray for Waleed, may Lord give him the strength to deal with a stubborn bitch like you. That guy is gonna have a real tough time getting you into bed with him", She said getting down from the bed.

I blushed at her mention of me being in bed with Waleed in that sense, images from the closet started flashing in my mind. What would his lips feel like on mine, I imagined his plump pink lips on mine, his teeth biting on my lip, his tongue battling with mine.

"Wait, what", I shook my head to get rid of that image from my mind.

Get your mind out of the gutter Mia, I thought bitterly. I was going crazy, how can I think about him like that, I never thought about

Imaad, though I was engaged to him for so long. And I did not even spend a whole day with Waleed and my mind was polluted with these dirty thoughts.

God help me, was it a sin thinking about someone in this way?

" He is your husband you idiot", Sheema scolded me.

What the fuck, was I thinking aloud? Ohh my God, I felt like jumping from my room window and killing myself. How much did I speak aloud? Even the kissing part?

"Mia we know it's tough for you, it's not easy to accept someone else in place of a man we have been engaged to and were going to get married. But honestly, Waleed is ten times the man Imaad ever could be. You should be grateful to God that he saved you from someone like Imaad who would have only hurt you and instead gave you to someone who cares about you", Sheema was again in her Hermione mode and for once I agreed with her.

Yes, Imaad would have only hurt me, think about his behavior in the past few weeks I realized he was not what I have thought about him. And Waleed was not what I have thought about him either. I have misjudged both of them, one had all the goodness and the other only appearance of it.

Chapter 16

R ameen

"Mia, what dishes does Waleed like?" Mom asked me when she saw me half inside the refrigerator.

I was searching for something that I could munch on, I was hungry. Sheema and Rania were still busy packing my stuff and I had told them I was going to the kitchen to grab something for us to eat.

"How would I know that?" I asked her turning to her in surprise.

"He is your husband", My mom said in accusation, she was trying to embarrass me.

Too bad I don't get embarrassed so easily, " Mom we got married yesterday, not a year ago. How will I know what he likes to eat".

"I was asking so I can ask the cook to prepare those dishes for the dinner, your dad had called and told him to dine with us", She replied thinking about something.

Ohh God, was he coming for dinner, that meant I have even less time for completing my packing because the moment he arrives my mom will make me give him company.

" And what is this you are wearing?" She looked at my clothes annoyed.

I looked at myself, I used to wear these clothes all the time before the wedding, at that she didn't have any problem with them. What was different now?

"You are an idiot Mia, you have just got married, you should dress properly so that your husband is attracted to you, if you will be wearing such clothes around him, it will be no surprise if he looks at other women", My mom gave me a long lecture, I don't agree with her on this but I didn't want to argue.

"Okay, I will change into something", I said avoiding more lectures.

"Come here, I will give you the saree I had bought for you, I had decided to gift you on your coming birthday but I will buy something else. You can wear it now", She said as she leads me to her room.

" I can wear the dress which I was wearing when I came", I said wondering why so fuss.

Mom didn't reply she went to her closet and pulled out a box and brought it to me. She kept it on the bed and opened it.

It was a silk saree in yellow and pink combination, it was beautiful. Mom walked to the safe and brought back a gold necklace and bangles.

"Wear this with it, they will look nice, now hurry up he would be here in an hour", She said pushing me towards the door.

I walked to my room with the saree and the jewelry, Sheena and Rania looked at the box with curiosity. I opened the box and showed them the saree.

" Wow!!! Your Mom is making sure you get laid tonight", Rania said with a mischievous smile.

I glared at her, but she ignored me and started looking at the jewelry.

"Pretty, you want help wearing the saree?" She asked me.

"I think I will manage", I know how to drape a saree, I have learned it from my aunt who was very fond of them and had taught me how to drape it when there was a traditional day in my college.

" You both keep working, I will get ready or mom will again start lecturing", I said as I walked to the bathroom to freshen up.

I changed into the saree, it had a pink blouse, Rania helped me with my hair and applied some makeup forcefully.

"Wow, you look hot in this saree, I hope Waleed has good restraint", Sheema said when she saw me after the makeup.

Mom called from downstairs, that Waleed was here and we should come down. The packing was almost finished, Rania and Sheema accompanied me downstairs.

They were sitting in the living room and as we entered and greeted, Waleed looked at me and I saw his grey eyes darkening as he checked me out from head to toe and nodded in appreciation.

I won't lie my heart skipped a beat and I felt that all my blood rushed towards my cheeks. He was still looking at me curiously, I knew every eye in the room was focused on us and I felt shy, this was the first time in my life that I was feeling shy.

I took a few quick steps and was going to sit beside my aunt when I noticed my mom glaring at me, I retreated and went and sat beside Waleed, mom looked satisfied after her mission was accomplished.

I couldn't believe my mom was teaching me tactics, to keep a man whipped. Maybe she was worried about our unexpected wedding and if Waleed liked me or not.

I could have shown her the hickey, which I was hiding beneath my hair to make her relax that her son in law, was a walking hard-on because of me.

Dad and chachu (uncle) were discussing business with Waleed, while Umair, Sheema, Rania and I were discussing the latest thriller flick.

Mom and aunt had left for the kitchen to look at the last-minute preparation for the dinner, they both were too anxious, the only son-in-law of the family was going to dine for the first time, which meant everything had to be perfect.

Waleed didn't look at me after that and was busy speaking with Dad and chachu (uncle), I was a little disappointed. I was getting used to his attention on me all the time.   He didn't even speak a word to me and I don't know why but my mood started spoiling because of lack of attention from him, I was grim even at the dinner table.

I barely ate anything at dinner though mom had prepared some of my favorite dishes, Waleed, on the other hand, was doing justice with each dish. Praising and complimenting while eating, mom looked quite happy by his praises and I felt her tense body relax and she started enjoying the dinner.

The only one not enjoying the dinner was me, I was mad at myself for giving him so much importance and letting him ruin my mood. When he was giving me his attention at the wedding I was mad at him and now when he was not paying me attention I was mad at him, Was I going crazy?

I mean why was I feeling the urge to be the center of his attention, why did I even care if he looked at me or not? I barely know him, maybe this is because of the Nikah. Mom used to say the two words of nikah, changed the woman's heart and life forever, it might be because of that otherwise there is no reason I was feeling like this.

One hour after the dinner Waleed asked me if I was ready to leave, I wanted to tell him I was not going with him and he can go to hell but I know everyone was watching so I just nodded in agreement.

Mom had already asked our manservant to keep my bags in the trunk of Waleed's car, I said goodbye to everyone. Rania whispered in my ear as I hugged her "Don't be a fool and give the guy the release he desperately needs".

I wanted to break the flower pot on her head, but I didn't my anger on Waleed was way more than it was on Rania and right now I wanted to kick him in his balls, arrogant asshole. What does he think of himself, I won't die if he doesn't pay me attention.

We drove home silently, Waleed tried to engage me in a conversation but I was not in the mood, I was too mad at myself, for giving him so much importance. Sensing my disinterest he turned silent and concentrated on his driving.

When we reached home, Dada had already retired to sleep, Waleed had said he was not feeling well and had not come to dinner for that reason. I went straight to the bedroom, Waleed followed me silently.

When we were inside the room and I was going to the closet to change Waleed held my arm and pulled me towards him, he then held my waist with both his hands. I felt like a jolt of electricity traveling through my body when his hands touched the bare skin on my waist, my breath hitched and my face flushed.

" What happened?", He asked.

"Nothing", I replied gulping the lump in my throat.

" Don't lie to me, you were okay when you came into the living room but afterward your mood changed, are you mad at me for something? I didn't even remember saying a word to you, so why are you upset?" He asked, his grip on my waist getting harder.

Now, what was I going to tell him, I was mad at him because he didn't say a word to me? Because I was expecting he might whisper something about how good I was looking or some teasing from him.

I didn't know what to reply so I just stood there looking at my hennaed hands which I had placed on his chest and through which I could sense his beating heart.

He lifted my chin so he could look me in the eye, I kept my gaze downward fearing he might find the answer to his questions in my eyes.

"Look at me", he said.

I kept looking at my hands, I don't know why I was afraid of looking him in the eye.

" Mia, look at me", This time his tone was commanding and his grip on my waist hardened.

I looked at him hoping, he was not good at face reading, and he won't find his answer on my face.

"What happened baby", He asked politely, I don't know what made him change his tone may be the expressions on my face.

My heart was beating in my ears when he called me baby, what the hell was happening to me, Imaad used to call me baby so many times but I never felt the way I was feeling right now.

" Mia", He whispered impatiently.

"I am tired", I lied turning my face to look in another direction.

" Maybe you should rest, I can understand the stress you have been through in the last two days", He said loosening his grip on my waist and pulling away.

My body protested at the loss of his touch and I got mad again, I had never expected my body would betray me so easily. I walked into the closet to change into something comfortable. Cursing myself, for dressing up like an idiot for him and he didn't even bother to give me a single compliment.

Waleed

Mia was sleeping beside me and I was watching her sleep, her eyes were closed and her lips were a little parted. Her black hairs were scattered all around her face, I loved her hairs they were so long and silky.

I had an urge to touch her hair and feel the texture of them, I carefully touched a lock of her hair, they were so silky soft. I leaned and smelled her hair, they smelled like apricots. I had seen her shampoo in the bath earlier it was apricot, her scrub, face wash, body lotion, and body shampoo were all in apricot. I think she is obsessed with apricots, and that's why she smelled like apricots, a little sweet and a little tangy.

I caressed her face carefully tracing my fingers on her face, she was beautiful, she was exquisite and she was all mine. She would have kicked me from the bed if she would have been awake right now. Last night I had convinced her with great difficulty that I would stick to my side of the bed and would not disturb her sleep or try to cuddle her.

But I never said I won't touch her, or that I won't kiss her, not kiss just a peck on her lips. She was looking so gorgeous and sexy in that saree it had taken all my strength to keep my hands off her.

I was meeting her family for the first time, the wedding day barely counted, as everything was so chaotic yesterday. I was speaking with her father and uncle when she had walked in that saree and Ohh my, I was barely able to breathe.

The yellow color of her saree was reflecting in her amber eyes and they looked like they were on fire, her perfect figure and gorgeous body looked so amazing in that saree. I wanted to pull her in my arms and make love to her till she screamed my name.

She blushed when she found me checking her out and it only added fuel to the already burning fire in me. I took my eyes off her with difficulty, I was glad when she was going to sit with her aunt, but then she turned and sat beside me.

I was barely hanging by a thread and her closeness and scent were driving me crazy, I tried not looking at her in fear I might do something stupid and embarrass her and myself in front of her family.

She looked cheerful talking about some movie with her friends and cousin, and I engaged myself in a dry business conversation with her father and uncle to keep my mind off her.

I noticed she was silent at the dinner table and was barely eating, I wanted to put some food on her plate but I didn't, fearing her reaction after what happened in the morning at breakfast. I was enjoying the food it was very good and was praising it because I had seen her mother and aunt nervous.

After my praise and compliments, Mia's mom looked relaxed and started enjoying the dinner. But Mia was still silent, I started getting worried about what had happened to her? One moment she was fine, chatting and arguing with her cousin, and the next I know she was grim.

She was silent on the way back home, I tried to start a conversation with her but she didn't look interested. I was wondering what was the matter with her? She was not the type to stay silent for so long. I wanted to tell her how beautiful she was looking today, and I had thought to try and seduce her while I was sitting in the sitting living room of her parent's home.

I know she was affected by me and she would give in with some persuasion, but her cold and distant behavior during the drive back home made me aware that at least today my seduction was not going to work.

When I asked her what was wrong she avoided answering and even avoided looking at me, I was worried was she regretting marrying me? Or was she missing her fiance? I didn't want to think about it but the thought kept crawling back to mind. What if Mia was not happy, marrying me?

I couldn't even think of losing her, in a matter of a few weeks she had possessed my mind and every thought of mine. Even imagining her with anyone else was enough to kill me, what if she asks me for divorce? What if she says she didn't want to stay with me?

I can't part with her now, she was mine though just in the name right now but that was enough for me. And I couldn't let her go now, it won't matter if I had to use force on her to keep her with me I will do that but I couldn't let her go. It was not possible, you marry Waleed Kamal, you fucking stay married.

I never use to share my things and she was not just a thing she was my wife, I could claw the men's eyes out who would even dare to look at her then how was it possible that I would let her go to be with another man.

No, this was not happening, she had to stay with me no matter if she loved me or not but she still has to stay with me.

I placed a soft peck on her lips, she stirred in sleep but thankfully didn't wake up.

"You are mine Mia, and I will make sure you always remain mine", I whispered and laid on the bed beside her a wall of pillows separating us both, I smiled, if I decided to take her this wall won't help her, hopefully, she knows that.

I went to my office the next day, I couldn't risk taking any more days off, there were too many projects lined up and I had to be there.

Mia was a little distant from me the entire week, she would speak to me but it felt like she was going through some internal struggle. I didn't want to push her for anything, so I just let her be, hoping she would come around and be normal again, but it proved to be my mistake.

She was a stubborn girl and she won't give me anything without a fight, I had to fight her even for an inch.

Chapter 17

Rameen

I was looking through my clothes to select a dress I can wear to the office tomorrow, it had been a week since we got married.

I was not going to sit idle at home to wait for him to come back from home, so I decided to go back to work.

Waleed was going office for the last I have been spending my time with Dada, but he also left today for their native village, he was worried about the school. It showed he cared about the village children and he didn't want to leave them to the teachers and the principal.

He was a loving and caring person and since I had known him from my childhood, we had bonded instantly. He had told me many things about Waleed, how possessive he was about all his things, even when he was a kid he won't let anyone touch his toys not even old and broken ones. If something was his it had to remain only his till his last breath.

He had shown me the room in which all his toys were still stored and all his other things, this was crazy. How can a man be so possessive about his things?

I selected a shirt and trousers and was looking for the accessories to pair them with when Waleed walked into the closet.

"Looking for something", He asked looking at me.

"Yeah, just picking clothes for tomorrow", I replied.

"Going somewhere?" He asked a little confused.

"Yeah, I am fed up sitting idle at home, so I thought of going to work", I replied, busy looking for matching shoes.

"Yeah, I will introduce you to everyone", He said as he pulled out a tee-shirt and sweats.

" Excuse me", I asked confused.

He had removed his shirt and was standing in front of me in just trousers.

"I will introduce you to our staff when we go to the office tomorrow", He replied looking at me in confusion.

" And who told you I am going to your office?", I asked placing my hands on my hips.

"You just told, you are planning to go to work", He said looking at me with suspicion.

" Yes by work I meant my job", I emphasized each word.

"You mean Daniyal's firm?", He arched his brow and asked me.

I was losing my patience now, what the hell was his problem? Didn't he understand simple things?

" That's where I work, I think?" I replied crossing my arms on my chest.

"You can't go and work in any other firm," He said enraged.

"And why is that?" I asked fearlessly.

He kept looking at me in anger, his grey eyes were burning with fury and it looked likes he was trying to control himself from lashing out at me.

"Because you are my wife Mia, and whatever is mine is yours including me. And I don't want you to go and work for anyone else", He said through gritted teeth.

" You want me to work for you?" I asked looking at him with a scowl on my face.

"I want you to work with me", He emphasized each word.

It softened my heart a little that he wanted me to work with him and not for him. But I knew no matter how much I work hard I would always be recognized as Mrs. Waleed Kamal and not as Rameen Shahab. I wanted to prove I was the best not because I was the wife of a billionaire, but because I deserved it.

" I am sorry Waleed but I can't work with you, I want my separate identity I just don't want to be known because I am your wife", I said in an apologetic tone.

"Mia, you are the best and it won't matter where you work, you will always be recognized for your talent and hard work and not because you are my wife", He said softening his tone.

" Then please let me work where I want to, please Waleed", I said in a pleading way.

He kept looking at me for some time as if he was trying to think of something that could make me change my decision.

"Why are you so stubborn?" He asked helplessly.

I felt like someone had gripped my heart in their hand, and I felt like telling him that I will work with him. But my mind stopped me, I can't give up now when I was so close.

"Please Waleed", I requested.

He took a deep breath and ran his fingers through his brown hair in frustration. Then he walked towards me and stopped when he was just inches away from me, I was puzzled. He was half-naked and was standing so close to me, heat radiating from his gorgeous body. I felt butterflies fluttering in my stomach.

He slid his arm across my waist and pulled me towards him till my body was touching his, I was standing there speechless with my eyes focused on my hands.

" This is what you do to me", He said pressing me close to himself.

I couldn't lift my eyes to look at him, all my senses were concentrated on the spot on my thigh where I was feeling his hardness.

"You drive me crazy Mia, so much that sometimes I just want to let go of all the restraint and claim you" He whispered in my ear, his lips rubbing my earlobe.

"Waleed, please", I was barely able to speak.

" Do you realize, how difficult it is for me?" He asked in a hoarse whisper.

I didn't reply and just stood there holding my breath, I didn't know what to do.

"And on top of that, you make it worse by arguing with me, why don't you just listen to me for once in your life?" He said, his lips rubbing on the side of my face playing havoc in my body.

"I-I do-don't want to argue" I replied stuttering.

He pulled his face away and lifted my chin with his fingers, his thumb caressing my lower lip. I kept looking downward afraid if I look in his intense grey gaze I will melt into a puddle near his feet.

"Look at me", He commanded." I want you to look at me when I am speaking to you".

I looked in his grey orbs with difficulty dreading I might drown into the storm that was rising in those grey eyes.

"I want to kiss you", He said in askance his gaze fixed on my lips.

" Waleed we can't", I mumbled terrified.

"Give me one valid reason, why I shouldn't?" He asked looking into my eyes.

My mind was in turmoil, how could I fucking think of a reason when I was barely holding myself from kissing him. I lowered my gaze to his chest and that was another mistake. His hard muscles on his chest were flipping my stomach into summersaults.

"I am waiting, Mia", He said, his thumb still on my lip, tracing it slowly.

" It's not correct, I am not ready", I whispered.

"I am not telling you to have sex with me, I am just asking you why I shouldn't kiss you now?" He was saying while his hand traveled from my face to the back of my neck.

Ohh my God is he about to kiss me? I thought half anticipating and half terrified.

"I think you don't have a reason and so I am going to kiss you", He said as he pushed me backward till my back was pinned down to the sliding door of the closet.

Why the hell does he always get turned on when we were in the closet, I will make sure next time to stay away from the closet in his presence.

His hand was still around, my waist, his body pushing me to the door while his hand pulled me into himself. I was finding it difficult to breathe.

And then he leaned and his fingers slid into my hair as he pulled my face closer to him, and he crushed his lips on mine. At first, I stood there without reacting, but he bit my bottom lip and pulled it demanding " Kiss me"

I started moving my lips with his, this was the first time I was kissing someone, and his naked torso pressing into my body was not helping. I slid my arms around his neck and my fingers into his soft brown hairs. I was touching his hair the first time, and let me tell you they were so soft for a man.

He was so beautiful, just like some Greek God, I just kept moving my lips with him, while he nibbled and pulled my lips, I was sure they would be swollen by the time he was done with them. Frankly, I didn't even know what to do I had seen kissing scenes in some movies but it was different now when I was witnessing live.

He pulled my hair and a cry came out of my mouth, using this opportunity he slid his tongue inside my mouth. His tongue moved in the inside of my mouth, it tasted like mint, I started moving mine with his, until they were battling with each other, he pulled my tongue and sucked at it earning a moan at the back of my throat.

I was trying to keep up with him but it was difficult I was too inexperienced, still, I tried to match his actions.

His hand traveled from my waist to my ass, he squeezed it, I groaned at his actions, my fingers dancing in his hair. He gave out a chuckle in my mouth at my groan, he was devouring my mouth.

I never had thought a kiss could blow my mind like this, the way he was kissing me, could have brought back the dead to life.

I don't know after how long he pulled back, but I sure was breathless, we both stood there breathing hard. Then he gave a small peck on my lips and pulled away saying.

"Do you know how many times I had fantasized this, Mia I can't tell you how good you taste and how hard it is for me to not carry you to bed right now?" He said, caressing my cheek as I looked into his eyes.

"Thank you", He whispered and left the closet.

And I stood there breathing frantically, trying to wrap my head around what just happened.

Waleed

I walked out of the closet with a proud grin on my face, I just couldn't believe I kissed her, not those pecks which I stole when she was asleep, but an actual kiss.

I was on cloud nine, I couldn't forget her taste, she was soo fucking sweet. I had kissed many girls before, but Mia she was so amazing, so innocent.

The way her gorgeous body molded with mine, the way she arched her back, without even realizing what she was doing. I was walking hard-on just because of her.

The way she looks at me terrified with her wide amber eyes, dreading and anticipating at the same time, just turns me on within seconds. I could understand, this was her first kiss, the way she was confused about what to do, and then gradually she started catching up and matching me, it was so fucking amazing.

I would teach her how to kiss and I am sure she will learn very fast, she is such an eager learner.

She came out after a few minutes, ignoring me completely. Her face was still flushed, and breathing uneven. She was standing in front of the dresser applying night cream on her face and body lotion on her arms.

" What's with you and apricots?" I asked out of curiosity.

She didn't reply to me and kept shooting daggers at me through the mirror, I hid my smile and stood up and took a step towards her. She turned towards me and yelled, "Waleed if you as much take one step towards me, I swear I will kill you".

The corners of my lips twitched, I was barely controlling my laughter, my fireball, so innocent and pure. She didn't even know how much she wanted me.

" Okk, I won't, just answer my question", I said raising my hands in defeat.

She kept looking at me suspiciously not believing that I couldn't stand down so easily, I wanted to tell her she was worrying for no reason, I got what I wanted right now and I won't disturb her for now, until my desire for her gets the better of me.

"What?" She asked confused.

"Why are you so obsessed with apricots?" I asked, pointing at the apricot lotion in her hand.

"I like the fragrance, and because I love eating apricots, dried or fresh", She replied.

" Plus this lotion is amazing, it softens the skin, like silk", She added.

"I wish I was apricot in your lotion", I said smiling mischievously.

She looked at me in confusion, like I was out of my mind, or something.

" What, why? She asked.

"At least then you might have allowed me to touch your body", I said with a smirk.

I saw her blushing, her cheeks turned red, the color of tomatoes, God help me, this girl had her pinky finger wrapped around my head.

She closed the cap of the bottle and threw it, at me in anger, I caught it easily with one hand and walked towards her and forwarded her the bottle.

She didn't take the bottle from me, instead turned and started brushing her hair, looking at my reflection in the mirror.

I bit my lower lip and looked at her in the mirror, she noticed my action and traced her tongue on the already swollen lips of her from the kissing. I was looking at her swollen lips pleased, she was never going to forget her first kiss ever, I had made sure of that. And now I would make sure she never forgets her other firsts as well.

" Waleed", She called me.

I was so busy with my thoughts that I hadn't noticed what she had said to me before.

"Huh?" I looked at her.

She turned and looked me in my eyes and then she closed the gap between us with quick steps, I was looking at her surprised, what was she planning?

"Thank you", She said as she tiptoed and kissed my cheek, and walked away.

Fuck me, what was she? I could never understand this girl, the moment I think I know everything about her, she does something completely out of the blue and shocks me.

I was the luckiest man in this whole world, I was sure I was never going to get bored in my life, this girl was always going to keep me on my toes.

Chapter 18

I was sitting on my desk, my cell phone in my hand texting in the group chat with Sheema and Rania.

Rania: Okay, I have got the popcorn so start spilling.

Sheema: Hey, wait let me finish typing this mail.

R: Sheema you can read afterward.

S: No way, I am not going to read leftovers.

M: Come on guys, my stomach is aching and if I didn't spill my guts, it's gonna burst.

R: She will die a virgin Sheema, hurry up.

I laughed at Rania's text, this girl was hilarious. She always had some non-veg references to everything.

S: Okay, I have finished typing, and go ahead.

R: Don't leave out any details okay.

M: Don't worry, I won't.

I replied smiling and then told them all about our kiss, I was dying to share this with both of them. This was my first kiss and it was mind-blowing. Or so I thought it was, I had never kissed before so I didn't have anyone to compare with.1

R: Wow, that's so amazing.

S: Did you like it?

M: Of course, I liked it.

R: Was he good enough?

M: How would I know, he is the only one I ever kissed.

R: You idiot if you had kissed Imaad, you would have at least known who was better.

S: Eww, why did you mention him.

M: I would never kiss that piece of shit.

R: Calm down bitches, I was just saying because Mia is inexperienced and how she would know he is a good kisser.

S: Point.

M: It felt good.

R: Tongue?

S:

M:

R: Good .

I laughed aloud, and everyone in the cubicle looked at me.

"Sorry", I mumbled.

R: So did you feel him?

M: Uh-huh.

S:

R: Is he?

M: You can't even imagine

S: Ewww

R: Sheema would you let two elders talk?

R: You should have boned him already.

M: I don't think I am ready for that.

R: You were not even ready to kiss? But didn't you enjoy it?

M: Kissing is a different thing.

R: It's just perception.

S:

R: Sheema stop sending those emoji's like School children.

" Mia, come to my office", Daniyal said as he was passing around our cubicle.

"Ohh shit", I thought, he saw me texting.

M: Boss alert. Bye.

R: We will text later, bye.

S: Bye guys.

This was the first day after our wedding that I had come to the office. And everyone was shocked to see me like I had grown horns on my head.

Then they said, they were expecting me to be on the honeymoon. I told them because of our sudden and unexpected wedding we couldn't because Waleed was very busy.

He would have taken me on honeymoon if I would ask him, but what were we going to do on the honeymoon if not sex?

I walked to Daniyal's office smiling to myself, I was euphoric, honestly, I never believed that just a kiss can make you feel so damn good. It was amazing, the feel of his lips on mine, the way he was demanding, it was like he was branding me, that I belonged to him and only him, and boy I wanted to be only his.

I knocked and entered Daniyal's office, he looked at me and smiled, and pointed to the chair across his desk for me to sit down. I sat on the chair smiling, at him.

" I didn't expect you to be back so soon, and frankly back to my firm", He said.

"Why?", I asked surprised.

" First it's been just a week since you got married, you still have three weeks' leave remaining and second I thought you would join Waleed's firm", He replied.

I know everyone was trying to figure out if our marriage was even real? And if it was then why we were back at work so soon.

"I would never leave my job Daani, I love working here. And I know I won't be pampered here as I will be in my husband's firm", I replied honestly.

" It's good to have you back Mia, I can only imagine how pissed he would have been because you didn't join his firm", He said smiling mischievously.

"Don't worry, I know how to handle him I replied", I said remembering the shocked expression on his face when I thanked him and kissed his cheek.

I could have done that for him at the least, he had been kind and loving to me, he cared for me more than anyone had ever, excluding my family. I had not joined his firm but I had the courtesy to at least thank him for the mind-blowing kiss he gave me, showing me what an important part of my married life I was missing.

One week passed since I joined back to work, we both have been so busy the entire week, that we just met at the dinner table and we both would be so exhausted that we would just stumble to sleep.

Saturday Waleed was having some business dinner, he asked me if I wanted to go with him, I declined him politely. I had to design a villa for Daniyal's friend and the deadline was fast approaching, I stayed home and worked on my design.

It was nearly midnight and Waleed was still not back, I shut off my laptop and went to bed, I fell asleep pretty soon, I was so exhausted I didn't even think about anything.

When I woke up, it was morning, I turned and looked to my side Waleed was not in the bed, I looked carefully, the pillow had an indentation which meant he had slept here, but where was he right now?

I tied the straps of my robe and walked out of the bedroom slipping my slippers on my feet, I was debating in which direction to go when I heard the sound of music, I followed it until it lead to the end of the corridor, the door was closed and the music was coming from inside, I turned the handle and it opened. I pushed the door and walked in, I was taken by surprise as I stepped into what looked like a gym, I still hadn't explored the whole house so I didn't have any idea that there was one.

And there he was in front of me, wearing just his sweats which hung low on his hips, his naked torso glistening with sweat as he was flexing his arms, his back was to me, he was practicing some moves of the king fu I guess, flexing his body and kicking a punching bag hanging in the middle of the room.

My, my what a sexy picture, I was licking the picture in front of me, his hard and broad back, the toned muscles of his arms, and his firm golden skin. How can someone be so hot and sexy, it should be illegal.

He might have sensed my presence because he turned and looked at me, his beautiful brown hair, were stuck around his face due to sweating, his chest was even more fascinating to see, I was sure I was ogling him with my mouth open.

He gave me a knowing smile, as he caught me eye-fucking him, I turned my gaze to look around the room when caught staring, there was all necessary equipment present, which had to be part of the gym if only I would had known, I could have hit the gym earlier.

" You woke up early today?" He said wiping the sweat with the help of a towel.

"I don't know, I didn't see the time", I replied, I was still embarrassed from being caught staring.

" Usually, you wake up after I finish the workout", He replied tossing the towel aside and walking to the refrigerator, and pulling out a bottle of what looked like an electrolyte drink.

"I didn't know you had a gym in your house, I would have done some cardio at least", I said walking to the treadmill.

" First of all, our house, and the second I love your body just the way it is, I think it's perfect", He said drinking the liquid.

I was astonished at his comment and my cheeks started getting warm, by just a mere mention of my body from him.

"I don't think a little workout will do any harm", I said trying to get over the effect of his comment.

" Of course it's your house and everything in this house belongs to you, you can use anything and everything as you please including me", He said with a wink.

I just blushed at his double-meaning comment, bastard.

"I will take a shower if you don't mind can you make breakfast? I don't call the cook on Sunday mornings, I make my breakfast", He said as he opened the bandages on his hand.

" I don't know how to cook, I hate cooking", I don't know why but I felt ashamed for the first time in my life, for not knowing how to cook.

"You don't know what?" He asked in shock.

"I don't know cooking okay, I can try but don't blame me if you don't like it", I replied getting mad.

" But all girls can cook", He said in astonishment.

"Not all girls, not the one clumsy like me", I replied ashamed.

He took some long strides and was in front of me, I thought he will say, how truly pathetic I was that I can't cook properly, but instead he placed his fingers below my chin and lifted it.

" Hey, it's okay, baby. This is nothing to be ashamed of, even I don't know how to do a lot many things, I can't design a house as you do, I can't sing, I am awful at poetry and you know what? I suck at drawing", He said, I thought he was just trying to cheer me up, but when I looked in his eyes I realized he was being completely honest.

"Freshen up, I will prepare the breakfast for you today, while you can sit and admire my body", He said with a wolfish grin.

He looked so cute at that moment, that I just lost control and tiptoed and kissed him, he was shocked at first, and then his hand traveled around my waist and the other in my hair above the neck he leaned and started kissing me back hungrily.

His warm naked torso pressing into mine, I could feel my nipples hardening against his chest, and I think he felt it too through the fabric of my robe as he groaned at the back of his throat.

This time I was more confident than the last, our tongues battling for dominance until I gave up and he ravished me. He broke the kiss and started kissing my jawline and then my neck, I arched my neck to give him access, he was kissing just below my ear then he bit my earlobe, a moan escaped my mouth and he smiled against my skin.

" I hope you know, what you started", he said sucking at my ear lobe but I was too ecstatic to think of anything.

The heat radiating from his body, the feel of his skin against the bare parts of my body. My mind was in a haze as his skilled mouth worked on my neck and then my shoulders. God, it felt so amazing, to be in his arms to be loved by him.

"Waleed" I cried in delight as squeezed my ass, and then my breath hitched as he spanked it, the pain felt so damn good.

"Did you like it, baby? Do you want more? Ohh Mia, if I could tell you what I want to do to you, how I want to devour you. You-drive-me-crazy-baby", He said between kisses.

He pressed his hips into mine, showing me how hard he was, inside his sweats, I blushed as I felt his hardness against my body. And he started grinding his hips against mine, it felt so fucking good.

"This is what you do to me, this is how you drive me crazy, I want you, I want you so badly that it fucking hurts so much", He said as he dipped his head to the swell of my breast and kissed just above my cleavage.

" Fuck, you are so soft" He groaned.

Then I felt his fingers working on the straps of my robe, and before I realized he untied it, I was wearing a tank top and shorts beneath it, His hands pulled off the robe and he looked at me with lust-filled eyes.

"You are so beautiful, you are so fucking beautiful", He said as he crushed his lips to mine, kissing me with more hunger and vigor than before.

His hands traveled to my sides under my top, his fingers caressing the swell of my breast gently and the truth dawned on me what was happening, I pulled away from him.

" Stop, we need to stop", I said panting.

I saw the shock and disappointment in his grey eyes for a second and then they change to something soft and warm.

"It's okay baby, I understand, you okay?", He asked looking at me with concern.

" Uh-huh," I replied unable to look into his eyes.

"You just have to say me to stop and I will, okay. I don't want you to rush into this if you are not ready, just take your time. I am always here for you", He said as he patted my cheek.

Why does he have to be so loving and considerate, it makes me feel guilty for not giving in to him. I was hating myself, but I just had panicked when I realized where this was leading and had acted on instinct.

My body protested as he pulled away from me, I wanted to tell him that I wanted him, but I was shy, I had lost the moment in panic and I didn't know how to tell him that I want him and I was ready.

Waleed

What the hell did I just say? I don't want to rush her into things? Was I out of mind or something? I wanted her, I want her, and I will always want her. And I told her it was okay if she didn't want to rush into it.

I am going crazy, she is driving me crazy. I banged the milk carton on the counter, where the hell is the pan now, I started banging the doors of the cabinet, I found it in the first cabinet.

I broke the egg so hard that the shells scattered in the bowl along with the egg, what the hell is happening to me? I can't even break an egg properly.

By the time I cleared the mess I created in the kitchen and had made scrambled eggs, coffee, and french toast, Mia walked into the kitchen fresh from the shower, her hair still wet and scattered on her back, her face devoid of any makeup, her lips swollen and a hickey on her neck, I gave her one more on the same spot because it had started fading.

"We need to talk", She said as soon as our eyes met.

"I am listening", I said arranging the plates and dishes on the counter.

"Waleed I am serious", She hissed through clenched teeth.

I looked at her, she was looking at me furiously, I wonder what I did wrong this time.

"You have to stop behaving like a vacuum, okay", She said pointing to her hickey.

I bowed my head and smiled so that she couldn't see I was smiling.

"I am talking to you", She sounded infuriated.

"I am the only one present here, other than you so I think it's common knowledge that you are talking to me unless you have a habit of talking to yourself", I turned and walked to the refrigerator to get some fruits.

Without even looking at her, I could tell her amber eyes must be on fire and if at all looks could kill, I would already have been dead.

"Why the hell, do you do this?, She asked, on the verge of breaking down.

"So that everyone knows you are taken", I replied honestly.

"What the fuck does this even mean?" She implored.

I looked at her while cutting cubes of the apple and peaches and tossing them into the bowl.

"I am sorry, I am too much fascinated with those werewolf books, and they kind of mark their mates on their neck so that everyone knows they are taken", I replied scratching the back of my neck.

She was looking at me with her mouth open and her eyes wide as saucers as if I was some alien who had just landed on Earth.

"You must be kidding", She exclaimed in disbelief.

And when I didn't reply and kept scratching my head, her expressions changed into astonishment.

"How old are you, five?" She asked, keeping her hands on her hip.

"Everyone has some fantasies okay, what if I am fascinated by werewolves and wish that I was one, what's so strange about it", I asked annoyed.

"My God, I can't believe this, The Waleed Kamal, CEO of KKC have fantasies of a four years old", She said dramatically.

I laughed at her tone, everyone has a child inside them, I may be a CEO but I still was human and I have my fantasies. I never told this to anyone before, but she was not anyone, she was my Mia.

"Do you shift on the full moon?", She asked teasing.

I just rolled my eyes and start putting food on my plate, she sat beside me on the barstool and looked around the table, and said

" Where is my tea?"

Ohh shit, I forgot she drank tea at breakfast, in my sexual frustration it slipped my mind.

"I forgot you drink tea, don't worry I will make it", I said standing from the stool.

She held my hand and pulled me down, making me sit on the barstool again.

" It's okay, I think I will try your coffee", She said smiling.

"You sure? It won't take much time to make your tea" I asked.

"It's okay, Alpha", She said with a mischievous smile.

Fuck, did she just call me an Alpha? I looked at her in astonishment.

"It's okay, we can pretend you are Alpha and I am your Luna", She said laughing.

"Mate", I replied laughing.

"Mate", She agreed.

We ate our breakfast discussing the werewolf stories we had read and the movies we had seen. It was fun, pretending with her to be the Alpha and the Luna.

"I want at least 6 pups, my Luna", I said teasingly.

She slapped my arm in fury, I liked teasing her, just to make her furious and watch her amber eyes turn into the color of fire, it was so fascinating.

Please dont forget to vote, comment and share. Do check out my other books as well.

Chapter 19

R ameen
    I was busy working on a project when my cellphone buzzed,
I looked at the screen it was a text from Waleed.

Hottie: What's up?

Yep, I saved his number as, Hottie, first I had saved it as, Arrogant
CEO, but since I had seen him work out in the gym last weekend, and
no matter how much I tried, I couldn't take out that sexy picture of
my mind, I changed it to, Hottie.

Mia: You just dropped me half an hour ago .

Hottie: So, can't I ask about ur well being?

Mia: Come to the point, will you?

Hottie: I am missing you.

A smile broke on my lip, what was I going to do about him, it was
too hard not to fall for him when he kept doing things like this.

"Mia, I want you to go to the resort site with Kabir, there is some
problem there, you need to sort it out, I would have come with
you, but I have an important meeting", Daniyal said standing at the
cubicle entrance.

"Okay boss," I said nodding my head.

"You leave in half-hour okay?"He warned.

"Yep," I replied.

Mia: I miss you too, ok. I need to go to the site there is some problem.

H: Who are you going with.

I rolled my eyes, this was not going as I thought.

Mia: Kabir

H: Why is Daniyal not going with you?

I was getting annoyed by his questions, was he going to poke his nose in my job all the time like this.

Mia: He has another meeting.

H: Don't leave until I tell you, okay.

Mia: I am leaving in 25 mins.

H: I told you not to leave until I tell you.

Gone was the charming man and the arrogant Waleed was back. Why does he always try to boss me around?

Thank God, I didn't choose to work with him, he would have driven me crazy. I saved my design and then shut down the system.

I went to the restroom to freshen up, and when I came out it was nearly time to leave, Kabir was already waiting for me near the cubicle.

" Hey, how are you?" He asked cheerfully.

"Fine," I replied picking up my handbag and cellphone.

"And your hubby?" He asked.

"He is good," I replied following him to the elevator.

Kabir pressed the button and we waited in silence for the elevator to reach our floor. I was looking at the screen flashing numbers of the floor on which the elevator was, impatient.

I would call Waleed on the way, I thought as the elevator reached our floor and the door started opening. And when I saw the person that walked out of the elevator my temper soared.

"Mr. Kamal, what a pleasant surprise," Kabir said forwarding his hand to Waleed.

"The pleasure is mine," He smiled looking at me.

I wanted to scratch the smile off his face, the possessive bastard was here just to stop me from going to the site with Kabir.

"I was here to meet Daniyal, you guys going somewhere?" He asked acting innocent.

"We were leaving for the site," Kabir replied, while I stood silent shooting daggers at him.

"Would you mind if I stole my wife for some time," Waleed said sliding his arm around my waist and pulling me towards him.

"Not at all," He replied.

Waleed lead me towards Daniyal's office, I wanted to pull myself away from him but I couldn't have done that without creating a scene in front of my colleagues.

"Hey Daniyal," He greeted as he entered Daniyal's cabin.

"Waleed, what a surprise man. I didn't remember we agreed to meet," He said smiling.

"I was thinking of visiting the resort site, and I was wondering if you can spare Mia for a day," He said still standing with his arm around my waist.

"Ohh sure, Kabir and Mia were on the way to the site and if you are going I think I will inform Kabir there is no need for him to go," Daniyal said as he picked up the receiver to call Kabir.

"Thanks, dude, I owe you for this. I hate driving alone, long distances," He replied smiling.

"No problem at all. Have fun you guys, I will be leaving for a meeting in a few minutes," he told dialing a number.

"Later then," Waleed said and turned around to leave.

"Later," Daniyal replied.

As soon as we were in the elevator alone I pushed him away from me, he just laughed looking at me.

"I was not going to let you go with any other man," He said in a serious tone.

" He is my colleague, we have been working together for more than a year," I said annoyed.

"I don't trust myself around you, there is no way I can trust any other man," He said.

"Pervert," I retorted.

"Trust me, baby, all men are perverts. They are just waiting for the right opportunity," He said with a smirk.

My heart leaped in my chest when he called me baby, why the hell does I react like this each time he called me baby.

"Last time you were alone in the car with me for so long, all I wanted to do was fuck you till you screamed my name. Do you think I would leave you alone with another man for so long in the proximity of a car," He said with his intense gaze piercing through me.

"As I said before, PERVERT," I emphasized.

The elevator door opened and he once again held my waist and strolled towards the exit of the building. He opened the passenger seat for me and walked around and slid into the driver's seat.

I was mad at him, I just ignored him and kept staring out of the window. He can't just walk into my workplace dictating everyone around.

After some time he took my hand in his and kissed on my knuckles. A jolt of excitement traveled through my body. Fuck I couldn't stay mad at him anymore, but I still had to pretend so that next time he won't demonstrate such machoism.

"I am sorry," He said.

I kept staring out of the window, though I was dying to look at him.

"Mia, look at me," He said.

I kept pretending I was mad at him, he needs to understand what he did, was against the ethics of professionalism.

He kept caressing the back of my hand with his fingers, making, butterflies flutter in my belly.

"Concentrate on driving, you will get both of us killed," I said bitterly.

"Such a killjoy Mia, I thought you will be glad to spend time with me, instead of your stupid colleague," He said annoyed.

Of course, I was glad, but I didn't want him to know, otherwise he would never take me seriously ever again.

"Didn't you have any work to do in your office today?" I said just as I remembered.

"Actually, had to reschedule a couple of meetings and cancel a few appointments", He said with a goofy grin.

"Waleed," I exclaimed in disbelief.

"What? My mind would have been diverted to you, what you were doing? Were you alright, or not? Or if your colleague was flirting with you? I won't have been able to concentrate on work either way. So I should be with you, at least I will have peace of mind," He replied in his CEO tone.

I hated it when he acted the cool and sexy billionaire, honestly, I loved it, it just turns me on and I was afraid of this fact.

"We can have lunch at Abdul's while returning," He tried to bribe me and my mouth water on the mere mention of the Dhaba (roadside restaurant on a highway).

"Okay, don't think I forgave you, I just don't want to die out of boredom in this long drive," I said suppressing my smile.

"Admit it you can't resist me," He said with a smirk.

"Cocky," I said rolling my eyes.

He chuckled at my response and left my hand as he diverted his attention to the heavy traffic.

We listened to songs while driving and Waleed now and then tried to talk me into giving him a smooch, which I declined, though I was tempted I knew one thing was going to lead to the other and I didn't want to lose my virginity in a car.

We reached the site in nearly two hours, taking a round of the construction going on, I was quite impressed by the speed of the construction, the last time when I was here the foundation was being dug up but now the structure above the ground was visible.

Waleed was very professional while dealing with the site engineers and supervisors, completely in his CEO form, it was kind of hot. I was looking at him mesmerized, the way he carried himself, with such ease and grace was amazing.

His firm tone and his don't mess me attitude was enough to make me drool, he was so hot and he was all mine.

It took nearly three hours to deal with the problems and to take a tour of the site, Waleed asked me if I wanted to take a walk on the beach with him. And how could I decline such a romantic offer?

We walked on the beach with his arms around my waist and my body pressed to his and my head on his shoulder and our spare hands intertwined with each other.

We didn't speak at all and were just drinking in the presence of each other, this was the most romantic thing I had ever done in my life and with none other than yours truly Waleed Kamaal.

I didn't want to leave but I was starting to feel hungry and my stomach, was growling.

"We need to get you something to eat," Waleed said smiling and kissing my forehead as we walked back to his car.

The food was better than I remembered, I had eaten more than I should have, and was barely able to keep myself awake.

We stopped at the village to meet Dada, he was still at the school, Dada showed me around the school enthusiastically. He asked us to go to their home with him but Waleed apologized saying he had a business dinner and we would come and visit him on the weekend.

Waleed

I was busy looking at some files from the finance department, it was Saturday and I had come early home, hoping to spend some time with Mia, but she had some different plans. She was going to a wedding reception and had asked me to go along with her.

I had also received the invitation to the reception, but I didn't intend to go, I was not a party person. On the other hand, Mia looked quite excited. While she was dressing up for the reception, I opened my laptop and started going through the emails and the documents.

She emerged from the closet after half an hour and when I saw her my breath stopped.

She was wearing a black saree, of all the outfits, she had to choose a saree and that too black. Honestly, I think Saree is the sexiest outfit in the world.

"Fuck," I cursed.

Maybe I should have agreed to go to the reception with her, but I never thought she could decide to wear a saree and look so hot in it.

The fabric was really thin, and the bare skin of her belly and waist was visible through it, which added to my misery.

She applied makeup expertly, combed, and left her hair open on her back, sprayed perfume, and was ready to leave. She came to me before leaving, gave me a quick peck on my lips, and said she would be back before midnight.

I sat there trying to concentrate on the document open on my laptop screen but all I could think of was her in that black saree, looking sexy as hell, and some guy flirting with her at the reception.

I cursed myself, took a shower got dressed, and left for the reception, there was no way I was going to leave her with vultures trying to claw at her at the first chance.

I was greeted by the host at the entrance whose son's reception was there, I wished and congratulated them and lol looked around for my wife. The reception was arranged on the lawn of a Five-star hotel and the guest list consisted of all the who's who of the town.

I found her speaking to a couple not far from me, I could see the way the men were staring at her. The possessive male inside me kicked in as I made my way towards her. Her back was to me and she had not noticed me until I slid my arm around her bare waist and pulled her towards me.

I could tell how shocked she was by my actions, she looked at me in fury, like she was going to kill me, but when she saw it was me who had the courage to touch her, her body relaxed and her expression changed to astonishment.

"Hey baby, sorry for being late. I hope you didn't have to wait," I said giving her a peck on her cheek

I was sure, she was gonna be mad as hell on this public display of affection, but I wanted everyone to know she was only mine, and no one should even dare to look at her.

"What the hell are you doing here?" She said through clenched teeth, a smile plastered on her face.

The photographers had approached us, taking our pictures, this was the first time, I was attending a public event with my wife after our wedding.

"Claiming my territory," I replied with a sweet smile.

"Waleed you have to stop, behaving like a werewolf, okay," She said in anger.

I know how mad she was at me right now, the way her amber eyes have turned into the color of fire and her whole body had stiffened in my arms.

"Sir, Mam, if you could look at the camera," One photographer said.

"Mam can you please get a little closer," Another called out.

"Please if you could turn a little to the left, yes, yes. Perfect shot," Another said.

We kept obliging to the photographers' demand, playing the perfect couple. A reporter from a tabloid approached us.

" How is your married life?" He asked us.

"Pure Bliss," I replied smiling and kissing her forehead.

"Waleed you have to stop the PDA," Mia whispered in my ear, in an angry voice.

" What is mam, whispering?" The reporter asked curiously.

"She was just saying, how hot I am looking," I replied smiling.

That earned me an elbow in my ribs from Mia, but I kept smiling to the cameras and the reporter.

"Your wedding was quite unexpected, how do you both feel about this, Mam, if you would answer this question," The reporter addressed Mia

"I am sure, I couldn't have gotten a better husband than him," She said as she gave a peck on my cheek, earning hootings and whistles.

Damn, this girl is so unpredictable, I thought fascinated. I was completely whipped, there was no chance of survival.

We excused after a few more photographs and walked to the Bride and Groom. After greeting them and exchanging a few words we walked to the buffet.

After dinner, we both met with some other guests and had some formal conversation.

By the time we returned home, it was past midnight, Mia looked quite exhausted, she had removed her Jimmy Choo sandals from her feet and was slowly massaging them sitting on the passenger seat.

When I opened the door of the passenger seat after parking the car she slid out with her shoes in one hand and her clutch in another, same as the day she was left behind on the site. The only difference was, she was my wife now.

I pulled her to me and carried her in my arms bridal style, ignoring her cries of protest. I let her down only when we were inside our bedroom, she was looking at me annoyed.

"You know you are a territorial and possessive brat," She said.

"Yes, and only for you," I replied in a husky voice.

" Waleed you need to stop behaving like this, I don't like when you act like this," she was saying something else but all my attention was focused on her lips, which were covered in red lip color and I swear I never have been turned on before like this.

Before anyone of us realized I had her pinned to the nearest wall and my lips were on hers and I was kissing her as my life depended on it. She was sure as a shock as hell at first, but then she gave in to the kiss.

I was holding her hands above her head, my other hand was around her waist, my body pressing hard into hers. I licked the entrance of her mouth and she welcomed with a moan. Our tongues battling with each other for dominance.

I pulled away when I was short of breath and started kissing her jawline, I trailed kisses down her neck and then to her ear, earning moans from her as I sucked, bit, and licked her flawless smooth skin.

Then I lowered down to her exposed belly, holding her saree, to bare her skin with one hand and stroking her skin with the other, as I kissed her belly button, her hands slid to my hairs and her grip tightened as she pulled them when my tongue started the onslaught of her navel.

"Aah Waleed," She moaned.

" Yes baby, sing for me," I said as I sucked and placed kisses on the bare skin of her waist.

My hand traveled up to her breast as I cupped her one breast, in my hand through the fabric of her blouse, she shuddered with delight.

"Yes baby only I can make you feel like this," I said as I pinched her hardened nipple below the fabric of her blouse.

She moaned and it was more than I could take, I stood straight and kissed her again on the lips, her passion matching mine as her fingers danced through my hairs.

I heard the ring of the cell phone, but I ignored it and kept kissing her jaw and neck, while she whimpered in delight. When the cell phone started ringing the second time Mia tried to push me away without any success.

" Waleed, someone is calling, it might be important," She said.

"Let them call, I am in the middle of something more important," I was still suckling at her earlobe.

The cell went silent to my delight and started ringing again after a few seconds.

" Dammit," I cursed as I pulled out my cell from my pocket taking a few steps away from her.

It was my classmate from the US, I wondered why the hell he was calling right now. I hit the receive button on the screen.

"Congratulations man, I just saw your pictures with your wife on the internet. Damn, she is hot as hell, you are a lucky bastard," He said laughing.

I cursed him in my mind, that fucker had ruined the moment with Mia, she was finally looking like she would give in.

"Thanks, dude," I replied cheerfully.

I saw Mia walk to the closet, as I kept speaking to my friend. She came out wearing a tee shirt and a pair of loose pajamas. I was disappointed, I should have told her not to change so soon.

The bastard nearly spoke for an hour to me and when I was finally able to say goodbye and disconnect the call, Mia was fast asleep. I once again cursed him with whole my heart.

Chapter 20

R ameen

    "Mia"

I heard someone call me, I turned and looked behind. This was the last person I wanted to see in this world.

He came beside me in a few long strides, I ignored him and kept walking.

"Mia, please can we talk", He said walking beside me.

"It's Mrs. Waleed Kamaal for you", I snapped and kept walking.

I had come for a meeting with the client and just had left their office and was on way to hire a cab. When I heard him call, seriously out of all people it had to be Imaad.

"Seriously Mia, we have known each other since childhood and we were", He was saying but I interrupted him.

"It's enough Mr. Imaad Hassan, I don't want anything to do with you, and please stop following me", I halted and snarled at him.

He stood in front of me, looking ashamed with his head bowed down.

"If you will please, let me explain", He said.

"I don't think there is any need of an explanation", I said and was turning when he grabbed my arm.

I looked at him furiously and tried to remove my arm from his grip, but he held it tightly.

"Leave my hand Imaad", I said through clenched teeth.

"Not unless you hear me out", He insisted.

I didn't want to create a scene in public, the photographs from the reception were all over the internet and tabloid if someone were to recognize me with a man holding my hand it would create a new controversy.

"Just leave my arm, and I will listen to what you have to say", I said trying to suppress my anger.

Imaad loosened his grip on my arm and retracted his hand, he pointed towards a coffee shop, I silently followed him, he walked to a corner table and seated himself, he asked me if I would like to have something, I declined and he ordered a coffee for himself.

" You have ten minutes, better start talking", I said looking at my wristwatch.

I don't know what I was doing, sitting with this man and why did I even agree to listen to him.

I had freaked out when he held my arm in broad daylight in the middle of a street, lately, I have been getting a lot of attention from the paparazzi, being a wife of the billionaire doesn't come easy. Waleed had tried to assign me with a guard cum driver but I had declined his offer.

Waleed used to pick and drop me to work and mostly I would go with Daniyal or Kabir to meetings. But today it happened that they both were busy and I had come to the meeting in a cab.

"Mia, I am sorry for what I did to you, but believe me, I am not able to forgive myself.

Our business had incurred huge losses in the last six months, we tried hard to control the damage but we lost a significant amount and were behind on the payment of the loans. I tried hard to get some money from money launderers but it happened that we even lost that amount.

We didn't have any option other than to ask your share of the business and then sell it to give back the money to the launderers", He said.

I was looking at him astonished, I couldn't believe what he was saying. Were they really bankrupt?

" If you really had financial problems you could have asked for help from Dad, he would have done everything in his power to help you", I said.

"You think they would have let us get married if they knew I was bankrupt", Imaad said furiously.

" I'm sorry, but there is no use digging old graves, I have listened to what you had to say, and that's it. Don't try to contact me again, I am happily married and I don't want to jeopardize my relationship with my husband because of you", I said standing from the chair.

"But Mia, we loved each other", He said trying to stop me from going.

" No, you loved me. I only love my husband", I stalled and left the coffee shop.

What the hell did I just say? I love my husband? Do I love Waleed? Ohhh my God what was happening to me? Was I falling for him?

I hired a cab and gave the address of our house, I texted Waleed that I was going home and he didn't have to pick me.

I didn't want to face Waleed right now, I was struggling internally, one part of me was telling me that I had fallen in love with Waleed, while the other was saying that I was just exaggerating things and I just have told Imaad that I loved my husband in the flow of the events and there was nothing significant about it.

I reached home, changed, and freshen up, I just wanted to forget what Imaad had told me, the fact was that he and his family were not worth it. He was trying to put the weight of his sins on my family saying if they had told the truth my parents would have called off the wedding instead of helping them, son of a bitch.

And on top of that, he had the nerve to tell me that we loved each other, I was fuming while pacing the terrace of our bedroom.

I came back inside after nearly two hours, Waleed was still not back, I started wondering why he was taking so long.

I tried calling him, but he didn't answer my call, it was getting late and still, he did not return.

I called him again and again, but his cell was switched off, all kinds of negative thoughts started crossing my mind, what if he was in an accident?

I didn't eat dinner and instead was calling every contact in the hope at least someone might tell me that he was with them, but unfortunately, no one knew where he was. His secretary told me he had gotten a call from someone and had left in haste.

My family was out of town, they had gone to attend a wedding, only Dada was at home, I thought of calling Dada but he would only get worried.

It was midnight and still, he didn't return home, I had started to panic by now, he always used to call or text me if he was going to be late.

I was really worried about him, and I was scared if anything happened to him. I was feeling guilty for keeping him waiting so long.

I was missing him, his smiles his concern for me, the way he flirted with me, and most of all I missed his touch. I wanted to be in his arms, kissing him and making love with him.

I realized how much I have got habituated to him, I hadn't realized when he was around and now when he was not there I was missing him and was wanting to be with him.

I prayed for his safe return to Allah, and I promised that I won't deny him his rights anymore. I just wanted him back safe and sound. Thousands of terrifying thoughts were crossing my mind.

I paced in the living room, and when my legs started hurting I sat on a sofa, my eyes were fixed on the clock it was two in the morning. It felt like I sat there for eternity dreading and scared.

And when I lost all hope of his returning I heard his car stop on the porch, I ran out to the main door and opened it, he was getting out of the car, when he saw me he stood still, his eyes studying my face, I had been crying and I was sure I looked like a complete mess right now.

Before Waleed could take a step I ran towards him and buried my face in his chest, inhaling the musky scent of his body mixed with the smell of his perfume and cologne.

He wrapped his hands around me and pressed me closer to him.

"Where have you been? I thought I lost you? I said between sobs.

I couldn't describe how relieved I was, to see him alright standing with his arms around me. At that moment I realized that I had fallen for him.

" I am okay, baby. I am absolutely fine", He replied rubbing his fingers in my hair.

"Why didn't you receive my call?" I complained.

"Let's go inside then I will tell you", He picked me in his arms and carried me to the bedroom.

He placed me on the bed carefully, then removed his jacket and loosened his tie, I was watching every moment of his, before today I had taken him for granted but not now, I want to cherish every moment I spend with him.

He opened his shirt buttons and tossed them aside as he went to the bathroom, he came out after a few minutes, towel around his waist and water glistening on his naked body I watched him mesmerized as he disappeared into the closet.

He walked out after some time wearing a tee and sweats, he came to the bed and sat opposite to me, and looked at me.

" Now tell me, why were you afraid?", He asked.

"You didn't return home last night, I was so worried for you", I said.

He took my hands into his and started massaging my knuckles. A jolt of excitement ran through my body by his touch.

" I was in the hospital, with your grandfather, his blood pressure shot up, I was wrapping up the last meeting when he called me last night.

I was really busy and that's why I didn't get the time to call you, and when your Dada called I left the office and took him to the hospital. His condition was not good, doctors told me a little more delay might have caused his life.

He had told me not to tell anyone that he was in the hospital except Umair, as you know your family is out of town attending a wedding", He stopped and looked at me.

"Why didn't you tell me? Is he okay now", I asked worriedly.

My Dada was unwell and hospitalized and no one told me, I was worried about Dada and whether he was alright or not?

" He is stable and out of danger now, that's why I came home, Umair arrived an hour ago and he is with him", He replied.

"I want to go to the hospital", I said trying to get up.

Waleed pulled my arm and made me sit on the bed again.

" You need to sleep now, I will take you to the hospital in the morning after breakfast", He said.

"Waleed, I have to go, I want to be with Dada", I tried removing his hand from my arm.

" Mia", His voice had a command and an authority.

I was quiet, he never raised his voice on me before, I knew he was right.

"Dada is sleeping due to effects of the drugs and will only wake up in the morning, there is no use of going there now, take rest we will go after breakfast okay?", He said.

I just nodded in agreement, he slipped on the bed beside me under the sheets and pulled me to him, I didn't protest at his attempt.

" I missed you so much, I don't know what you have done to me", He whispered as he snuggled me into his arms and placed his face on the crook of my neck.

I was too exhausted to think of anything else, and I fell asleep instantly.

We visited Dada after breakfast, Waleed left me at the hospital and went to his office. Dada looked like he had aged ten years overnight. His face had lost color and he looked weak.

I stayed in the hospital, with him, Umair was there with me. He was discharged after two days, we took him to our home, I had asked Daani for one week leave.

The week passed very fast with Dada and Umair around, he had returned from the wedding lying to my family, and some internal exams had come up.

Waleed was very nice with Dada and Umair, he gave them company every evening after he returned from work. I was really glad that he just didn't love me but also cared about the people attached to me.

My feelings for him had gone a transformation in the last week, I was glad that I had finally realized how much I wanted him and loved him. He was a true gentleman and the way he cared about Dada showed it.

Dada went back home when my family returned from the wedding, though Waleed and I insisted he stay with us, he said he was missing home and will come and stay with us again. Dad and Chachu were mad at us for hiding that Dada was unwell. Mom and aunt went to the extent to scold me and Umair for not informing them and were only calmed when Dada told them that he had told us not to inform them.

Chapter 21

Waleed

I had come to another town for a business meeting, I was going to stay overnight, but when the meeting was over and the deal was finalized I felt the sudden urge to go back to Mia.

I had called and told her in the afternoon that I would return tomorrow, but as I had wound up all the work today I went to the airport and returned home by the next flight.

I had told the driver to pick me from the airport and not inform Mia of my return, I wanted to give her a surprise, the last week was very busy with her Dada and Umair around.

They had just left yesterday, and I had a flight last night so I didn't get any time to spend with her. She was opening up to me I have seen the change in her in the last week. She was trying hard to be close to me and I was happy she had finally accepted me with her whole heart.

As I sneaked into the bedroom my jaw hit the floor, she was standing in front of the dresser wearing a pale pink-colored cute baby doll nightdress that ended just below her hips. Her shoulders were bare, only two thin straps of her nightdress covered them.

I could see her cleavage through the deep neck of her dress, her long pair of legs were bare and were enticing wicked thoughts in my mind, She was applying the apricot lotion on her arms and neck, I was watching as her hands traveled on her body and I wished it were my lips instead of her hand.

The bottle of the lotion dropped from her hand as she noticed me standing in the door with my jaw hitting the floor and my eyes fixed on her.

"Waleed" My name left her lips in the form of a whisper.

I shut the door and closed the gap between her and me, she was looking at me in the mirror, anticipating my next move. I leaned and picked up the bottle of the lotion from the floor near her feet and stood up.

I forwarded my hand to her and whispered: "Allow me".

She turned and looked at me, debating with herself whether to take my hand or not.

" Trust me", I took her hand in mine and walked towards the couch, I made her sit on the couch and sat on the floor near her feet.

I placed my hand on her feet, I was looking at her feet so close for the first time, and I must say they were beautiful. Manicured nails of her toes were covered in a deep burgundy nail color.

Her toes curled as I touched her feet, I looked at her, she was looking at me mesmerized, her amber eyes wide with anticipation.

I poured some lotion on my palm and started applying it on her feet slowly and gently as I had all the time in the world when I finished applying the lotion on her feet, I proceeded to the calf, of her long slender leg, her complexion was white, with a hint of golden. It was like a layer of milk over a layer of honey.

I massaged her legs as I kept applying the lotion, maintaining eye contact with her, I could see the havoc my touch was causing to her, in her eyes. When I finished massaging her feet and calf, I raised her foot a little till it reached my mouth and gently placed kisses on her toes without breaking eye contact.

I felt her shiver, she was barely holding, I could see the need building inside her, but I didn't want to rush. I had waited so long for her and I wanted her to find out how difficult it had been for me to resist myself from taking her.

I did the same on her second leg, starting from her feet and moving up to her knee, the dimple in her knees were provoking me to move upward on her thigh but I resisted and when I finished the massage, I kissed her toes in the same way like the first leg, looking directly in her eyes.

Then I sat on my knees and lifted her hand in mine, I applied the lotion in the same manner first on her hand then her forearm then upward on her elbow and hind arm, kissing each of her fingers when I finished.

I could see how desperate she was by this time, she was breathing fast and I could sense that her pulse had risen.

I continued the same torture on her second arm, I saw her clenching her thighs when I kissed her fingers and sucked at her pinky finger this time. My lioness was aroused, I patted myself, for displaying such patience. Not so easily, my love, I addressed her in my mind.

I stood up and went behind the couch with the bottle in my hand as she watched me alarmed why I was leaving her. I came around and poured the lotion on her bare shoulder and she shuddered. I had a smirk on my face, if she was a lioness then I was a lion, and I love playing with my prey.

I spread the lotion gently on her skin, massaging along as I went, first her shoulder then her neck, I was glad she had fixed her hairs in a bun, so I had easy access to her neck without her hairs disturbing me. Apart from a few loose strands that hung around her face and neck.

I placed a kiss on the back of her neck, on her spine, just as I finished massaging her neck. I slid the straps of her dress gently down her arm, and she placed her hands to stop me from sliding them further.

"Shh, tonight you play an obedient wife", I slid my hands out from below hers.

" Waleed".

"Not today, my darling wife", I whispered as I sucked at her ear lobe and she moaned.

I barely controlled myself from giving in, then I applied lotion on the exposed area of her back gently moving towards her shoulder then her collar bones, and down to her cleavage. I halted and felt her breath hitch, I slowly started massaging in a circular motion as I touched her skin just above her breast, she leaned back, resting her back against the couch, allowing me full access, but I had something else in my mind.

I stopped and pulled my hands from her body and closed the cap of the bottle as I walked to the dresser, I felt her staring at my back with astonishment. When I placed the bottle and turned around she was still staring at me.

I removed my jacket and tossed it aside, as I was about to loosen my tie, I saw her approach me, not breaking eye contact. She was in front of me within seconds, she raised her hand and kept them on mine which was loosening the knot of my tie.

"Allow me", She said in the same tone as mine.

It was my time to be shocked, she gently removed my hands from the tie and loosened and opened the knot leisurely, like she had all the time in the world, and tossed aside my tie.

Her fingers then started working on the button of my shirt, one at a time slowly, still maintaining eye contact as she reached the last button she pulled the shirt tucked in my trouser and discarded it on the floor below.

She then started working on the belt of my trouser, she slowly opened the buckle and pulled it from my trousers, and then she passed it through her fingers slowly, very slowly biting her lower lip, as the woman in the movies or commercials does with a whip, and I can't describe how fucking sexy she looked at that moment. This girl was driving me crazy, with her teasing.

She put the belt around my neck and pulled me towards her with it, Lord I was whipped completely there was no doubt in it.

"Would you like to take me on the bed or the couch?" She whispered in my ear.

Fuck.

I couldn't control myself, any longer. I pulled her to me and crushed my mouth on hers, biting her lower lip and pulling it, she moaned in my mouth and I slid my tongue inside her, she was so sweet, fuck I love her taste, I love everything about her, she drives me crazy.

I put my hands on her hips and hoisted her up as she wrapped her long legs around my waist, carrying her to the bed without breaking the kiss and laying her on it, I quickly positioned myself between her legs.

I leaned and placed a kiss on her jawline and then bit it, a giggle escaped her mouth, I trailed down to her neck placing kisses and licking her smooth skin. Tonight, I would own her in every possible way.

_____

We laid there on the bed our limbs entangled with each other, as we came down from our high, her face was flushed and her breathing was fast from the ordeal I had made her go through.

"You okay?", I asked her.

" Uh-huh", She replied nodding.

"Are you sore?" I asked looking into her eyes.

"A little".

" I will run a bath for you, it will help soothe the pain", I slid out of the bed and strolled into the bathroom.

When I came back she was sitting on the bed wrapped in a sheet, her hairs were plastered on her face due to the sweating.She turned her gaze when she saw me, I smiled at her embarrassment and went into the closet and slid into a pair of sweats.

"You like to eat something?" I asked her, I was feeling hungry after the lovemaking we did.

She nodded in reply, I opened the bedroom refrigerator and retrieved two cups of Greek yogurt in apricot flavor. Yes, apricots were my favorite now, since I found out how much she loved them.

I walked towards her and sat on the bed opposite her, peeling the wrapper from the cup and filling the spoon with the yogurt, she tried to take the cup from my hand but I pulled it away from her and instead offered her to feed myself. She opened her mouth without protesting and I fed her till the cup was empty, then I picked her in my arms and carried her to the bathroom.

The bath was filled, I slid her down on the floor and turned off the tap, adding a bubble bomb to it, which exploded immediately and bubbles started to emerge on the surface. I added a few oils to the bath which fastened the healing process.

"I will wait outside, let me know when you are finished", I told her and went out of the bathroom giving her privacy.

I didn't know when I fell asleep waiting for her on the bed, but when I woke up she was snuggled close to my chest. It was still dark outside I pulled her to me and buried my head in her hair and fell asleep again.

Rameen

I woke up to a beautiful morning, the sunlight was straining through the curtains, I could hear the chirping of the birds from the cages that were present on the terrace.

Waleed was very fond of birds, he had many different kinds of birds in his collection, he had shown me the birds enthusiastically and had narrated to me their names and the countries from which he had imported them, and I hardly remembered any of those details.

I turned and looked at Waleed who was sleeping behind me, his arm wrapped around my waist, his face resting on the crook of my neck.

I slowly unwrapped his arm from around me and tried to slide out of bed, but before I could do that, his arms were around me again and he pulled me towards him, slamming me with his chest.

" Where do you think you are going?" Waleed inquired as he nuzzled my neck.

"Good Morning", I taunted.

" I told you my morning will be good if you kissed me", He said as he dipped his head and kissed me on my lips.

I kissed him back, it was a gentle kiss with no tongue or teeth involved just our lips sliding on each other.

"Last night was great", He whispered to me as he pulled from the kiss.

I just nodded shyly to him as the images of last night passed through my mind. I couldn't believe I behaved like wanton pressing him closer to me and asking him to be rough.

" Mia, look at me", He commanded as he noticed my embarrassment.

I was feeling mortified, I didn't know what he thought about me? That is how I behaved like a cheap slut.

"Mia", He whispered as he pushed back a strand of my hair behind my ear from my face.

" Mia, baby, I don't want you to ever be embarrassed with me. Babes, I am your husband and it's my duty to please you in every possible way. So never feel embarrassed to tell me what you want, okay?" He was looking in my eyes, with a storm of emotions filled in his grey orbs.

"You are so amazing baby, I don't know how was I able to stay away from you for so long", He pulled me close to him.

I felt his hardness against my thigh, and a blushed appeared on my cheeks as I felt the moisture pooling between my legs from his arousal.

" Are you still sore?" He asked me with concern in his eyes.

I nodded and replied in a no, I was surprised by the way my body wanted him again. I felt so whole and complete with him, he had filled the hollow of my body.

"You want me?" Waleed teased

I blushed at his words harder, I felt his gaze on my face staring at my staining cheeks.

"Ohh Mia", He rasped helplessly.

" You drive me, crazy baby, I can't tell you how much I want you. When I didn't have taken you, I thought the feeling will subside after I had you, but now when I have got a taste of you I want more", Waleed sighed and buried his face in my hair.

"You know we can-n if you wanted", I stuttered.

He chuckled when he found me stuttering and immediately ceased it as I glared at him.

" Not now baby, you need to heal. But don't worry once your soreness is gone you will have to forget about resting", He winked at me.

I punched him in his chest with all my strength, but it didn't feel like it affected him. His body was hard, his golden skin stretched on his firm muscles, all that workout he does daily ought to have this effect on his body.

"I will take a shower, I have to go to the office, there is a lot of pending work", He got out of the bed kissing my forehead, and strolled into the bathroom.

I thought of calling in sick to work today, I didn't feel like going to work, I texted Rania and Sheema to check if they could meet me, Rania replied she was at home resting as she had the flu, and Sheema told me she will take a half-day leave.

Chapter 22

Rameen

"Twice", Rania looked at me in disbelief.

"Uh-huh", I replied with a nod.

"You are one lucky bitch, you know, I got my first when we were doing it the fifth time," Rania announced sipping her saffron milk.

Sheema choked on her diet coke, while I who was eating roasted cashews, dropped the packet from my hand. Rania probably realized her mistake, she looked at us both aghast who was looking at her in astonishment with our eyes wide as saucers.

"Rania you are not even married," Sheema was barely controlling her astonishment.

"How could you do this without getting married?" I asked in disbelief.

"Before you both, start judging my character I want to tell you, I and Asjad have been married for a year now," She murmured with her head bowed.

I couldn't believe what I heard, maybe I was in need of an ear check-up, this was not possible.

"You have been what?" Sheema exclaimed in disbelief.

"It was really tough, we had dated for a year and tried convincing our families for another but they didn't agree. The sexual tension and temptation between us were only growing with time, and when we both couldn't cope with it we decided to get married discreetly," She said.

"You both got married so that you could bang each other," I looked at her in shock.

"We got married because we love each other and we want to spend our life together," She asserted through clenched teeth.

"And bang each other," I said teasing her again, well I get very few chances of teasing Rania, mostly it is the other way round.

She pulled a cushion and threw it at me, I dipped a little and it hit Sheema, spilling the coke on her lap.

"Bitch," She cursed.

I gave Sheema an appreciative nod, she was getting better in our company.

"Why should we believe you? Maybe you both are just sleeping with each other," I asked, with suspicion.

"Waleed and Saad were the witnesses in our wedding," I choked on the water I was drinking.

"You mean my husband knew you both are married and he didn't bother to tell me?" I was beyond shocked.

What else was Waleed hiding from me? I was an idiot, I never asked him anything about his past other than the one time when we were returning from the luncheon.

"Actually, I and Asjad didn't want anybody to find out about our marriage until we convince our families," Rania replied sighing.

Rania was a small-town girl from a respectable family, she was a software engineer and was working in an IT company in our city. She had told me that she met Asjad at a friend's wedding and they both have hit out well and then started dating. But Asjad's family didn't agree to the match because Rania's family was not that rich and Rania's family was against the match because Asjad's mother had insulted them once when they had come to meet them at Asjad's home on his insistence.

I never understood why people think money was more important than happiness? Was Asjad's family blind that they couldn't see how happy he was with Rania. Why did they want him to marry a girl from a rich family, who most probably would be a plastic bimbo?

"Anyways, we were talking about your sexcapade," She said changing the topic.

"He is my husband," I threw back the cushion at her.

"Look who is talking now, as I remember he was pompous, arrogant, asshole, cocky," Rania rolled her eyes.

She would have continued with the list of abuses that I had hurled at Waleed in the past if I would not have thrown another cushion at her which hit her directly on her face.

"Will you both stop bickering, and Mia, would you continue with what happened next," Sheema complained.

"Well nothing, he fed me Greek yogurt and then ran a bath for me," I said with a shy smile, remembering how considerate he was after he had literally fucked my brain off.

"Wow, can you exchange him with Asjad? Asjad is always in a wang bang thank you, Mam, mode," She said joking.

"Rania", I cried in disdain.

"What, really I remember the first time we did it Asjad was more nervous than I was, and when it was over he ran from here as if I had a contagious disease," She was laughing hysterically.

I remembered Waleed, he was not nervous at all, instead, he looked confident and was in control.

"Do you think Waleed might have slept with someone before?" I gave my thoughts a voice. "I mean he didn't look nervous, instead he knew very well what he was doing."

"Ohh, come on Mia, don't be an ass. You should be grateful he is your husband, that guy gave you two orgasms on your first time. What else do you want from him?" Rania didn't like my question a bit.

"I am not complaining about his skills in bed, okay, I am just curious how does he know all this if he never slept with anyone," I said annoyed.

Rania replied laughing, "Thank pornhub, baby."

" Yikes," Sheema and I yelled in unison.

I don't know why but I never found it in me to see a porn video, I and Sheema had tried many times but whenever we used to play a video the feeling of nausea, would overcome us within seconds, and then we would shut the laptop. After a few attempts, we decided it was not our cup of tea, and we never tried watching porn again.

My cell buzzed, I looked at the screen it was a text from Waleed.

Waleed: I am hungry.

I smiled I knew what he was referring to but I wanted to play innocent.

Mia: Go have your lunch.

I texted the reply smiling.

Waleed: You are not on the menu.

I am sure I blushed at his reply, I never thought I would be sexting in my life.

Mia: Waleed.

Waleed: I want you.

To be honest, I was aroused just by his text, I mean that man didn't even need to touch me to turn me on.

Waleed: I want to devour your beautiful body until you scream my name for the whole world to hear.

My God, how kinky. I never had imagined Waleed Kamal could be sending someone such texts from his office.

"Are you sexting Waleed?" Rania gave me a suspicious look.

" No," I replied too quickly.

"Don't lie, I know those expressions," She said trying to snatch the cell from my hand, which I hid behind my back immediately.

"Liar," Rania hissed.

"Tell your hottie to teach Asjad a few tricks," She teased.

"No way I am telling that to him," I snapped back.

"I knew you were sexting him," Rania said with triumph.

"Bitch," I cursed her.

The cell buzzed again with a series of text.

Waleed: I am coming home.

Waleed: Wear that red nightwear set I bought for you last week.

He had gifted me that nightwear set the day after the reception when we almost had slept together. But unfortunately, Dada fell ill and I never got the chance to wear it.

Waleed: I am having a hard-on just imagining you in that dress.

Waleed: Fuck, Mia, I am leaving.

I panicked, I was here at Rania's apartment. I had told him in the morning that I was going to have lunch with Rania and Sheema he might have forgotten that.

Mia: Waleed, I am not at home. I told you I was meeting Rania and Sheema.

I ignored Rania and Sheema's hooting and waited for his reply hoping he didn't leave his office.

Waleed: Fuck, Mia. I want you so badly.

I was just about to type a reply when he texted again.

Waleed: I am coming to pick you.

I really freaked out, he must be joking if he came here to pick me Sheema, and Rania will drive me to hell teasing.

Mia: You won't even think about it.

Waleed: I want my wife and I am coming now.

He replied, asshole, I cursed him. There was no way I was going to let him come in the middle of the afternoon to pick me just for the sake of banging me.

Mia: Waleed if you come now, you will have to remain celibate your whole life.

I hope my threat would work, I could just pray, how could you stop a hot blooded horny alpha male from fucking his wife?

Waleed: You have 15 minutes to come up with an excuse. I am on my way.

Shit, I was screwed, Rania will torment me to my grave fr this.

Mia: Waleed please, if you don't come now I will give you a BJ tonight.

This was the best excuse that I could have thought that could save me from the embarrassment.

Waleed: Are you sure?

I know he was just as shocked as I was, what the hell was I thinking to get into this? I had never ever touched that thing in my life, how the hell was I going to do it? But I couldn't back off now, he would think I am afraid.

Mia: Yes.

Waleed: You don't know, what you have gotten yourself into.

Of course, I know what I had gotten myself into. I was striking a deal with the devil himself, what could be worse than that. "Ohh God, just make me vanish from the face of Earth, anywhere would do even Pluto," I prayed.

What the hell was I thinking and how the hell was I going to fulfill my part of the bargain?

Waleed

I was going through the meetings, half-heartedly, all I wanted to do was spend the day in bed with my beautiful and sexy wife. I was having a hard-on just reminiscing the images of her naked body whimpering below me in delight.

I was barely hanging by the thread, and when I texted her and she tried to play innocent and I snapped, I wanted her then and there. She told me she was with her friends and still, I wanted to pick her up and go home and make love to her till she screamed my name to heavens.

She declined to come with me even threatened me with celibacy, I knew she was just bluffing. I have seen how her body was turned on just by a flicker of my gaze. God, she was sexy and her body was way too sensitive, the way she reacts to my simple caress.

All I was thinking was how her skin felt below my lips, she was so fucking soft and luscious. I loved her, I still could remember her taste on my tongue, she was sweet with a little hint of tangy. God, I wanted her, I wanted her real bad.

I had left my office and reached the parking when she texted she would give me a BJ if I didn't pick her up right now.

I couldn't believe what she had texted, I never expected this from her. But she was so fucking unpredictable, and it made everything more fun. She would shock me at every turn and render me speech-less.

I texted her back if she knew what she was getting herself into and she replied,

Mia: I know you will teach me how to do it, and I am looking forward to learning.

This girl would be the death of me, she will just kill me someday from a heart attack with some shock. I know she was fire, I had sensed it long ago, the way she responded to my touch, and there was no denying the chemistry between us. I don't know how I went back to my office, my Secretary was surprised to find me back, I had told her to cancel all my appointments after lunch today.

I don't know how I spent the remainder of my time in the office, it was like walking on burning coal. It felt like the hands of the clock were crawling today, I left my seat as soon as the clock struck five.

I drove to Rania's apartment directly, Asjad had rented that apartment for her after they got married, before that she used to stay in a girls hostel. It had been a year since they got married, still, they hadn't made any progress with their families.

I really felt sorry for Asjad, I don't know how he copes with staying away from Rania, I can't even imagine not looking at Mia for one whole day, and now after last night, I had doubts if I would ever want her to be out of my sight.

I need to keep a check on myself otherwise I could scare her by acting horny all the time, but how was I supposed to have control. I couldn't think about anything else than her, and the moment her thoughts occupied my mind I got turned on, fuck she didn't even need to raise a finger to turn me on.

Maybe I should take her on honeymoon, not long but at least a week so that my body would calm down a bit. I was a hot-blooded male after all and for how long could I control myself. I never was affected by any girl in this way and trust me, I had dated a lot of girls but I never allowed myself to go further than the first base, but Mia, I wanted her since I saw her.

I hated her at the time but I still wanted her, I still remember how fucking hot she was looking in that peach blouse and cream skirt outside the coffee shop. Why her why only her I couldn't understand?

When I reached Rania's building I called Mia and told her I was waiting below, she came out after a few minutes, looking breathtakingly beautiful in a skirt and a simple blouse.

Her perfect hourglass figure, her beautiful amber eyes, her long hair, and her smile, her million-dollar smile, which was just for me.

She opened the passenger seat and slid in the passenger seat, I looked at her and beamed, she was mine, this sexy as hell woman was all mine.

"Hey gorgeous," I took her hand and placed a kiss on it.

"Hi," She mumbled.

She was nervous, my fierce lioness was nervous, and that too because of me, I felt proud of myself.

I didn't say anything to her while we drove home, I wanted to give her time to settle. When we reached home and changed, I asked her if she wanted to watch a movie, she was surprised by my suggestion, I was surprised myself because the whole day in the office I was fantasizing how I was going to rip apart her clothes when I see her, but when I saw her nervous in the car I calmed, I didn't want to scare her.

I want her to be her fearless self, not a nervous wreck. I could wait until she was back to normal again. Till she came to me willingly like last night, though I know I could seduce her easily but I wanted her to seduce me.

"So which movie do you like?" I asked as we entered the theater room.

"Do you have any good romantic movies?" She asked me in reply.

I don't know maybe I had a few, I was never a fan of romantic movies I had just bought some for the sake of collection. I went towards the shelf where all the CDs and DVDs were stashed and started checking the romance genre, she came and stood beside me and started looking at the names.

"La la land, we can watch this one, if you have not watched this before," she pulled a DVD.

I looked at the DVD, in her hand and the sparkle in her eyes, I was sure she liked that movie, I was not a fan of musicals but I decided to watch this movie just for her sake.

I don't know why but I was enjoying the movie, it reminded me of me and Mia, and tell it a coincidence the female lead in the movie was also named Mia. She and the male lead Sebastian don't start on a good note with each other just like us but as the story progressed they get along and then fell in love, but I didn't like the ending.

They don't end up together, in the end, though, they get what they dreamt of in life but had to give up their love for their careers. I mean what kind of love story is that? Give up the true love of your life just so you could pursue your dreams. I didn't agree with it, and I told Mia what I thought about the ending.

And she laughed and told me that's what separates this movie, from other love stories, it was not cliche. It was more realistic and close to life.

"Will you give up your love for your career," I asked her as we entered our bedroom

"You know, I don't believe in love," She rolled her eyes.

"Will you give up me, Mia?" I asked looking into her amber eyes.

She kept looking at me her eyes filled with thousands of different emotions, but I was searching for only one and I saw it, I know she is still afraid to accept it but I know she loves, I was seeing it in her eyes right now, overpowering all her other emotions and coming out victorious above all.

"Never," She said as she pulled me towards her holding the neck of my tee shirt and crushing her mouth on mine.

I was dying for her touch and as soon as she kissed me, I slid my arm around her waist and pulled her to me, as I pushed her to the wall and pinned her to it, without breaking the kiss, I stumbled on the straps of her robe and loosened it, I pushed it down from her shoulder and to the floor while kissing her.

Then I broke the kiss and looked at her, she was wearing the red three-piece nightwear set I bought for her, it was made up of lace, her golden-white skin was visible through it, and I can't describe how fuckingly beautiful it looked on her.

It just ended below her hips, I was drinking in every inch of for beautiful body visible through the nightdress.

" Fuck."

I pulled her to me and picked her up in my arms and walked towards the bathroom, she looked at me in surprise.

"Waleed the bed is," She was saying and stopped as I blurted out.

"Not now," I interrupted her as I entered the bathroom and walked to the shower stall, sliding the door aside and slowly putting her down.

I adjusted the pressure and temperature of the shower as I turned it on, I was still fully dressed in sweats and tee and they got soaked within seconds, I pulled my tee-shirt above the head and tossed it outside.

"Do you remember your promise babes?" I whispered in her ear-biting on the neck just below it.

She shuddered, remembering what she had promised me, I didn't waste any time and pulled her to me as I locked my lips with her, the warm water trickling down our bodies and the feel of her bare skin on mine, it was the best feeling in the world.

We both came together and I rested my face on the crook of her neck as we both came down from the high panting heavily.

"That was great," She whispered as she kissed my cheek.

I smiled against her neck satisfied, after the amazing sex I had with the most amazing woman in the world.

Chapter 23

Waleed

"Would you like to go on a honeymoon?" I asked as we walked out of the restaurant.

I had brought Mia for dinner to celebrate the three-month anniversary of our wedding. The last three months were the best time of my life, Mia had changed my life for the good. I was whipped to her to an extent that I found it difficult breathing without her.

"Depends on which destination you suggest?" She snuggled closer to me due to the chilly air outside.

I had wanted to go earlier, but I was too busy with my company and Mia was busy working on different projects.

"Bali?" I asked.

She shook her head in disagreement.

"Australia?"

"No".

Now I was thinking, what place would she want to go? What could be her dream destination?

" Europe?" I asked.

"You are close".

" Swiss Alps?" I asked with a glint in my eyes.

She nodded shyly, I kissed her on her head as we approached our car in the parking.

"Did you hear it?" She asked suddenly looking around.

"Hear what, love?" I asked surprised.

"Shhh", She gestured me to be silent as she moved her head around as if to catch signals.

She then hurriedly walked towards the bushes planted on the side of the parking and crouched and picked something from the bushes as she stood up.

" Well, Hello", She said smiling as she held a red-colored kitten in her hands.

I felt my stomach churn, keep it between us but I was afraid of cats, my mom had gifted me a cat when I was 6 years old and I was very happy taking care of her until one day she bit my hand and scratched it, and from that day till today, I hated cats.

And right now as I saw Mia holding that kitten and looking at it like some prized possession I didn't get any good vibes.

"Mia, be careful it could bite you", I said anxiously.

" It won't, look she loves me", Mia purred along with the cat.

Shit, this was not good.

"Mia we are getting late, I have an early morning meeting tomorrow", I was annoyed.

" Okay".

She was still holding the kitten in her hand and didn't look in a mood that she would let the kitten go.

I pointed to the kitten in her hand, "Where do you think you are taking that?"

" Home" She replied easily.

What the fuck, she can't be serious about this, I can't tolerate a cat in my house.

"No, no, no, no, that thing ain't going home with us", I shouldn't have said this that early.

She looked at me with suspicion, her amber eyes fixed on me.

" Are you afraid?"

Dammit, I should not have reacted in such a hurry, now she won't stop until she finds out, and I didn't want my wife to think I was afraid of anything.

"Of course not, those things are gross, they can give you asthma", I said with a scowl.

She laughed at my words and said, " That is a myth, do you really believe it".

"And how can we leave here alone, she might die, " She added.

"She won't die, her mother must be lurking around somewhere, she will take care of her", I mumbled in a bored tone.

Who cares what happens to that thing, it was the least of my concern, I didn't want my beautiful wife anywhere around it. She might give her scars for a whole life.

" I am not living it to chance, she is going with us or I might as well stay with her", She replied stubbornly, stomping her feet on the ground.

She looked so cute at that moment, stomping her foot on the ground that I could not decline any further.

"Okay, but only on one condition. You won't bring her into the bedroom", I gave up.

She asked impatiently, " I won't, now can we go?"

I got on the driver's seat while Mia followed on the passenger seat, the kitten still in her lap.

"If it moves as much as an inch, I can't guarantee you your safety in this car", I warned her eyeing the kitten.

Mia just smiled at me and held the kitten tightly in both her hands, I could see how hard she was trying not to laugh.

"I have decided, I am going to call her, Red", She said in excitement after some time.

"That's not a cat name", I retorted.

"It is from now", She replied in her signature stubborn way.

"Red, do you like the name baby", She lifted the kitten and brought her to eye level as it meowed.

"Hi, I am Mia, Miiiaaa", She was talking to the kitten like it was a baby.

I started wondering about how our baby will look in her arms, I need to talk to her about our own children. I know Dada had always wanted to see his great-grandchild and there was no reason to delay it.

"Meoww", The cat purred.

Mia laughed at her and said " Not meow, Mia".

"Meow", The cat purred again.

" Mia", She pronounced each letter.

"Stop it, Mia, it's not she is gonna start talking", I was annoyed at her childish behavior.

" You are mean", She replied.

"I know", I shot back.

" I hate you", She said furiously.

"Feeling is mutual babes", I retorted.

" I don't want to talk to you", She started looking outside the window.

I suppressed my smile at her childish declaration, I know as soon as I just look at her in a particular way, she was going to forget everything and will come running in my arms. That's how insatiable she was, my fireball.

If that bloody kitten would not have been on her lap, I would have taken her hand in mine already. I looked at the kitten with jealousy, it was sitting on my territory, anything that gets Mia's attention more than me made me jealous even if it was a damn cat.

I just wanted her all to myself, to love her to cherish her, and to prove to her no one in this world can love her more than me.

"Mia, look at me", I called after some time, I couldn't bear to be ignored by her when all I wanted was her to take her in my arms and kiss her till she was short of oxygen.

She ignored me and kept looking out of the window, damn kitten, I was already hating it.

" Mia", I called out again.

Still no response, I think she was really very mad.

"Mia"

"Don't Mia me, Waleed", She shot back.

I smiled, at least she said something which meant she was going to be normal after some persuasion, I didn't want to ruin my night because of that kitten.

"Baby, you know, how much I love you, right?", I said looking at her.

"You are not getting it tonight", She looked at me with fire in her amber eyes.

I suppressed my smile, she knew I was trying to sweet-talk her so that I could get what I have been fantasizing about since morning.

"Red baby, what would you like to eat?" She asked cooing to the kitten.

I sighed, she didn't look in a mood to forgive me, now I was thinking of ways in which I could get rid of that kitten.

"Waleed", She called out.

I looked at her in surprise, why the hell does she always prove me wrong when I thought I was starting to predict her.

"Thanks," She said.

"For what Mia?" I asked her.

She kept looking at me, then she smiled and kept her hand on mine, which was on the steering wheel.

"For loving me", She replied.

Damn, this girl. She would kill me someday.

"Come here", I pulled her towards me, not before checking the kitten, which was fast asleep on her lap.

Mia shifted closer to me and kept her head on my shoulder, while I intertwined my fingers with her.

I was definitely going to get it tonight, I thought with a wolfish grin.

Rameen

"Waleed put me down", I cried as he carried me into the house in his arms.

Waleed had picked me up from the office and we discussed our day as we drove home, this was our daily routine. When we got out of the car on the porch, Waleed lifted me in his arms and carried me inside. He would do this quite often when he was in the mood and we would end up in bed.

"No way, I have been thinking about this since morning. Damn it kills me when you are on your period. Isn't there any medicine that could shorten the duration", He said nuzzling my neck.

I giggled in his arms, as his nuzzling sent a tickling sensation throughout my body.

"Why don't you make such a drug, I am sure it's gonna be a great hit among all the horny husbands like you", I said poking a finger in his chest.

"You are going to get fucked, really hard today, Mrs. Waleed Kamal ", He teased biting my ear.

I slapped his arm on his comment, as we entered the living room. Waleed nearly dropped me on the floor and halted a few steps inside the living room.

"Jeena", He exclaimed, as he gently slid me down from his arms.

" Wal".

She cried out, as she came running to him and hugged him.

I was looking at them shocked, who was this girl? And why the hell was she hugging my husband? And why was my husband hugging her back?

They broke the hug after a few seconds and Jeena checked Waleed out from tip to toe.

"Still handsome huh?" She said with a broad grin.

I felt my temper searing as my husband kept looking at her with admiration, it was like I had gone into the background suddenly.

I checked out Jeena, she was not too bad, she was nearly identical to me in height and physique. Except for the fact she had chocolate brown eyes and brown hairs with golden highlights. You might call her beautiful, but right now I couldn't help but feel jealous by the mere thought that Waleed was so close to some girl, that he had hugged her in front of me.

"Jeena meet Mia, my wife. Mia this is Jeena, my cousin. Our moms are sisters", Finally Waleed remembered to introduce me.

It was as if Jeena came out of some trance, she looked at me startled, and then she flashed me her beautiful smile.

She hugged me and cried, " Ohh my God, I am so happy to meet you. Finally, a girl has conquered the mighty Waleed Kamal".

I just smiled back in reply, Waleed slid his arm around my waist pulled me near to him, and gave a peck on my cheek.

"Yes, my heart and my love belong to her and only her", He said beaming at me.

I snuggled closer to him, claiming my territory.

" Lucky you, she is beautiful", Jeena declared in excitement.

To be frank, I was not expecting a compliment from her, I was thinking maybe she might be mean to me. But she had surprised me, I felt ashamed for feeling jealous. Maybe they were just close friends and I was getting jealous for no reason. Ali and I are close too, and honestly, we were inseparable.

"So what's up for you?" Waleed asked her as he directed her to the sofas in the living room, while he, lead me with his arm around my shoulder to one of the sofas.

"I have a few meetings with some publishers for my new book. And so I thought to crash at your place while I am in town. I hope, I am not disturbing your privacy", She said the last sentence looking at me.

"Of course not, Waleed, and I would be glad if you stay with us", I replied smiling.

"Thanks, Mia, I am really glad. It's been nearly two years since we have seen each other", She replied gratefully.

I noticed Waleed shift on the couch, maybe I was imagining things. Jeena looked sweet and I was glad that I will have company in this huge house.

" You are always welcome here, Jeena", Waleed smiled at her.

I rose from the sofa excusing myself, I needed a shower desperately. I had been on the site for two hours with Daniyal and the sunlight was too harsh today.

Waleed would have joined me in the shower if we would have been alone, shower sex was the favorite of both of us (blush). The feel of the warm water splashing and trickling down our bodies as we pleasured each other was just beyond description.

I had discontinued my pills from the last month after we had discussed having kids. It was bound to happen someday hence we decided the sooner the better. We both were the only kids of our parents and missed having siblings, at least I had Ali and Umair but Waleed had a lonely childhood especially after his parent's death. Though Dada took good care of him and raised him into a wonderful human being, still the loneliness of not having any siblings was there in his heart.

Waleed was disappointed when I had my period last week, he was expecting I would get pregnant in the first month itself. And after my period started he was determined to get me pregnant this month.

I was in the shower when I heard a knock on the door as he entered the bathroom, I saw through the fogged glass of the shower stall he was just wearing his sweats. The door slid and he peeked inside.

"I thought you might wait for me", He was looking at me hungrily.

" It's still not late, you can join me if you want", I giggled shyly.

As if he was just waiting for my offer he entered the stall and stood behind me.

After the shower, we got dressed in a hurry and joined Jeena in the dining room for dinner.

She was cheerful and talkative, narrating a lot of incidents from their childhood with enthusiasm she kept the conversation alive throughout the dinner. I found it difficult not to warm up to her, she was too nice and I genuinely liked her.

Waleed didn't participate in our conversation, he kept to himself and only spoke when Jeena asked him something or reminded him about some incident of their past. I, on the other hand, was enjoying her company. After so many months, there was someone in the house apart from us.

Of course, I enjoyed spending time with Waleed but sometimes I felt lonely, I was from a joint family and always was surrounded by people, but now it was just me and Waleed. All the more reason I decided to have kids so that there will be someone else other than us in the house.

Chapter 24

Waleed

"Wal," Jeena called as she entered my office.

I was busy looking at the plan of a commercial complex, which my firm was starting the work on when she came along, all happy and cheerful.

"Hey Jeena," I replied smiling.

She was looking beautiful as always, she smiled at me as she sat on the chair across my desk.

"So what brought you here?" I asked curiously

"I just wanted to speak to you in privacy, and at home, it's really difficult with Rameen always around and it would look rude if I ask you to speak in private," She replied anxiously.

I was trying to figure out, where this conversation was going, I liked her no doubt she was my cousin and a good friend and at one point in my life, I was considering marrying her.

"Have you told Rameen about our past?" She asked me.

I looked at her surprised, why was she interested in knowing what I had told Mia or not?

"No, I still haven't but I will soon," I replied studying her.

"I would prefer if you won't," She said.

I looked at her with my brow arched, trying to understand what she was implying.

"Actually, Rameen and I are getting along well, and if she knows that we had a relationship in the past, I don't think she will ever warm up to me," She added.

"First of all, Jeena, we were never in a relationship, yes, I was inclined to marry you because I thought we had a good understanding, and second I don't prefer to hide things from my wife," I replied, to her honestly.

Hell, how can she call it a relationship? Yes, I liked her we had a good understanding and I was considering her as a potential match. But, I never had any commitment to her and when Dada had told me that he didn't think she was the right girl for me, I had never looked at her as more than a friend.

"Sorry, I just got carried away, yes we never were in a relationship except for the fact that we wanted to get married," She replied.

"Jeena, let me make myself very clear, I was just considering you as a potential match and nothing more," I was annoyed.

"Right," She said with a scowl.

I looked at her, truly I was not comfortable with her staying at our home, but before I could have said anything, Mia had gone ahead and told Jeena that she could stay with us, as long as she liked.

It was not that I didn't trust Jeena, it was just that I was overprotective of Mia, and I didn't want her to be hurt in any way. And I was worried if she found out that once I have considered marrying Jeena, she would truly feel insecure in her presence.

What I had with Jeena was a truly calculated decision, I was a jerk before Mia. I always used to date the perfect kind of girls, those who were accomplished in everything, I don't know if they were accomplished or not but they posed that they were and the fool that I was at that time I used to go after them in search of a perfect life partner.

The one who would look after my home, throw parties, and played the perfect hostess. And all her decision would be calculated and she would always be smiling and taking care of my every need.

But, Mia didn't have any single quality that I had wanted in my wife, instead, she was the opposite. She never cared to impress me by showing how accomplished she was or how good she was for me. She never acted or faked what she was not in front of me, she was just what she was and I was crazy about her.

If only six months ago, someone would have told me that I would be completely smitten by a girl like Mia, I would have surely suggested to them, to find refuge in an asylum.

Mia, she is just different what could I say about her, I can't even describe how she makes me feel. It's just that I feel alive around her, I don't have to be the cold-hearted CEO in front of her, I am just Waleed with her just a normal 28 years old guy without a worry in this world.

She is so fierce so unpredictable that she keeps me on edge always, making me think about what she might do next? She is not like the plastics bimbos, she is charming, alive, cheerful, and wild.

"Please Waleed, I would appreciate it if you don't tell Rameen anything, I like her and I want her to be my friend. You know very well, that I never had any friend other than you," She said rotating the paperweight with her fingers.

I looked at her thoughtfully, the look on her face was genuine. We had always been good friends since our childhood and I knew she had feelings for me in the past and she was the one who had proposed to me.

I was shocked at first at her preposition at that time, I mean yes I liked her as a friend and after she had suggested we get married, I had given it a thought and had discussed it with Dada, who had said that she was not the kind of girl that I needed as a life partner. He had told me I needed someone who would bring the thrill in my life and will make me feel alive.

I remember Dada had suggested to me at that time, that he had a perfect girl in his mind for me to get married and had asked me if I wanted to meet her, at that time I hadn't understood his logic. But Dada knows me better than I knew myself, he knew exactly what was missing in my life.

Yes, I was a successful businessman, I had girls that used to swoon around me and my life was perfect in everyone's eyes, but I knew how lonely I felt after the death of my parents. Though Dada had given me all the love and affection, still I felt a void in my heart. And

I use to think that a perfect life partner would fill that void one day. How stupid I was at that time if only I had known that no amount of perfection in a girl would fill the void inside me.   Mia always made me behave differently, I was different around her, always my true self. I was not afraid that she might judge me for my imperfections, I could never imagine sharing with someone those things about me that I had shared with Mia.

That girl, she was living, thrill, joy, and she was what I had always needed, a reason to live. And now I can't imagine living a single day without her.

I love her, yes I Waleed Kamal the control freak and arrogant CEO, was conquered by a girl. But she was not any normal girl, she was Mia, my Mia. I wanted to scream and tell the whole world how much I loved and wanted her.

"Waleed, can you do this for me? Just for old times sake?"

Jeena's voice brought me back from my thoughts, she was looking at me with hope-filled in her eyes.

"Okay Jeena, if you insist," I replied giving up.

Jeena could be really persuasive when she wants to.

" Thank you, thank you, thank you so much, Waleed," She giggled in delight.

She then started telling me about her meeting with the publisher and left when I had to go for a meeting.

Rameen

"Hey Rameen, can you get down here," I heard Jeena's voice from downstairs.

I pulled from Waleed and looked at him, we were in the middle of a make-out session. I was sitting on his lap, my arms were around his neck, while he was holding me by the waist.

"I am gonna throw her out if she keeps interrupting us like this," Waleed said brooding.

I gave him a quick peck on his cheek and got up from his lap, wondering why Jeena could be calling me?

As I walked down the stairs, I saw Jeena pacing in the living room nervously. She looked as if she was going somewhere out.

"Everything okay?" I asked her.

"Yes, actually no, I don't know," She replied intertwining her fingers.

I looked at her curiously, I thought she was a confident girl, but looking at her now felt like she was as vulnerable as others.

"What is it?" I asked.

"Well, I met this guy a few days back and he asked me out today, and I don't know why but I am freaking out. I have not been on a date in ages," She replied anxiously.

"It will be okay Jeena, just take deep breaths. You are looking absolutely gorgeous, just try to be yourself," I rubbed my hand on her shoulder, trying to give her a boost.

She looked at me gratefully, then she looked at her watch and sprang in panic.

"I am late, thanks Rameen for helping me calm down. I will leave now," She said collecting her clutch from the table.

" Have a good time," I said to her and wished her luck.

When I walked back to the bedroom, Waleed was looking at me with his brow arched.

"She is going on a date and was just freaking out," I told him.

" It's unlike her," Waleed replied.

"Maybe she likes the guy," I said thinking about Jeena's behavior.

Waleed just nodded and called me to him by flicking his finger. I was too eager to continue from where we left. But I remembered I had not fed " Red".

"I need to feed Red," I told him as I left the room and Waleed kept calling after me in frustration.

I came down to the kitchen, put some cat food in the bowl for Red, and walked back to the living room, I called "Red" a few times, meowing a few times. And she came running out of somewhere and leaped into my lap. I picked her up, kissed her head, and gently placed her in front of the bowl.

I watched her as she hungrily ate up all the food from the bowl, I played with her for some time. She then ran away, I walked back to the kitchen and washed and put the bowl back into the cabinet, beside the cat food.

I opened the fridge and pulled out the tub of my favorite Almond and Chocolate fudge ice cream, I took a spoon and dug into it. I was busy eating, and along with it moaning when someone gripped my shoulder and pulled me towards them, slamming me into their chest.

I screamed in shock and the tub of ice cream slipped from my hand, then I heard the chuckle beside my ear. I turned and slapped him on his chest with all my strength.

"When the hell, are you gonna stop sneaking up on me, I could have gotten a heart attack," I yelled at him.

Waleed smiled and pulled me into his arms, he tried kissing me, but I pushed him away and turned and picked up the ice cream tub and stormed out of the kitchen, leaving a frustrated Waleed behind me.

I came to the bedroom terrace and sat on the swing, gulping down the ice cream in anger, Waleed had to stop sneaking up on me like this, he used to do this every time I was busy with something, and was unaware of the surrounding. And the asshole was so good at it, that he won't even make the slightest sound like some fucking ninja.

I heard the stereo play " You have lost that loving feeling," by Righteous Brothers, before I saw him walk out of the glass door of the terrace, with a mischievous smile on his lips.

And when the lyrics came to

But baby, baby I know it

You lost that lovin' feelin'   Whoa, that lovin' feelin'   You lost that lovin' feelin'   Now it's gone, gone, gone,

He was on his knees in front of me and was singing, on top of his lungs along with the Righteous brother.

I forgot that I was mad at him and started laughing, I placed the tub aside and held his hand and he stood up, pulling me towards him and dancing with me, holding me close to him.

"I wanted to dance with you, since the moment I saw you dancing in that white gown at Sheema's birthday party. I am surprised why didn't I do this earlier," He said as he turned me in his arms, then pulling me close to him, as my back touched his chest. He wrapped his hands around my waist and rested his face on the crook of my neck, inhaling in my scent.

I felt his breath on my neck, a shiver ran down my spine and its intensity only increased when he sucked on my neck and bit it gently.

"Waleed", I whispered his name as I bent my head and gave him more access, sliding my arm around his neck, and tugging at his hairs, as he continued his sweet torture on my body.

"I love you," He said leaving a trail of kisses along my neck.

My heart leaped in my chest, this was the first time he had said the " L" word. And I knew he meant it.

"I love you so much, baby," He whispered in my ear as he bit my ear lobe.

" Waleed, I-I," I didn't know what to say, I was still not sure of my feelings.

"I know baby, you still have not figured out your feelings, but trust me, I don't want to push you. I want you to take your time and find it out yourself," He said stroking my neck with his nose.

I wanted to say to him that I loved him, confess that I had fallen for him, my subconscious was laughing at me, how proudly I used to say that I didn't believe in love and that I would never fall in love with anyone. And now here I was standing in the arms of the man I had despised more than anyone a few months ago hopelessly in love with him.

I had fallen in love with Waleed Kamal, the control freak and arrogant CEO. I wanted to tell him, but I don't know what held me back. If only I could have told him that day, how much I loved him our life would have been simple.

Chapter 25

R ameen

"It's been so many days since we have gone out together, what do you say about dining out in the new Thai restaurant?" Waleed asked me while driving home.

"Yeah, I have been thinking about that too," I replied to him.

Since Jeena had come to stay with us, we rarely got time alone with each other. I hadn't thought she might stay for such a long time.

She always hung out with us and used to keep us busy with something nearly every evening. We only were alone when we retired to the bedroom for sleeping.

"I wonder when Jeena will leave, I like her but that doesn't mean that my personal life is being overlooked because of her," Waleed said in an annoyed tone.

I didn't reply to him because I was thinking the same thing. Her presence was getting unbearable for me right now, but I avoided voicing my opinion, to Waleed, she was his cousin and good friend and I didn't want to offend him.

"I think we both need a break from work and the city," I told Waleed.

"Yeah, I was feeling the same thing, what do you say we go to our beach house this weekend?" Waleed asked after agreeing with me.

I looked at him startled, did he own a beach house? And why the hell he didn't tell me that before?

"Don't be mad at me babes, I am sorry it slipped my mind, it's an hour's drive from the city and you are going to love it," He stroked my thigh with one hand while holding the steering with the other.

How could I stay mad at him, when he was doing that to me? My anger had vanished and all my senses were concentrated on the movement of his hand on my thigh. I know Waleed had sensed how I felt and he teased me further by moving his hand upward on my thigh.

I didn't even realize we were home and Waleed had parked in the garage, my mind was still on the way his hand was moving above the fabric of the dress on my thigh.

He pulled me towards him and leaned and captured my lips, I was more hungry for him than I realized. He traced his tongue on my lip asking for permission to enter, which I granted gladly, he lifted me from my seat as if I weighed like a feather and placed me on his lap in a straddling position, as he pushed his seat behind.

We pulled as we both were short of breath, Waleed didn't lose any time as he started trailing kisses on my neck and jawline, I giggled as his stubble tickled my skin.

"Waleed, you need to shave, honey. Your stubble is spoiling the mood, though you look hot with it," I giggled again.

Waleed didn't pay me any heed and continued sucking at my neck, his hand traveled from my waist to my hips, pressing me closer to him.

I involuntarily started grinding against him, the friction felt so good, a groan escaped from his mouth, he was enjoying my actions.

"Waleed, stop it," I said giggling as he kept rubbing his face on my neck and cheek.

"Mia it's been so long when was the last time? Last weekend?" He said against my neck.

"I think so," I replied, his actions were making it difficult for me to concentrate.

"God, you smell so fucking good, I can never get enough of you," He said as he opened the topmost button of my button-up shirt.

I held his hand, no matter how much the idea excited me, I didn't want to be caught in the act by the house staff. Waleed looked at me with narrowed eyes, clearly annoyed by me, stopping him.

"Waleed, anyone can come here, I don't think it's a good idea," I said as I struggled to keep the hold on my shirt.

"The glasses are tinted, no one can see us," He nibbled on my lower lip.

"Ohhh really, even the front glass?" I asked in sarcasm.

"Mia, I just want to kick Jeena out, it's been two months now. When the hell is she planning to go back?" He leaned back and rested on the seat.

I was still sitting on his lap in a straddling position, and my back resting on the steering.

I cupped his face in my hands, he was frustrated, he had always got what he wanted, and whenever he had wanted. But Jeena was proving to be a pain in the ass.

"I am fed up too, but she is your friend, you just can't ask her to leave. Honey, I think we need to slow down, maybe it's a good thing. This keeps the fire in us burning, otherwise, we could get wearied of each other," I said gently stroking my thumb on his cheek.

"Mia, I can never get wearied of you, you don't have any idea how I feel about you, and how much I want you. I just can't get enough of you baby. I am taking you on a honeymoon, once Jeena leaves. No work, no commitments, and no relatives, just you and me," He leaned and kissed me.

His kiss was gentle as if he had all the time in the world, slowly moving his lips on mine, gently tugging and nibbling at my bottom lip.

He pulled from me after some time, though I wanted to keep going on, we would get late for dinner if we didn't stop. He gently placed me back on the seat as he removed his seatbelt and walked out of the car coming to my side and opening the door for me.

We walked in and were glad when we didn't find Jeena in the living room, it was a relief. We both hurried to the bedroom took shower and when we came back downstairs Jeena was waiting for us in the living room.

"You guys going out?" She asked as soon as we reached the bottom of the stairs.

"Yes, for dinner, it's been quite a long time, since we went out together," Waleed told her, pulling me closer to himself.

"But I told you that I was cooking the dinner for you," Jeena said furiously.

I passed Waleed a glance at her words, had Jeena told him and he forgot? Or was he deliberately trying to avoid her?

"Oh, I am sorry Jeena, it completely slipped from my mind," He replied blankly.

Jeena didn't say anything, she just ran up to her room, I called after her but she didn't stop. I heard the door of her room slam loudly.

"What the hell Waleed, how can you forget? I need to talk to her," I said as I left his side and started walking up the stairs.

"Mia, she will be okay, I think we should go," Waleed called after me.

I turned and gave him a sharp look, how can he act with such hostility. Jeena was his cousin, and best friend and she was our guest.

I saw Jeena crying as I entered her room, she was sitting on the edge of the bed, her eyes and nose were red due to crying, I felt guilty after seeing her like this, though I had nothing to do with it.

"Jeena, I am sorry, I didn't know that you had planned to cook dinner for us. And I had asked Waleed if we could go out for dinner. It has been a long time since we went out together," I don't know why I took the blame for the whole thing.

"It's okay, Mia, I can understand I have been staying for too long here, anyone would have got tired by now, you two are a newly married couple. I should have thought before I decided to stay with you," She replied wiping her tears.

Her words only increased my guilt, if only I had known that Waleed was deliberately trying to avoid her.

"Jeena it's not like that sweety, we enjoy your company. I had been so lonely before you came to stay with us. I am glad you are here, and you know Waleed is planning to go to the beach house this weekend. He is feeling guilty, that he couldn't spend enough time with you," I knew Waleed was going to hate me for this, but I didn't have any choice.

"Really?" Jeena asked me suspiciously.

"Yes, of course, I am going to ask Rania and Sheema to come along so that we could have a girl's night," I lied, after sensing her interest.

It was the least I could do for her, for how Waleed had behaved with her, a complete jerk. Even I knew how to behave with guests better than him, he was an arrogant asshole like before, the only difference was that I am in love with that asshole now.

I told her some jokes to cheer her up and after nearly half an hour I was able to convince her for dinner. We came to the living room, where Waleed was busy on his cell phone, with a bored expression on his face.

I gave him a death glare as we descended the stairs, his expressions changed immediately and he tried to look cheerful. He joked with

Jeena as I went into the kitchen and told the maid to set the table for dinner.

"Jeena, the food is amazing, I can't tell you how much I like it, " I praised Jeena while eating.

She had made a lot of dishes, all favorites of Waleed, I felt even Waleed was enjoying the food, though he was upset that we couldn't go out for dinner but was acting normal because of Jeena.

"Thanks, Rameen. It's not a big deal, it must be known how easy cooking is, " She said humbly.

I laughed at her words and narrated my experiences in the kitchen with my mom and aunt. She looked startled to know that I sucked at cooking.

"But, Waleed loves homemade food, he is such a big fan of my mom's cooking," Jeena said looking at Waleed in a surprised tone.

"Yeah, that's why I have hired the best chef in the town," Waleed said as he shrugged his shoulder.

Her words stuck in my mind, I know Waleed is a foodie and I had never made him breakfast. Before Jeena was here he used to make breakfast on the weekend, and since Jeena was staying with us we have asked the cook to make breakfast on weekends.

"But Waleed," Jeena tried to say something but was interrupted by Waleed.

"Jeena," His tone held a warning.

I saw Jeena give a cold stare and then she focused her attention on the food. I was feeling a little awkward, I know Waleed had stopped

Jeena from making any comment on me but I still was feeling degraded.

I realized my mom was right that I didn't have a single quality that was required to be a good wife. And I don't know why Waleed loved me? Did he love me or was it just an infatuation?

I agree we have great chemistry in bed, we both love experimenting and I was as insatiable for him as he was for me. But was it enough for a wife to be just good in bed? What else did I have in me to be married to a man like Waleed, who was nearly perfect in everything?

He was better than me even in cooking, and I didn't find even a single quality in me of a good wife. Is Waleed really happy with me? Will his love wear off as his desire for me to die?

There were so many questions in my mind right now, I felt like I was looking at Jeena for the first time, she was a walking example of how a girl is meant to be.

She was beautiful, qualified and today I found out she was a wonderful cook, she was amicable and well behaved unlike me. She made friends easily and was so charming and bubbly. Waleed should have been with someone like her, who would have taken care of him and his home, who would have cooked for him and have raised his kids to perfection.

I was feeling self-conscious for the first time in my life, Jeena and Waleed tried to engage me in a conversation but I excused myself saying that I was having a headache.

Waleed came to the bedroom after nearly half an hour, he looked at me carefully as I lay on the bed wondering for how long will Waleed be attracted to me, and after that what will happen?

"Mia, baby you okay?" He asked me as he sat on the edge of the bed beside me.

I looked at him, he was truly beautiful, his grey eyes were fixed on me, as he tried to search my face for any expression. I tried to keep my face as blank as I could, but I know it was difficult to hide my feelings from his intense gaze.

An unknown fear of losing him gripped my heart, I had not realized till that moment how much I loved him and how terrifying the thought of losing him was.

"Baby, I love you, for what you are," He held my hand in his.

He pulled me on his lap and wrapped his arms around me, he didn't say anything just kept inhaling my scent. I didn't realize but tears had started gathering in my eyes and were soaking his shirt. He pulled me away from him and looked at me startled when he felt the wetness on his chest.

"I am sorry, I know I am not good enough for you," I said looking at my hands in my lap.

" Mia my love, you are the best thing that ever happened to me, I am so lucky that I have someone like you who is so pure so innocent. I can read all your feelings on your face. You never pretend to be what you are not, like other girls, you are too honest for your own good, do you know that", He said the last sentence with a mischievous smile.

I smiled back at him, how did he know how to say all the right words to make me feel better?

"Baby, always keep smiling like this, I love my bubbly and stubborn Mia," He pinched the tip of my nose.

"Waleed, I asked Jeena to come to the beach house with us, I also told her that I was going to invite Sheema and Rania too. She was hurt by your behavior, and I thought that it was the best way to cheer her up. I am sorry I ruined our plan," I said with guilt.

" It's okay Mia, Jeena already told me about it after dinner, I think you are right, I shouldn't have behaved with her like that, but I am not used to being nice when I am frustrated," He replied honestly.

I took his hand in mine and gently massaged his knuckles, I knew he was habituated to get what he wants, but due to Jeena, he was getting frustrated.

"What do you say, I give you a BJ to decrease your frustration," I asked teasing him.

"Only a saint won't get tempted by an offer like that," He replied smiling, keeping his hand on his heart and faking to fall on the floor.

Waleed

I had come to pick Mia up from her office and was waiting in the parking lot, across the street, when I saw her coming out of the building. She was about to cross the road when a guy approached her, she cried in excitement when she saw him and nearly threw herself on him.

I was shocked and beyond furious, the territorial and possessive male surfacing from inside me and he didn't like what he saw. She had pulled away from him after a few seconds, but I still didn't like that she hugged a man that was not me.

I slid out of the car slamming the door in anger and my eyes fixed on Mia and that guy. I don't know how I crossed the street and reach them, because all I was seeing was red.

Mia saw me when I was a few feet away from them, her eyes went wide, I always used to wait in the car for her, but today I had come out, she was sure to get startled.

"Babes," I exclaimed as I pulled her to me sliding my arm around her waist and kissing her forehead.

I didn't care if she shot me afterward, there was no way that I was leaving her side until this male was standing with her, whom she had hugged a few minutes ago.

" Riyaan, this is Waleed, my husband, Waleed this is Riyaan, my childhood friend and classmate," She introduced us.

I didn't like the reference childhood friend a bit, they were the ones to look out for. And the way he was looking at Mia, I wanted to snap his neck.

"Hello," He smiled, forwarding his hand to me.

"Hey," I replied dryly ignoring his hand.

I saw a look of embarrassment pass his face, Mia elbowed me in my ribs, to which I replied with another kiss on her cheek and pulled her closer to me.

"So Riyaan, never heard or seen you before," I sized him up.

He was a good-looking guy with an Athletic build and light brown eyes, his brown hairs were curly and he had grown them long, he was sporting a beard and he looked quite similar to Jon Snow from thrones.

"I was in the UK, doing my PG," He replied smiling with a British accent.

That explains it, the guy was Kit Harrington's fan, the character I disliked in thrones. For me, it was Jamie Lannister all the way.

"Well congratulations on your wedding, you stole the hottest girl from our batch," He gave Mia a wink.

If only Mia was not with me right now, I would have killed this bastard right then and there.

"Riyaan, stop teasing my husband," Mia replied laughing.

She knew how possessive I was for her, and I was sure she sensed my anger on the douche bag standing in front of us.

"Baby, we are getting late," I said, as I turned to face her, for the first time moving my eyes from that son of a bitch who was still ogling my wife.

"What about coffee, I hope you can spare time for at least a coffee," Riyaan interrupted us.

"Bastard," I thought bitterly.

"Actually, some other time. Right now we are getting late and we have some commitment for the evening," I replied before Mia could say anything.

"Lunch then, tomorrow? I will pick you, Mia," He had a wicked smirk on his face.

"Sorry, but we are meeting with a client tomorrow for lunch," I said in a cold tone.

The guy was not backing off and neither was I. She was mine and he had the nerve to ask her for lunch in front of me. I don't know what they had in the past, but now she was my wife and in no way, I was going to allow this man around her.

"Riyaan, I will give you a call when I will be free, then we can catch up on the past two years," Mia spoke, sensing the rising tension between us.

"Very well then, take care babes," He said, as he took her hand in his and gave her a handshake.

I wanted to snatch away her hand from him. I wanted to give the guy credit he had balls, to touch my wife in my presence.

"See you then, love," He said as he waved and walked away from us.

"You are not seeing that man ever again," I snarled to Mia as soon as he left.

She looked at me annoyed, but I didn't care a bit. I was beyond furious, she was my wife and there was no way I was letting her keep any kind of contact with that fucker.

"Waleed, he is my friend and he was just teasing you when he saw you getting jealous," She said in annoyance.

"Mia, this isn't up for discussion," I replied in a cold tone as I guided her to the car, with my arm still wrapped around her waist.

"You are a complete jerk, you can't just dictate me like this", She slammed the door of the passenger seat as I entered the car, in anger.

I didn't reply to her, she was a fool if she thought that guy was just her friend because he considered her more than a friend. I have seen it in his eyes, the way he looked at her. I was a man and I could recognize in an instance in what way was any other man looking at a woman.

And I didn't like it a bit, the way he was looking at Mia, and I was surprised how didn't Mia notice that.

"That guy considers you more than a friend," I said sighing after a few minutes.

"Waleed, you are mistaken, I have known Riyaan since childhood, he is just a good friend and that is what he thinks about me," She replied frustrated.

"Mia you don't understand, the way he was looking at you is not supposed to be the way a friend should look," I said agitatedly.

"And how do you know that?" She asked turning to face me.

I took a deep breath, trying to calm myself, I didn't want to argue with her, which could lead to a fight.

"Because it is the way I look at you," I said running the fingers of my left hand through my hair.

She didn't say anything for a while and just kept looking at me stunned, I was sure she was not expecting this answer from me.

" I am so sorry Mia, but it's the truth and I don't know why you didn't notice that yourself," I added.

"You are just imagining things, you are just being possessive and territorial. The Alpha male inside you is making you imagine all this stuff," She replied after some time.

"Mia it's not my imagination, believe me, that guy thinks of you as more than a friend," I softened my tone, careful not to offend her.

I didn't want any kind of bitterness between me and Mia because of that guy, I couldn't live without her even for a day. I felt like my breath would stop, if I didn't speak to her on call every hour when we were at work, no matter how busy I was, I would at least text her every hour.

"I don't know Waleed, I have never thought of him as more than a friend and I never thought he could think about me in any other way than that," She sighed.

"Baby, you are too innocent, you can't see the masks people put on their faces in this world," I replied stroking her cheek with my hand.

Chapter 26

R ameen

"Waleed, have you seen Red?" I asked Waleed who was busy typing a mail on his laptop.

"You know Mia, I try to stay as away from that thing as possible," He replied with a smirk.

"She has a name you know, you don't need to call her thing," I replied irately.

"Whatever," He just shrugged his shoulder.

I came back into the bedroom from the terrace, I had last seen Red last night when I fed her when in the morning I looked for her before going to work she was nowhere in the house.

It was unusual, Red never used to leave the house, she always stayed indoors because of the dogs. Did I tell you, Waleed had five pet dogs, can you imagine? Who keeps five dogs?

I never liked dogs, they terrified me, once in my childhood our neighbor's dog chased me and he had bit my calf. I still shudder when I remember the injections I had to take afterward because of it. His teeth had torn through my skin and I still had the bite mark on my left leg.

After that day, I tried to stay as away from them as was possible, I don't know how Waleed tolerated them and that to so many.

Xander was his favorite one, he was a double coat German Shepherd the size of a wolf. And hairs long and thick, when he roared it felt like the walls were vibrating. He was a nasty beast and he terrified me more than that bitch in the movie Grudge, with black hairs and pale face, just crawling out from everywhere.

I shivered even thinking about her, she was evil and she gave me creeps. I walked back down the stairs to the living room, I checked the kitchen and other rooms but I didn't find Red anywhere.

"Jeena, did you by any chance saw Red?" I asked Jeena who was in the kitchen, busy baking apple pie.

"You mean your cat?" She asked me with wide eyes.

"Yeah, I haven't seen her since morning, I am worried about where she is, she is always around somewhere," I replied to her.

I looked around the kitchen, making cat sounds and meowing, hoping she might come running to me from somewhere, but there was no sign of her.

"Ask Waleed, maybe he knows, the reason your cat is missing," She said in a hushed and mysterious voice.

I looked at her, she was looking at me with an unknown expression on her face, what was she trying to imply?

"What do you mean, Jeena?" I asked dryly not liking a bit her mysterious ways.

"He hates cats, doesn't he?" She asked coyly.

Was she suggesting, that Waleed had done something to her? But why would Waleed do anything to Red? She has been with us for three months now, and I had seen he was getting used to her.

"Waleed adores Red," I answered furiously.

"Does he, really?" She had that mysterious smirk on her face, which I wanted to scratch from her mouth.

"I will ask the maid to look for her," I said leaving the kitchen.

Within half hour the whole house staff was looking for Red, the security guards and the driver were looking in the grounds, while the maids and the cook were looking in the house.

Waleed had joined the guards to look for her, he was worried after seeing my concern for Red. I was pacing on the porch when I saw Waleed coming towards me from the driveway. I looked at him, with hope, he shook his head in a no.

He wrapped his hands around me when he came close to me, I didn't say anything just placed my face on his shoulder. I was getting more and more afraid with each passing minute.

"Sir," A guard called Waleed, he had just come from the backside of the house.

Waleed pulled away from me and looked at the guard, I noticed they were having a silent conversation, Waleed then turned and looked at me and said.

"Mia, wait here," He said squeezing my shoulder.

"What happened?" I looked at Waleed and then at the guard.

The guard gave Waleed a pleading look, and he followed him towards the back of the house, my sixth sense was telling me something was wrong, I followed in the direction they both went.

When I came around the house at the back, the two guards were standing beside Waleed looking at something on the ground, when Waleed saw me approaching them, Waleed took a few long strides and was in front of me within seconds.

"Mia, come with me, you don't want to see it," He grabbed my hand and started pulling away from there.

"Waleed, what is it you are hiding?" I asked hastily.

"Mia, please don't," He kept pulling me away, I twisted my hand in his grip and freed it, my karate training coming in handy.

And before he could hold me again, I ran and was beside the guards, and when I looked at the spot they were staring at a few minutes ago, a scream left my mouth.

There lying on the ground was bloodied and immobile body of red, her stomach was slit and her entrails were hanging out.

Before I could look anymore, I was engulfed in a hug and was been dragged away from the spot. I wanted to throw up, bile was rising from my stomach to my throat, and tears were flowing from my eyes.

I pushed Waleed away from me and I bent as my mouth filled with vomit, I was spilling my guts on the lawn, Waleed was holding my hairs at the back of my neck and was rubbing my back affectionately.

"Mia, I told you to stay there," He said wiping my mouth with his handkerchief as I leaned back up.

I had emptied the whole of my stomach and was now feeling dizzy, Waleed picked me up in his arms and carried me inside the house. I was too exhausted to protest, he placed me on the couch in the living room gently.

He sat beside me and pulled me in his arms, I was a complete mess at that moment, my mind was trying to figure out, who could have done that to Red?

My thoughts were going back to Jeena again and again, the way she was looking at me, her mysterious smile, and her hints regarding Waleed hating cats.

"Who could do this to Red? She was so adorable," I said looking at Waleed, my gaze fixed on him to catch any clue from his expressions.

"It could be the dogs," He replied.

I noticed he was in deep thoughts, his usually calm composure looked rattled, I saw he was also sick to his stomach, by the sight of Red's body.

"Waleed you know it, that it wasn't the dogs," I said emphasizing each word.

"Who do you think can it be?" He asked looking at me alarmed.

"You think I wouldn't have killed that person by now if I knew who did that," I asserted.

"I will ask the security to look at the CCTV footage," He said, standing from the couch.

I was still not able to divert my mind from her body, she was so small and harmless, what kind of monster might have done that to her?

I was stinking from the vomit, I stood up and went to the bedroom to take a bath, I was soaking in the warm water in the bathtub when Waleed came into the bathroom.

He sat on the edge of the bathtub, his eyes fixed on my face, he was trying to know what I was thinking from my facial expressions.

"They are checking the footage, we will find out soon who it was," He said as he caressed my face with his knuckles.

I didn't say anything to him and just nodded in reply, I don't know why but I had the feeling that we won't find anything from the footage. Whoever it was would know the estate was under surveillance by the cameras 24X7, there was no way an outsider could breach the security of this place. It was a fortress, guarded by arm guards and trained dogs.

It had to be someone from inside, and whoever it was I wasn't able to figure out.

Waleed

My senses were rattled, I could not figure out who could have killed Red? And why? She was a harmless animal who could be so cruel as to kill her.

Mia was shaken by her death, a week had passed but still, she had not recovered from it, and I could understand if it was a natural death, she might not have been affected this much, but some had murdered her in cold blood.

Nothing was recorded in the CCTV, it just showed someone throwing out her body from a room on the first floor, but the person was careful enough not to step in the window, they just had tossed it aside.

Jeena was worried about Mia a lot, she had seen how attached Mia was to Red and was trying her best to cheer up Mia, but Mia had distanced herself from everyone like she was unable to trust anyone.

I couldn't blame her, I would have done the same thing if I would have been in her place, thankfully, the time the CCTV showed when Red's body was tossed outside I was with Mia, so she was at least not suspecting me.

I wanted to cheer her up really bad, I was missing her, I was missing her smiles her playful banter with me and of course, I was missing our lovemaking. It's been a week since I kissed her, and it's been the longest since we first made love.

"Do you like any particular color, sir?" The salesman asked me, as I was looking at the kittens in different cages.

"I don't know, which one is the best breed and rarest color?" I asked him.

I had come to a pet shop to buy a kitten for her, Don't be surprised, I don't believe this either, that I am standing in a pet shop and buying a cat.

"The things we do for love," I understand the meaning of this famous quote right now. Poor Jamie Lannister had to go through so much for the woman he loved.

"This is the Persian breed and the coloring pattern is called Chinchilla, this one is the best we have got. It's a pure breed and is trained for the best homes," He replied pointing to a cat.

" Is it a male or a female? I asked looking at the fluffy cat.

"It's a Tomcat," He replied.

"Does it have a name?" I asked again.

"He is named, Greyson, but we call him Grey," He replied with a smile.

"Great, I think I will buy Grey, "I said to him.

The salesman picked up the cage and carried it to the counter.

"Do you want to gift it to someone?" He asked me, clearly he understood I was not into cats.

"Yeah, my wife, do you have anything fancy to pack him," I told him looking at the ugly cage he was in.

I heard a laugh from behind me and turned, a lady walked up to me and smiled.

"I am Claire the owner of this pet shop, I don't think I can pack him up, but surely I can arrange something presentable," She said looking at me with curiosity.

"I suppose you don't like cats," She asked me.

Was it that obvious? That everyone understood by taking a look at me that I didn't like cats?

"Do you want to buy cat food and shampoo for him?" She asked pointing at Grey.

"Yeah, if there is any favorite of his, I would like to buy that," I replied pulling out my wallet to pay her.

She swapped the card I forwarded to her then went inside an adjoining room, she came out with a basket, which had a red ribbon tied to it, she placed a blanket in it and then pulled Grey out of his cage and gently placed him on the blanket.

She stashed some cat food containers and cat shampoo in a bag and forwarded it to me along with the basket. I was debating whether to hold the basket or not, I mean Grey looked like a decent cat to me, but how to make sure he won't bite me the moment I hold the basket.

"Don't worry he won't bite," Claire smiled and said.

At her assurance, I held the basket in one hand and the bag of the other accessories in the other. And carefully carried it to my Range Rover. I placed the basket on the backseat and slid into the driver's seat.

I drove to Mia's office hoping that Grey will cheer her up a little and I will have my wife back, my mind was still caught in the death of Red.

I called Mia, as I reached the signal near her office to come down, she said she will be there in a minute, avoiding parking in the lot, I waited on the side of the street for her.

She came out of the building as soon as she saw my car, her beautiful face was still engulfed in sadness, her amber eyes had lost the sparkle.

"Hey, beautiful," I greeted her as she opened the door and slipped on the passenger seat.

"Hi," She replied with a sad smile.

I felt someone punch me in my gut, my beautiful wife was depressed because of some fucker, and I was not able to do anything to find and punish them.

"Close your eyes," I said to her.

She looked at me surprised but silently obeyed as I told her and closed her eyes. I carefully took the basket from the backseat and placed it on her lap. I was glad that Grey didn't make any sound, otherwise, my surprise would have been spoilt.

"Now open them," I said looking at her.

She slowly opened her eyes and looked at the basket on her lap stunned, then she squealed in delight.

"Ohh my God, Waleed, this is a Persian cat with a Chinchilla pattern, do you know how rare they are."

"Not as rare as your smile, I have been dying for one," I replied caressing her cheeks with my fingers.

"I have missed you, Mia," I said to her who was looking at me with moist eyes.

She opened her mouth to say something but choked, I knew she was overwhelmed with emotions.

"The fun part is, he already has a name and it is exactly according to your taste. Meet Greyson, but he likes to be called Grey," I pointed towards Greyson, who was now looking at Mia with his wide eyes.

"He is beautiful, I love him, thanks," she spoke finally.

She pulled Grey, out of the basket and then tossed it on the backseat, as she settled him on her lap.

"Hello Grey," she purred.

I looked at her satisfied, at last, I was able to break the shell of sadness surrounding her, she was now busy stroking Greyson's fur with affection.

"I can't believe you got a cat for me, you actually went and bought one," she said with her beautiful smile.

"You know, I can do anything for you baby, but I just want my Mia back, do you think I will get her back?" I kept my hand on her and asked with hope.

"I am yours, Waleed, now and forever," she exclaimed, placing her head on my shoulder.

Chapter 27

Rameen

"Is this the last one?" Waleed asked me pointing to the bag.

I nodded in reply, he pulled the handle of the travel bag and dragged it out of the room, where the manservant was waiting. He gave him instructions as I picked my handbag from the center table and checked my cell and sunglasses when I was sure everything was in place I walked out of our room.

Waleed locked the room behind us and we descended the stairs, I checked Grey, he was sleeping in his carrying basket. I was not going to leave him behind while we were gone for two days.

Jeena was waiting for us on the porch, she was looking a little nervous. She had invited the guy she had gone on date with for the weekend, they surely were a thing now.

"Jeena, you sure he is coming?" Waleed asked her.

"Don't worry, you guys go ahead, he will be here soon. You have sent me the location right? We will follow the map," She replied giving her hair a flip.

"Okay, then we will meet you at the beach house," he said as he walked to his black Cadillac Escalade and opened the door to the driver's seat.

It was a beast and I loved it. This was the first time he had taken it out of the garage after our wedding. Usually, he used his Range Rover or his Lamborghini among the many cars he owned, I still have to learn their names. Boys and their toys. One thing I had learned is that he loved driving himself.

"Do you like it?" He asked excitedly as I slid into the passenger seat.

"Yeah, she is a beautiful beast," I replied smiling at his boyishness.

"Don't call my baby a beast, would you like if I called Greyson a beast?" He asked looking annoyed.

I just rolled my eyes and connected my cell to the blue tooth, so I could hear my playlist. The weather was beautiful, a little cloudy with moderate sunlight and a cool breeze, Greyson slept silently in the basket. He was a darling, a well-trained, and a decent cat.

Even Waleed was getting fond of him, he didn't even protest when he slept in our bed a few times, though he got jealous sometimes when I gave Greyson more attention than him.

After an hour and a half long drive, we reached the beach house, it was beautiful, the location was exotic the interior was lively and elegant. The walls were plush white, the flooring was wooden, with floor-to-ceiling windows. It had a deck at the back and its private beach.

The perks of marrying a billionaire. Waleed gave me a tour of the house, it had six bedrooms, a living room, kitchen, gym, recreation room, where I saw a pool table. After giving me the tour of the whole house he took me to the master bedroom.

By the glint in his grey eyes, I knew that it was something special and he was excited for me to see it. As he opened the door and I stepped inside I was beyond shocked. There was a swinging bed in the middle of the room, and a glass wall behind it, which opened up on a terrace and it had an infinity pool. Someone pinch me please, I hope it's not a dream.

Waleed pulled me to him as he strolled towards the bed, and dropped on the bed dragging me with him. I tumbled beside him on the bed and the bed started swinging with the impact of our fall.

Waleed rolled to his side and propped up on his elbow, he looked down at me with mischief in his eyes and his lower lip, tugged between his teeth.

"This is amazing," I said looking at him, as my body adjusted itself to the swinging motion.

"I knew you will love it," He said leaning as he kissed me.

Before we both knew, we were tearing out each other's clothes. Waleed hovered over me, teasing me with his mouth and lips.

"Ohh God Waleed, this feels so amazing," I moaned in excitement.

As if his torture was not enough for my body, the swinging bed made it unbearable, he restrained me by the cuffs attached to the chain by which the bed hung. I was struggling to free my hands so that I could hold on to something as he was driving me crazy with his skills in the bed.

I never could have imagined, how fuckingly amazing sex could feel when I was suspended in the air on a swinging bed with my hands tied.

"Waleed," I cried as the orgasm raced through my body and he followed me after a few seconds screaming my name.

"This-this was the best sex I ever had in my life," I told him as he withdrew from me and uncuffed my hands, and slipped to the floor.

"Pleasure is mine babes," He said with his cocky smile.

Right now, my mind was still in a haze and I couldn't even give him a witty response.

"Hurry up, take the shower, they will be arriving soon. I will use the bathroom in the next room. Make sure you don't exhaust yourself today because I am gonna fuck you there tonight," He said pointing to the pool beyond the glass wall.

I turned and looked at the pool and then at him who was looking at me with a promise in his eyes, and I knew at that moment that I was fucked.

By the time I took a shower and got dressed, everyone has arrived downstairs apart from Jeena and her beau. I was looking forward to meeting that guy.

Waleed was already present in the living room speaking with Asjad and Saad, and Sheema and Rania were busy discussing the latest fashion trends as I entered the living room. They both looked at me with knowing smiles, heat-blasted on my cheeks as I looked at Waleed, who was looking at me and winked when our eyes met.

"God, this man would get me killed someday," I thought helplessly.

I took quick steps and dropped on the couch beside Rania, who elbowed me in my ribs and smiled teasingly.

"We know you just got laid, don't even try to deny it," She said in a whisper that only we could hear.

I grinned at her, well I was not going to deny the fact that I just had the best sex of my life with the hottest guy in the town, who was, fortunately, my husband.

I showed Rania and Sheema their rooms, Rania was obviously going to share one with Asjad, while Sheema and Saad had to do with different rooms until they got married.

"Our rooms are good enough, I hope you guys didn't bang in any of these rooms you are alloting us," Rania said as she looked at the bed carefully, for any sign of crinkled bed sheets.

"You idiot, why would I want to bang in here, when I have the best bedroom," I said smiling mysteriously.

She and Sheema then demanded to be shown our bedroom and when I lead the way to our bedroom and they entered and saw it, they were wearing the same expression as I was, when I first saw the room.

"What the fuck is this place?" Rania asked looking impressed with what she saw.

"If I would have not known that you both just spilled your nectar on this bed, I would climb into it," Rania said looking at the bed eagerly.

"Rania," Sheema and I exclaimed at the same time, on her obscene use of language.

"What did I say wrong?" She said looking at us annoyed.

"Do you guys have any plans for the pool, if yes, I would like to take a dip before you pollute it," She asked giggling?

I threw a cushion at her from the couch and thankfully it hit her head directly.

"Geez, Mia, are you horny again? Do you want me to send Waleed upstairs," She teased me. A pillow fight started between us, which only interrupted with Asjad calling Rania downstairs for somethin g.We walked into the living room panting, all the three guys looked at us in surprise.

Before they could ask us anything, Jeena entered the living room with a guy and greeted, and when I saw his face I was bearly able to suppress my laughter as I looked between Waleed and him.

Waleed

I was looking at the guy in front of me with disdain if he would not have been with Jeena I was surely gonna beat the shit out of him. But because he was accompanying Jeena, I needed to calm myself. If he made her happy that was enough for me to tolerate him, but if he made one move towards my wife I was going to forget he was with Jeena.

"Riyaan this is Waleed, my cousin, and best friend," Jeena introduced me to him, though I knew he didn't need any introduction.

The bastard smirked at me as he greeted everyone, and when he hugged Mia, I was barely holding by a thread.

"Wow, what a coincidence that you both know each other," Jeena said excitedly when that asshole told her he and Mia were classmates.

I walked to Mia and pulled her to me snaking my arm around her waist. I kissed her head inhaling in her scent to calm my senses.

"She is mine, she is just mine," I reminded myself.

But the territorial caveman inside me was still not convinced, he didn't want this guy anywhere around Mia. I didn't like the way he was looking at her right now. Like he was eye-fucking her, or maybe I was just imagining things.

"Riyaan, me, and Sheema are schoolmates," Mia told Jeena.

I looked at Sheema then back at Riyaan, but he was barely paying Sheema any attention, his eyes were fixed on Mia who had snuggled closer to me, I smiled knowing that she couldn't resist me.

"Imaad beat me to her, otherwise it could have been me holding her in my arms," Riyaan told Jeena with a teasing smile.

"I am glad he did," Jeena said as she wrapped her arms around his torso.

"And I am glad I beat you both to it," I smirked at him as I gave Mia a peck on her cheeks.

I saw Asjad and Saad shifting on the spots they were standing, surely they have sensed the tension between us.

"The game still isn't over," he retorted.

"Riyaan, enough of your teasing, don't try to make my husband jealous. He is the only one for me," Mia shrieked at him, as she wrapped her arms around me.

I was planning to lunge at him and claw his eyes out but suddenly felt like someone had brought me into a cool shade from the scorching heat.

"I like when he goes all jealous and starts planning to murder me," he replied chuckling.

I wanted to punch his teeth into his guts, that sight would be funny to laugh at.I saw Jeena getting a little uncomfortable with his constant flirting with Mia. He was too brave or rather foolish, to hit on my wife in my presence and expect to get away with it.

"Mia, no matter how beautiful you are, Jeena is the only one for me," he said pulling Jeena closer to him.

I saw Jeena smiling as she tightened the grip across his torso, Mia offered to guide them to their bedrooms, which I wanted to protest but didn't have any choice as they were our guests. Rania and Sheema joined them and I was left with my friends.

"What's up with you and that guy?" Asjad asked as soon as they were out of earshot.

"I don't want him anywhere around Mia," I told them honestly.

"Cool down Wal, the guy was just teasing," Saad said as he sensed how pissed I was at Riyaan.

"I can't believe you and Mia lasted this long, remember what scene you created on Sheema's birthday," Asjad said laughing.

I smiled remembering my second meeting with Mia, and what disaster it turned out. We both honestly had come a long way, thinking about the few initial meetings with Mia, I still couldn't believe that we are happily married.

"And the way he was pissed when she blew her date with Maram," Saad reminded.

I was glad that things didn't work out between me and Maram who knows if they had, I would have been with her right now, and I could imagine how boring my life would have been with her.

I can't even imagine my life without Mia, she was oxygen for me and I just couldn't get enough of her. I was impatient to start a family with her. We had been trying for a few months now and still hadn't conceived. We even consulted a gynaec who ran some tests and assured us that everything was fine and soon we will get the good news. She had prescribed some pills to Mia, which helped in conceiving and I made sure she took them on time.

When the maid announced that the lunch was served we left for the dining room as the girls and Riyaan joined us for the lunch. I was surprised to see Riyaan had shaved his beard in the meantime. Not that it concerned me, but I was still curious to know the reason. He was looking quite ridiculous sporting his Jon Snow hairstyle with a clean shave.

He didn't flirt with Mia during lunch and was busy chatting with Sheema and Jeena all the time, while Rania and Mia were busy speaking to each other in hushed voices, I wondered if she was discussing our lovemaking from a couple of hours ago.

"If you guys wanna hit the beach now is the time, I have asked the cook to arrange a BBQ in the evening and the weather gets cold in the evening, so it's better to take a swim when the weather is still warm," I said as we finished our lunch.

To my surprise, everyone agreed with me, even the girls, they hurried to their rooms to change into their swimming clothes.

I came into the bedroom to find Mia in an orange sleeveless one-piece bathing suit which ended on her calf, I didn't like it a bit. Though it covered all her body it fitted her like a second skin and I didn't want anyone else taking pleasure from the sight she was right now.

"You are not leaving this room in that dress," I announced the first thing.

She looked at me as if I had lost my mind, but I didn't care a bit about what she thought, I was not backing down.

"Waleed I love this swimsuit, and I am not changing it," She said in a firm voice.

"Too bad, then you are staying here," I shrugged my shoulders.

"Waleed, you can't decide what I am going to or not going to wear," She glared crossing her arms on her chest.

My mind was diverted a little by the outline of her breast in the swimsuit, but I quickly looked away from her bosom to her eyes.

"Mia, for once please don't argue and listen to me," I softened my tone.

I knew there was no way she was going to back down if I ordered her, so I changed my stance and thought of sweet-talking her into changing the dress.

"Waleed this is my favorite, I bought it, especially for this trip," She said stubbornly.

"Baby I will buy you more, for when we go on our honeymoon or come here alone, but please change it now, please for me," I couldn't believe I was pleading to a girl.

She kept looking at me for some time and then raised her hands in defeat as she pulled out another dress from her bag and stormed into the bathroom. I congratulated myself, for successfully changing her mind without a fight or argument.

We left for the beach as she walked out of the bathroom, this time wearing a tee shirt and a loose cotton Capri, I heaved a sigh of relief. At least her perfect figure was not on display in this outfit.

"You owe me for this," she said walking with me towards the beach.

"I owe you my life," I replied smiling.

"Charmer," she replied rolling her eyes.

Everyone had already come to the beach, I saw Jeena stretched on a chair, while Rania and Sheema were busy in a discussion, Asjad, Saad, and Riyaan seemed to warm up for the beach volleyball.

Mia walked up to the girls as I sauntered to Asjad's side, they had already decided the team's, Saad and Riyaan were standing on the opposite side of the net from Asjad and me.

"You think you are up for it," Asjad asked looking at me.

"Fuck off Asjad," I snapped.

"You are pissed at the guy and your reflex is clouded when you are pissed," Asjad said eyeing up Riyaan.

He had a good physique, no doubt about it, but that was not my concern right now, I just wanted to see how good he was at volleyball.

"Hey, you think you can make room for me?" Mia asked strolling towards us.

"Real-life partners can't be in the same team," Riyaan announced.

I looked at him, really? I mean was there any limit that this guy was not ready to go to be around my wife.

" Fuck off Riyaan, I am playing on Waleed's side," Mia replied to him before I got a chance to react.

"I know you always have been a cheater," He teased Mia.

"Riyaan, not one more word," She hissed in fury.

"Ohh really doll? What are you gonna do about it?" He asked standing in front of her, too close for my comfort.

"You know I can kick your ass whenever I want," She replied with her brow arched.

"What about a match?" He asked with a smirk.

I walked up to Mia, there was no way I was letting that bastard get into her head, the way they were looking at each other made me jealous like they shared some chemistry.

"Mia, let's take a swim, we can do snorkeling if you are in for some fish sighting," I pulled Mia by her arm.

Mia looked at my hand on her arm and then in my eyes, she then looked back at Riyaan, who still had that awful smirk plastered on his face.

"Give me five minutes Waleed, I will just kick his ass, it's been a long time since I got to kick one," She said flexing her arms.

"Maybe your husband is afraid, you will embarrass him by losing," He gave me a wicked smile.

I know the game that bastard was playing, and I was afraid, Mia was falling right for it. She was looking at him with fury, the same expression she had on her face in our initial meetings when she was up for a challenge.

"Mia you don't need to prove anything to anyone," I said through clenched teeth.

I was worried she was going to accept this challenge, and it was the last thing I wanted right now.

"Challenge accepted," She declared calmly.

I wanted to punch that bastard until his ridiculous face was bruised, who was looking at me with a triumphant smile, saying now try and keep your wife away from me.

Mia walked across the net where Asjad was standing with the ball, she took the ball from him and got in a position ready to hit. Saad and Asjad took a few long strides and were beside me, while Mia and Riyaan were ready to start the game.

Mia hit the ball with her intertwined hands and Riyaan easily hit it back to her, I was not interested in looking that asshole play with my wife, I turned around and walked up to Jeena and dropped on a sun lounger beside hers.

"They seem to have a strong bond, don't they?" Jeena said looking at them with interest in her eyes, as they both were trying hard to outdo each other in the game.

"I wonder what would have happened if you didn't have married her, maybe they would have been a couple," She added.

I was trying hard to control myself, as I watched Mia, laughing and teasing Riyaan every time he missed a hit. They were so engrossed in each other, oblivious to what was happening around them.

"You love her don't you?", Jeena asked again looking at me.

I didn't reply to her yet again, my eyes were fixed on Mia who was now mimicking a dance move after Riyaan missed yet another hit. I don't know if she was the better player, or Riyaan was missing the hits willingly.

"Does she love you?" Jeena asked again.

And for the first time in the entire conversation, I looked at her, I don't know why, but her question has dug its claws in my mind.

"Do Mia love me?" I asked myself.

I know she liked me and she wanted me, but does she love me? What were the chances that she would stay with me if by any chance she falls in love with someone else?

"She loves me Jeena," I replied to her, but I felt like I was trying to convince myself more than I was trying to convince her.

"Does she?" Jeena asked arching her brow.

I stayed silent and kept looking at Jeena, trying to figure out what she was trying to imply.

"If she did, she would be beside you right now, enjoying the limited time you got off from work, especially when this is your first trip after your marriage. Not playing volleyball with her childhood friend trying to win a childish bet," She gave me a smirk.

I snapped, I was afraid to admit she was right, this was our first trip after our marriage and I wanted to spend the time with her, she had already ruined the trip by inviting Jeena and our other friends and now she was more inclined to win a stupid game against that bastard than spending the time with me.

My mood was ruined, and I just wanted to get out of this place, I got up from the chair and walked back to the house, I was disappointed to find out Mia didn't even notice me leaving.

.

Chapter 28

R ameen

I hit the ball and leaped into the air with joy as Riyaan missed again this time, I always knew I was the better player. I had been playing volleyball since childhood on my school team, on a national level. Though beach volleyball was different from it, I still had practiced it with Ali and Umair.

I missed Ali, it had been a couple of weeks since we spoke, he was busy with his last semester and as scheduled he was coming back next week. I was looking forward to his return, it will be the first time we will meet after my wedding. I just hope Waleed would get along with him.

I suddenly remembered that Waleed was not here celebrating my win with me, as Asjad, Saad, Rania, and Sheema congratulated me on winning. I looked around but didn't find him anywhere on the beach.

Jeena was spread across on one of the sun loungers, but Waleed was not with her. I looked around again to confirm he was not there, then

I turned and looked at the sea to confirm if he had gone for a swim, but he was not there.

"Have you guys seen Waleed?" I asked them.

They all shrugged their shoulders in reply and looked around the beach. I felt a little guilty, he was so excited about this trip, and what had I done? I was busy trying to prove myself better at a stupid sport than spending time with my husband.

I knew how possessive and territorial he was and I still got carried away by Riyaan's teasing, I always had a love-hate relationship with Riyaan. One moment we were best friends and the other we were ready to kill each other.

Riyaan had always been a part of my life since my school days until he went abroad for his Masters. My relationship with him was completely platonic but Waleed didn't know that. And of course, when people looked at me and Riyaan they thought we were together, but the truth was we were just frenemies.

"Jeena have you seen Waleed?" I called out to Jeena.

She raised her head to look at me and then shook her head in a no. I was getting anxious now, I was sure Waleed was upset because I ignored him and preferred to play with Riyaan.

"He might have gone to the house, to fetch something," Saad said looking at me sympathetically.

"I don't think he liked the idea of you playing against Riyaan," he whispered.

I had figured that out by myself, that he was upset with me. I apologized to the others as I made my way to the house, hoping that he would forgive me.

I found the living room empty, I checked the bedroom and he was not there, I looked on the terrace, the gym, and other rooms to find them empty.

I came to the recreation room and found him playing a game on his Xbox, this was not what I had expected him to be doing.

"Hey," I said as I dropped beside him on the couch.

He didn't reply to me, his eyes were focused on the screen where a car was running on a race track with lightning speed.

"I am sorry," I said keeping my hand on his shoulder.

Waleed still ignored me and brushed aside my hand from his shoulder, I never imagined that he could be so mad at me.

"I know you are mad at me, but I am sorry," I said with guilt choking my words.

"Finally, you got the time to think about what I was feeling," He snapped at me.

I hadn't expected this answer from him, this was the first time he was upset at me so much that he didn't even look at me once.

"Sorry na Waleed, " I whined like a child.

"Mia, I don't want to talk about it right now, so please just leave me alone, " He said in a cold voice, which I had never heard before.

I looked at him, his eyes were still fixed on the screen, his face as hard as a stone, and his grey eyes burning with fury. The vein on his temple was throbbing as it would burst. I had never seen him this much enraged in my life. No matter how pissed he was at me, his eyes were always glued to me, even in our first few meetings.

I had never witnessed this side of Waleed before, and I don't think I ever want to, he was scaring the shit out of me. I was accustomed to his teasing and his loving tone, but this side of him was something new and terrifying.

"Waleed, I just want to say," I tried to explain to him but he interrupted me.

"I said, enough Mia, just leave me the fuck alone," He thundered.

I looked at him terrified, with my eyes wide, as he looked me in the eyes for the first time, I saw his eyes warming up a little after seeing the moistness in my eyes, but I didn't wait there, I sprung to my feet and ran out of the room.

I tried to calm my senses as I wiped the tear that had rolled on my cheek, this was the first time we fought, I know I had made a mistake by ignoring him but I apologized. I still couldn't understand what made him so mad at me that he didn't even want to forgive me even after my apology.

I came into the kitchen, I needed tea, my head had started pounding and I knew it would lead to a headache. I had a migraine and a little stress could trigger a headache.

I had on the electric kettle and started adding sugar and tea to the water heating in it. I poured milk into the cup as I stood there waiting for the tea to lose its color and flavor in the boiling water.

I sensed his presence in the kitchen, I knew he would come to me when he realized he had hurt me, but I didn't turn to look at him, in my fury.

I felt his breath on my neck and the heat radiating from his body, I wanted to turn around and suck the air out of his lungs, kissing. I could have easily because no one was there in the house apart from us two, and there was no fear of someone walking upon us, but I still waited for him to make the first move.

I closed my eyes when I felt his arms snake around my waist as he pulled me to him. His scent invaded my senses calming my chaotic mind. He gently placed his lips on the crook of my neck and a moan escaped my mouth.

I slid my arm backward to wrap around his neck, and I froze in that instance because I knew that it was not Waleed who was holding me in his arms, but it was someone else because Waleed's hairs were short at the back and whoever this was had long hairs. And before my mind was at the conclusion that it was Riyaan who was holding me I heard Waleed's voice.

"Get your hands off her."

I was petrified, it was as if someone had knocked the air out of my lungs, I just wanted to die at that moment, because I knew what it would look like to any person and what must be going on in Waleed's mind at this moment.

I opened my eyes as Riyaan turned me along with him to face Waleed, his arms still around my waist, and his chin resting on the crook of my neck.

"I said get your fucking hands off her," Waleed snarled.

I was looking at him with my eyes petrified, his lips were pressed together in fury, his jaw clenched and his grey eyes filled with hurt and rage were fixed on me.

I felt Riyaan pulling away from me, as he slid away, his hands from around my waist and then he stepped beside me. Waleed was looking at him with hate and blood in his eyes.

"I think your wife likes my hands on her," Riyaan said with a smirk, and I couldn't believe what he was saying.

Riyaan was my friend, my childhood friend and how could he do anything like this, I looked at Riyaan who was looking at Waleed with triumph on his face. I couldn't let him do this to Waleed, I couldn't let him do this to us.

"Waleed I can explain," I blurted out as I took a step towards him.

He held his hand in front of me to stop me from getting closer to him.

"Just stop Mia, I think I know what I saw," He said in a voice barely audible.

He looked at Riyaan and roared "If you are not gone from my house within the next five minutes, I swear to God I will kill you."

Riyaan didn't reply to him and just left from there, knowing what he wanted was accomplished. Before I could say anything in my defense, Waleed turned and climbed up the stairs to the first floor. I followed after him and saw Jeena standing in the doorway and by her facial expressions I knew she had heard and seen everything.

She had a smirk on her face, I ignored her at the moment and climbed the staircase after Waleed, by the time I reached the bedroom door, he had already locked it. I knocked on the door and called him to open it, but was shocked as something smashed on the door and broke with a loud noise.

I was standing there still as I heard him throwing and breaking everything inside the room, I knocked again and kept calling him to open the door but he didn't, and kept breaking the things in the room. Then there was silence inside, maybe he had nothing more to break in the room.

I heard the ruffling of clothes and the voice of the zipper being pulled, and a few seconds later the door opened, Waleed was standing in the door, with his hand on the handle of his bag and his other hand dripping with blood, I looked at the blood oozing out of his hand in panic. He might have cut it, while he was on a rampage to break everything.

I tried to grab his bloodied hand, but he shoved me aside and walked past me to the staircase with his bag, by the time I came out of the shock and understood that he was leaving he was already at the bottom of the staircase.

"Waleed please wait, where are you going," I ran after him.

He didn't even turn back to look at me, as I ran after him, he was out of the main door before I reached the foot of the staircase and kept calling and running after him.

I saw him dumping his bag in the trunk and taking long strides to the driver's seat before I reached the car he was already on the seat and had turned on the engine.

"Waleed you can't leave like this, at least give me a chance to explain," I called as I saw his Escalade skid on the driveway.

He sped out of there before I reached the spot he had parked his car without even giving me a look. I stood there defeated, as the dust settled back on the road again.

Jeena

I smiled as I saw her run after Waleed terrified, I can't say for how long I have been waiting for this day and how joyous and triumphant I felt right now, after seeing that bitch grieving.

I had loved Waleed since childhood, he was the only one I had ever wanted and desired. And I knew he loved me too and he wanted me, but that old man had brainwashed my Waleed into believing that we were not good for each other.

I have hated Waleed's grandfather, more than I hated anyone until Mia came along. That bitch, she thought she could take away Waleed from me? Never, I would let any girl take my Waleed away from me, he is mine and we belonged together and no one can take him away from me, I would never let that happen.

I always knew what type of girls Waleed liked and I had shaped my personality into the exact type that he wanted. We have been friends and there was nothing that I didn't know about him. Apart from the last two years, when he had drifted away from me because of his

Dada. Still, I had not given up on him, I used to call and text regularly just to know what was going on in his life.

I always dreaded the moment, when he would find a girl for him, but it never came because I knew the type of girl he preferred didn't exist in this world, they were hypothetical and the closest anyone could get to it was me, because I knew what he wanted and I acted accordingly in front of him. It was a matter of time before he would give up his hope to find that perfect girl and come running back to me.

But his Dada had ruined that chance for me, he had made him marry a girl that was the complete opposite of the type of girl Waleed liked. I was busy with my examination when they got married, and I had seen their pictures on social media from some reception they had attended.

The way he was looking at her, the way he was holding her, made me want to burn that bitch alive. I knew she was beautiful, and that she had Waleed wrapped around her pinky finger.

I started stalking her on social media, trying to find anything and everything about her.

I wanted my Waleed back from her at any cost and I was glad to have found the one thing I had been searching for. I found Riyaan's profile on Mia's friend list. Riyaan's profile picture was of Mia and him, Mia was holding his ear in that picture and was looking furiously at him, while he was looking at her with puppy eyes.

I sent him a friend request and a direct message, from a fake profile asking him if he wanted the girl in his dp all to himself. He was shocked at first, even threatened to report me, but I knew deep down that he wanted Mia and I was not going to let this chance go.

I brainwashed him for nearly a month until he finally, agreed to help me with my plan. When a month was left for him to return from the UK, I went to Waleed's town. Riyaan and I planned everything to the end, how he would meet her randomly to avoid any suspicion. The way I should pose is that I was dating someone and was into him. When I found out about the trip to the beach house. I knew this was my chance.

Riyaan and I decided on the course and I bought him the Cologne Waleed used. So Mia would get distracted because of the similar smell. Everything worked out perfectly and I can't help but rejoice, knowing that Waleed was finally going to be mine.

It was the most difficult thing I did in my life trying to be friends with the woman I wanted to kill. As I started to get to know her and find out about her personality, I was shocked completely. She didn't have a single quality that Waleed desired in his wife, yet he was so smitten with her. She had become oxygen for him, and it was impossible for him to keep his hands off her.

The thing that most shocked me was that she had brought a kitten home, and Waleed was even getting fond of that stupid cat. I remember in my childhood he had made me give up my cat when he had come to our place to stay during the summer vacation. And I had gladly given away that cat because I loved him and I didn't want anything in my life that Waleed didn't like or detested.

I was waiting for a chance to kill that cat so that Waleed won't have to bear her presence. I know my Waleed didn't like cats and I will do everything to keep him happy. I was happy when I killed that stupid cat, it had been easy, I just stabbed her with a knife and threw her body out of the window, cleaning the blood with the help of bleach.

I knew Waleed and Mia were distracted at that moment, I had heard him say to Mia, that he wanted a BJ in the shower that night, and looking at Mia's face she looked quite eager for it.

The nights were the most difficult for me, the thought that Waleed was with that bitch rather than me and was pleasing her the way I wanted him to please me. Sometimes I wanted to barge into their room and just kill that bitch.

I hate Mia, I hated her more than anyone in this whole world, she doesn't deserve Waleed, she doesn't have any right to be with him. She doesn't love him, she is incapable of taking care of him. She is so pathetic that she can't even cook.

Ohhh my poor Waleed, he didn't need to worry for long, I will get rid of that bitch for him, and then I will take care of him. I will love him and will treat him as he deserved to be treated just like a king.

I knew he will forget her the moment she is out of his life and he will realize that I am the one for him, that I was the only one for him. No one can love my Waleed as I do, especially Mia, she doesn't know, how lucky she is to be with Waleed, but she doesn't give a damn about him. She argues with him, she makes him miserable by her stubbornness.

My Waleed is not weak but around her, he is a completely different person. I had never seen him bending to anyone's will, but he is on his knees in front of Mia.

And I can't describe how much it hurts me to see my Waleed, being so crazy about her, it kills me, it's as if I am walking on hot coal, barefoot.

But not long now, I will have my Waleed back, I will snatch him away from Mia and she won't be able to do anything. Now when Waleed had seen what a whore she was, he won't take a minute to throw her out of his life.

He will come back to me, he will be mine forever, and no one will ever take him away from me. I heard Mia asking Waleed to open the door, as far as I know, Waleed, it's a matter of time he will leave Mia here and I have to get the next part of my plan ready.

I went into Riyaan's room, he was ready to leave, I told him I was going along with him. He looked at me shocked, for some time, and then said.

"What about Waleed? What will he say if you go with me?" He asked me.

"Waleed won't even notice, he is beyond furious and his mind doesn't think rationally when he is angry," I replied with a smirk.

I knew Waleed better than anyone in this whole world, I know how his mind works in different scenarios and I used it to the fullest.

"Okay then let's leave," He said.

I pulled my bag out of my room and followed him, I know the drama that could unfold after we left, but I was hoping Waleed to react in the way I know he will.

Waleed came exactly half an hour later to his house after Riyaan dropped me off, I was hoping to speak to him, but he ignored me and went straight for his room. He came out of his bedroom exactly an hour later with a servant carrying his black leather luggage bag.

I was puzzled, was he leaving for somewhere? I took a few quick steps and was beside him. He didn't halt and kept walking and I tried to match his steps.

"Waleed, where are you going?" I asked him, worried.

"I am leaving for the US, I need to get out of here, otherwise I would kill that fucker," He hissed but didn't stop.

We were on the porch in a few seconds, where his driver was waiting for him, he opened the door to the backseat as soon as he saw Waleed.

"But Waleed, what about me?" I asked him hopefully.

"You can go back to your house Jeena because I am not coming back soon," He replied in a cold tone.

I watched helplessly as he got into the car and left before my eyes, I couldn't believe he could leave me alone just like that after what happened. I thought he would need me to comfort him, to tell him how much I loved and wanted him. But nothing as such happened he just left, without even thinking about me.

My hate for Mia only increased by his hostile behavior, it was because of that bitch that he was behaving like this with me.

Chapter 29

Rameen

As soon as I entered the house I got the feeling Waleed was not there, I don't know why I felt like this, but I knew that he was not in the house.

Jeena and Riyaan had left before Waleed, good for them otherwise I would have beaten the shit out of both of them. She was mistaken if she thought me to be some damsel in distress. I knew how to fight and defend what was mine, I was not going to let her take Waleed from me, he was mine as I was his and no one in this world could ever change it.

I had told Rania and Sheema what had happened between me and Waleed after Waleed had left. They were shocked beyond doubt, I told them about how Jeena was looking at me when I left the kitchen, and all about Red's death.

If I doubted before that Jeena had been the one to kill Red, now I was certain that she was the one who killed her. I was not going to forgive that bitch, she was going to pay for it.

It took us nearly an hour to wind up our stuff and leave the beach house. I don't know what Sheema and Rania had told Asjad and Saad, but they had assured me that they both will always be there to help me. Asjad told me that Waleed had once told him that Jeena wanted them to get married, but his Dada didn't want Waleed to marry her, and now I understand why he didn't want Waleed to get married to Jeena.

I was shocked that Waleed had not mentioned anything about it to me, did he hide that from me on purpose? But why would he want to hide it? He had told me a thousand times that he loved me then why didn't he tell me about Jeena. Did he still have feelings for her? How close were they in the past?

I didn't want to think about it, but still, my mind was occupied with the thought that they were having any sexual relationship? Did he make love to Jeena the way he loved me? For fuck sake, Mia, stop thinking about that and concentrate on how you are going to clean this mess.

I handed Grey, to the servant who came to me as soon as he saw me get out of the car, he held Grey in one hand and my bag with the other. Rania asked me if I wanted her to come with me. I politely told her that it would be better if I handled it alone, I was not sure how Waleed would react and I didn't want any scene in front of my friends.

As I entered the living room, I saw Jeena sitting on the couch, she was the last person I wanted to see right now, and I think I was the last person she wanted to see, because, the moment her gaze fell on me she shrieked.

"How dare you step into this house?"

Saying that I was shocked by her words would be an understatement, she was standing in my house and asking me, how dare I step into this house?

"Excuse me, did you just address me?" I asked crossing my arms on my chest.

"You are not to enter this house," Jeena snarled.

I was not allowed in this house? And who gave her this authority, to tell me that I was not allowed in my own house.

"And who gave you this authority?" I asked arching for my brow.

"Waleed," she replied immediately.

"Then let him tell me, that I am not allowed in here," I said fearlessly.

She was a fool if she thought I would take her word for it, she could have deceived me once it won't be happening twice.

"He is on the flight to the US, and he had asked me to not allow you in the house," she spat at me.

I felt like someone had squeezed my heart with their hands, I can't describe how hurt I was to find that my husband had left without giving me a chance to explain myself to him.

"I think you have forgotten Jeena, but let me remind you, I am his lawfully wedded wife, and I have equal rights on everything he owns till I am married to him. And neither you nor he can make me leave my house," I took a few steps and stood in front of her.

I knew she was lying, there was no way Waleed would tell her to not allow me to come into the house. Or did he? Fuck him if he did, I was not leaving my house until he divorces me.

"He will come back to me, he loves me he just needs to find it out, and once he does he will throw you out of his life and marry me," she hissed through clenched teeth.

I chuckled at her declaration, fucking bitch if she thought it will be easy for him to just throw me out of his life and marry her then she was in for a surprise.

"What do you think I am, Jeena? A damsel in distress, that will stand aside and let him marry you? I will drag him to courts and shred his reputation to pieces if he even thinks of divorcing me and marrying you. But as far as I know, he won't do any of this, because the moment his anger cools down and he is in his right mind, he will come crawling back to me. Because it is me he loves, and me he wants, not you," I said calmly looking in her eyes.

"You bitch."

She screamed raising her hand to slap me, but I was fast enough, I caught her hand before it could come in contact with my face and twisted it, as I turned her around and slid my other arm around her neck.

Jeena tried hard to loosen my grip and get away from me, but I was strong, all those years of karate training had come in handy for me at this moment, and I know she didn't even know, how to punch. I bet she was too busy all her life trying to be the perfect girl, which by the way she was far from. She was screaming and struggling hard but I only tightened my grip around her neck.

"It would just take a little movement for me to snap your neck, and you will be dead like Red. Would you want to join Red, Jeena? I know it was you who killed her, you can't fool me Jeena, not twice," I whispered in her ear.

I felt her body stiffen and then she went rigid in my grip, Bitch, now she will know that I am the Queen Bitch here, and it won't turn out good for her if she messes with me.

I loosened my grip on her neck and pulled my arm back, keeping her in place with my hold on her arm. I kicked her behind her knee and left her arm, I smirked as I saw her fall on the ground and turn and look at me.

"This was just a trailer Jeena, if you don't leave within an hour from my house, I will throw you out myself, and I am sure you know, I am capable of it," I said in a voice as cold as ice, looking in her eyes without blinking.

I didn't wait after that to look at what she does, taking quick steps towards the staircase I climbed the stairs without halting.

My heart was beating as if it would jump out of my ribcage, but I was proud of myself that I didn't let myself get intimated by that bitch. She might have caught me unawares once but I will not let her exploit me ever again.

Waleed

I felt like the whole world was burning and I was the only one left alive, the smoke was suffocating me, and I was finding it difficult to breathe.

I just couldn't take the image of Mia in his arms, his lips on her throat, and her arm wrapped around his neck, out of my mind. No matter how much I tried not to think about it, my mind kept going back to it again and again.

I had broken everything in the bedroom that could be broken, and still, the rage inside me was amassing with every passing minute. I wanted to kill that fucker, I wanted to flay him and then burn him alive. And for Mia, I don't know what I wanted to do to her, I just couldn't make up my mind.

The sane voice inside me was telling me to let her in and allow her to explain, but the caveman within me just wanted to kill her along with that fucker. I knew if I stay around here, I might do something that I would regret later, the moment this thought came into my mind, I stuffed my things in the bag and closed it pulling the zipper.

Mia was standing outside the door as I opened it, she looked at me with terrified eyes, and the moment her eyes landed on my bloodied knuckles I saw her flinch. She tried to grab my hand, but I pushed her aside, and taking long strides and jumping three steps at a time reached the bottom of the staircase.

I heard her call my name, but I didn't stop to listen to what she was saying, I hurried out of the house to the driveway where my SUV was parked, I nearly threw my bag in the trunk and was on the driver's seat within seconds as I turned the key in the ignition, bringing the engine to life I saw Mia, through the rearview mirror hurrying out of the house.

I didn't lose any time and put my feet on the accelerator, the SUV moved ahead with a jerk. My eyes were fixed on the mirror, where I saw her coming to halt on the spot my SUV was parked earlier. She called me again, but I knew if I stayed a minute longer there, I was going to kill somebody.

I called my Secretary to book a ticket for tonight on the US flight, I had a visa for ten years to the US, and it was the only place where I knew would be the best for me to wait up the rising storm inside me. I didn't want to think about anything right now, making a decision about my marriage was the last thing that I wanted to think about in this state of mind.

I reached home and was surprised to find Jeena present there before me, I would have given the thing thought about how she came back before me, but right now I had a flight to catch in a few hours. Ignoring her, I went to my room and just tossed my clothes and other stuff in a luggage bag as fast as I could.

I made a few calls to Tariq to tell him that I was leaving for the US and putting him in charge of the office. He asked me when I was going to return, I told him I was not sure and called me only if it was extremely essential.

I made a few more important calls, and the last call I made was to Dada, to tell him that I will be in the US for some time and if he wanted he could contact me on my US cell number.

He asked me if I was taking Mia with me? I told him, that she had some crucial projects going on and she couldn't go with me. He sounded disappointed to know I was leaving her behind.

Jeena tried to speak to me as I was on my way to the car to leave for the airport. I told her that I was leaving for the US and that if she wants she could go back to her home.

I don't know what she was trying to tell me, and I was least interested to know anything. I just wanted to leave that place as soon as I could.

I didn't even know why I was running and from whom? Maybe I was afraid, afraid to know that Mia didn't love me. And that she loved someone else, and desired someone else.

I don't know what I will do if she decides to leave me and go to that son of a bitch. I will kill him, I will kill that fucker if she as much thinks of leaving me.

I needed time and space to think clearly, and I knew she needed space too, to figure out if she wanted to be with me or if she wanted to leave me.

I just wanted to be away from her, till I was able to think rationally so as not to hurt her in my rage and not make any decision that will only come to haunt me later.

As I boarded the flight, I switched off my cell, there were nearly a hundred calls from Mia, which I had ignored.

I was awake for the whole flight, I couldn't sleep for a moment, the moment I closed my eyes Mia's image in Riyaan's arms would start flashing in my mind. I kept myself busy, reading the project files on my laptop.

The moment I entered my apartment in Chicago, I was completely exhausted. I took a shower and stumbled to bed and thankfully I was so tired that my mind couldn't think of anything else and drifted into darkness soon.

Chapter 30

Rameen

It had been a week since Waleed left, I had tried calling him many times but it would just go to voicemail. He didn't even read my text messages, it was as if he had blocked me completely. Whatever I heard about him was through Dada.

Dada had told me that he was in Chicago and Dada was thinking he was gone because of some business. Waleed had invested in a hotel chain in the US, and everyone thought he had gone to the US for that purpose.

Jeena had left the same night, Waleed went to the US, and that was the last I saw her, and I wanted it to remain like that for my whole life, I had no interest in seeing the woman who tried to steal my husband from me ever again.

If I could only share with anyone what was going on between us, my parents knew that he was in the US and mom was insisting I come and stay at their place while he was gone.

I couldn't make up my mind to go and stay there, I was hoping that he might come back one day and if he would not find me home, he might imagine all sorts of things, and I didn't want any more misunderstandings between us.

I missed him, I missed him so much that it hurt, I didn't even realize how addicted I was to him. He was like a drug to me, and now when he was not here, I was unable to function properly. I was going to work daily, I even went to his office in the evening to make sure that everything was running smoothly in his absence, I didn't want anyone to think there was something wrong between us.

It was the first weekend after he left, I had just finished my breakfast and was feeding Grey in the living room when Ali walked in.

Shit.

I had forgotten that he came back from the US last night, and I didn't even call him. I had to stay in Waleed's office a little late because of some problems with a client, by the time I had sorted it out it was nearly midnight, I came home and just stumbled to bed, without having dinner.

When I woke up in the morning, I for the first time realized how lonely I was in this house, at least going to work kept my mind off many things, but today being the weekend I had to stay in the house. Thank God, the cook had come today, it saved me from making breakfast, otherwise, in absence of Waleed, I would just have to eat cereals.

"Mia, I can't believe this, you didn't come to the airport to receive me, and you did not even bother calling," Ali boomed as soon as he saw me.

I kept my head low trying to keep my tears from flowing out of my eyes, seeing Ali my best friend and confidante after so many months, and in these difficult times in my life had made me lose control, and before I realized I was a sobbing mess. I was trying to act strong since the last week and I think I was reached my limit today.

"Hey, Mia, what happened sweety?" Ali asked, his voice full of concern for me.

"He left me, he left me and went to the US," I said between sobs.

Ali let me cry my eyes out and when I was tired of crying and no more tears left my eyes, he poured me a glass of water, which I drank in a single gulp.

"Now tell me, what happened?" He asked in a gentle voice.

I placed my head on his shoulder and narrated the whole thing to him beginning from Jeena's arrival to Red's death and to the day Waleed left.

"I am going to kill that fucker, Riyaan," He fisted his hands.

I shot up a look at his face, he was barely controlling his anger, his usually soft features looked as if carved in stone. His brown eyes filled the rage.

"Lee, relax, I am not concerned about that asshole, what worries me is Waleed, he is not answering my texts, my calls go to voicemail. I have no idea how I am going to contact him," I replied sighing.

"Mia, pack your bag, you are leaving with me now, there is no way I am leaving you here alone in this condition," He said determinedly.

"Lee, what if he comes back," I asked him caught up in an inner turmoil.

"I don't care if he returns, he knows our address, and if he wants to find you. Listen to me let him rot alone for some time, he will come back to his senses," He said pulling me from the couch and towards the staircase.

He made me pack my clothes, not listening once, to any reason that I told him. I accompanied him unwilling to our house, everyone was glad that I had come to stay there.

Mom hugged me and patted my back saying, " I am so happy you came to live with us, Mia, your Dad, and I missed you a lot."

It felt a little different at the start but as the days went by, I came back into the routine. This time I made use of my time in the evenings, seriously trying to learn cooking. And I was glad that I had learned to cook a few of Waleed's favorite dishes.

I hate to cook, but still, I wanted to do it for Waleed. I didn't want anyone to think that I was incapable of keeping him happy. I had made a resolution that I will try to become a good wife, like my mom and my aunt.

I tried hard to change myself, I watched my mom and aunt as they went around the house taking care of everything and everyone and I started making notes in my mind to follow them in my house.

Nearly four weeks passed and there was still no contact from Waleed, and it panicked me. I had thought that his anger would subside in a week or two but it had been nearly four weeks and there was no sign of him.

I left him text messages and voice mail, in the hope that he will respond eventually.

Ali was trying hard to cheer me up, he was the only one who knew what was going on, apart from Rania, Sheema, Asjad, and Saad. I too tried to focus on reforming myself rather than thinking and worrying about Waleed and our marriage.

I was hurting from inside, it had been so long since I heard or seen him, and I was missing him very much. I tried hard not to think about him and not to miss him, but I was failing miserably. The few months I had lived with him were the best months of my life.

I was missing his smiles, his teasing, his concern, the way his grey eyes sparkled whenever they looked at me. I missed the way he touched me, the way he kissed me, and the way he made love to me. I missed waking up to his warm body, I missed sleeping in his arms at night, I missed the way he bathed me, the way he made me snuggle close to him when we slept. I missed his breakfast every morning, God, I was going crazy thinking about him.

I was mad at him, to be mad at me, I wanted to fight him and argue with him, till I drove him crazy that he lost his control and would want me like never before.

"Ohhh Waleed, what have you done to me?" I thought with help-lessness.

And finally the text I was waiting for came, it was short and to the point.

Waleed: I will be home tonight, if you could come over, we need to talk.

I felt such relief reading that text that I can't even describe. I packed my bag immediately and left for my home, informing everyone that Waleed was coming back.

It was still afternoon but I wanted to surprise him by cooking dinner for him. I had another surprise for him and I was sure after finding it out he would be overwhelmed with joy.

Waleed

Nearly four weeks had passed since I came to Chicago, I had made myself busy here with the meetings with different investors who were interested in investing in my business.

I had done a little research into prospects that looked good for investment in the US. I was planning to expand my business, and I had started acting on my plan two years ago when I had invested in a hotel chain in the US.

I didn't limit it there, over two years I had successfully invested in restaurants, real estate, and a clothing line.

At least these last weeks I was busy and was fortunate enough to make some good deals, Mia still occupied my mind most of the time, it was nearly impossible for me to not think about her.

It was like she possessed me, and no matter how hard I tried I couldn't keep my mind off her. My anger was slowly subsiding and I had started thinking from different angles now.

I had been foolish to not trust Mia and listen to what she had wanted to say, but I had been so furious finding her in the arms of that man I hated the most that I had lost all control and at least I was sensible to leave from there without doing anything stupid which I would have regretted my whole life.

I was not oblivious to what Mis was doing, I had her followed by a private detective who gave me a report regarding every small thing she would do in a day. I was impressed by the efficiency of the detective.

I even had her cell hacked to install spyware in it, through which I got every information about what she was doing. I could listen to her conversations through the microphone or watch her with the camera on her cell phone.

Whenever I saw her sad my heart stirred in my chest, I wanted to remove the sadness from her life and make her smile again. But I was waiting, I wanted to make sure that she was not involved with Riyaan, and that she had been loyal to me.

By the time four weeks passed, I became restless, my body ached for her, I wanted to touch her to love her, to feel her walls around me, it had been so long that I was inside her, the last time had been at the beach house before all this drama had unfolded.

When I could bear no more I booked a ticket home for tonight and boarded the flight, there was no use sitting here, we needed to have a heart to heart, to know where we stood, and to decide what we were going to do with our marriage if either of us was not willing to go ahead with it.

I texted her from London, when I boarded the flight after a halt, that I would be home tonight and I wanted to talk to her. I knew she was at her parent's home so I asked her to come over to our home.

I was nervous as to what she was going to decide if she wanted to stay with me or if she wanted to be with Riyaan. But one small part of me was excited to be able to see her again in flesh after nearly a month.

When I entered my house and was passing through the living room, I was shocked to find Mia asleep on one of the couches. I walked toward her and was beside her within seconds like she was some magnet and she was pulling me.

I looked at her, she looked pale, the color in her cheeks was lost, there were bags under her eyes, which exhibited the lack of sleep. She even had dark circles around her eyes. I looked at her with a sad smile on my face.

Had my absence affected her so much? I felt a little guilty to have made her go through so much. I traced my finger on her cheek and tucked a strand of hair behind her ear, which had fallen on her face.

She opened her eyes and looked at me stunned as if she was trying to believe that I was there and that it was not just a dream. She then raised her hand and touched my face, and when she felt my warmth, she sat up with a jolt.

"Waleed," She murmured in her sleepy voice.

I felt like someone was tugging at my heart, I wanted to turn away from her, storm out of this place again, but I didn't do any such thing. I just kept looking in her beautiful amber eyes, resisting the urge to pull her in my arms and suck the air out of her lungs, kissing.

"You must be hungry, I will set the table, why don't you freshen up in the meantime," she stood up smiling at me.

I just nodded in reply and she went to the kitchen, to arrange the table for dinner. I was tempted to do as she had instructed me, but instead, I went to the kitchen after her.

I saw her heating the food in the dishes one by one in the microwave and arranging it on the kitchen counter. She placed two plates on it and turned and was startled to find me standing in the kitchen.

"Ohh God, you gave me a scare, I thought you would be in the shower," Mia exclaimed as she tried to calm her breathing.

I kept looking at her, without speaking a word, I knew she was getting anxious by my constant starting and silence.

"I hope you are hungry, you might not believe this, but I have cooked the dinner tonight," she was trying to divert my attention towards the food.

I stayed silent and kept staring at her and noticed the way she shifted uncomfortably on the spot she was standing.

"I haven't eaten, I was waiting for you. I thought we could eat together, it's been a month since we had dinner together," she rubbed her palms on the fabric of her sweat pants.

I walked up to her and halted a few inches away from her, my shoes touching her flip-flops. I felt her breath hitch, I was glad to know that my proximity still affected her in the same way as before.

"Waleed I have something to tell you," she spoke with her head bowed down and her eyes fixed on the floor.

"Waleed I am pregnant," Mia raised her head and looked into my eyes.

I couldn't believe what I was hearing, did she just tell me she was pregnant? Was she pregnant with my child? Or was it someone else who was the father, and Mia wanted to be with him.

What if Mia wanted to end this marriage? What if she realized she didn't love me and she didn't want me anymore. What will I do if she decides to leave me? There were so many questions in my mind, but I didn't know where to find the answer. I decided to ask her.

"Who is the father?" I asked in a cold voice, without any emotion or expression on my face.

I didn't have any idea at the time, how my words were going to shake the foundation of our marriage.

Chapter 31

Rameen

"Who is the father?" He asked in a cold voice, his face was devoid of any emotion.

I was looking at him with disbelief, did he just ask me who the father of my unborn child was? When he fucking knew he was the only man I had ever slept with. Or did he think I have been sleeping with men other than him? What does he think I am, some bitch? Who didn't know who the father of their child is?

I have been through so much in the last month, from being away from him, from having to stay lonely dreading if he would ever come back to me? Being betrayed by someone I had thought was my friend.

To find out that I was pregnant with Waleed's child. I had not told anyone about my pregnancy, because I wanted to share it first with Waleed and then with everyone else.

Little did I know, instead of being overjoyed, he will ask me who was the father of my child? My temper soared and I snapped at that moment.

I didn't think about the consequence of my action and just slapped him hard on his face. Now it was his time to look at me in disbelief if he thought that I would plead or beg him to believe me that the child was his, he was in for a surprise.

"You are truly pathetic, and I am happy to know that you and Jeena deserve each other. You both are heartless monsters, who don't give a damn about other people's feelings.

I am glad that I have seen your true face now, and believe me, you are the last person that I want around me or my baby," I said enraged, my eyes were locked with his and I was observing the battle going on inside him.

"What does it have to do with Jeena?"

"Ohh really?" I taunted.

"Your precious Jeena is waiting for you to dump me and marry her, she was the one who killed red. She was the one who planned everything with Riyaan," I lashed out.

Waleed's face paled for a second, but he recovered soon. I am sure he would never have suspected Jeena could be behind all of this.

"When I came back home that night after you left for the US, Jeena told me you didn't want me in the house. She was foolish enough to think that I would give in to her threats. Let me tell you, Waleed Kamal, if you think you can get away with this it will prove to be your biggest mistake. I will make your and Jeena's life living hell. I am not someone you can trample and walk away," I was shaking with fury.

The audacity of this man to ask me who my child's father was? I had never faced such humiliation ever in my life. No one had ever dared to question my character and I wouldn't let Waleed get away with this.

"Why should I have your child? When you don't even want to acknowledge that it's yours. I don't think I am obliged to keep it inside me for nine months and bring it into this world risking my life.

I am going to abort it the first thing tomorrow, and please don't try to contact me, my lawyer will contact you very soon," I hissed and tried to walk past him but he grabbed my arm immediately.

"Mia, listen to me," He murmured with guilt covering his features.

"Waleed, leave my hand, nothing you say or do is going to compel me to stay with you," I said brushing his hand aside from my arm and walking out of the kitchen.

I grabbed my bag which I still hadn't unpacked along with my handbag and walked to the main door. Waleed was following me, pleading trying to tell me he was sorry and not thinking of aborting the child.

He even blabbered about how much he loved me and missed me, but whatever he said now was not going to make any difference. Though I was shocked at what made him change his mind, one minute he was accusing me of sleeping with some other guy and the other he was begging me to not abort the child.

I walked to the porch and thankfully the driver was still there, he opened the door of the backseat as soon as he saw me walk out with a bag. Waleed still followed me, but he fell silent in the presence of the driver.

I slid into the car and slammed the door on him, "I was not going to forgive him, I would drag him to court and shred his ego and reputation to pieces, " I thought to myself.

I asked the driver to drop me at Rania's apartment, I didn't want to go to my parent's place, because it would just create a scene. They knew Waleed was returning from the US today and if I go to their house tonight they will know that something was wrong.

I rang the bell to her apartment waiting for her to open the door, but when Asjad opened the door instead of her, I was a bit surprised.

"Mia," He exclaimed in surprise.

"I am sorry to have interrupted you, but I need a place to crash tonight," I shoved him aside and entered the apartment.

Rania was standing in the living room, she looked at me with her mouth wide open, I knew Asjad would be having the same expression on his face, but right now I just didn't care.

"I thought Wal came back tonight from the US," Asjad asked from behind me.

"Sorry to disappoint what came back is a dick and not your friend," I taunted.

"What?" They both looked shocked at the choice of my words.

I couldn't help it, that's what he deserved to be called, after the way he behaved with me.

Asjad's cell started ringing at that moment, he looked at the screen and excused himself, and walked to the bedroom.

"What happened Mia?" Rania asked gently keeping her hand on my shoulder.

I hugged her and broke down, I had been holding my tears for so long, I couldn't believe Waleed would think of me like that. I hadn't spent a single night away from him since we got married till the day he left for the US and he was suspecting me of adultery. Well, maybe he thought I did the deed in the daytime in my office, hours, what other explanation could there be other than this.

"He accused me of cheating on him, he thinks I slept with someone else behind his back," I said sobbing, my head still on her shoulders.

"Shhh, everything will be fine Mia, come here, we will sit and talk," Rania said rubbing my back, and guiding me towards the couch.

She sat beside me and poured me a glass of water, which I drank in a single breath. I still couldn't believe this was happening to me, I had been so happy, just a month ago. Everything had been so perfect between us, Waleed was an ideal husband till the time Jeena and Riyaan had walked back into our lives.

"You okay?" Rania asked wiping the tears on my face.

"I don't know," I replied honestly.

I had told Waleed that I was going to abort the baby, but I knew I would never be able to do that, we had been trying for the last few months and when it had finally happened, everything had changed. I had thought Waleed would be so happy after knowing about the baby that he will forget the little episode between us, but I was wrong, instead, he had accused me of infidelity.

Asjad walked back into the room, his eyes were fixed on me, he checked me out from head to toe, like he was searching for something, and then what he said startled everyone.

"You are pregnant?" He asked.

"Ohh my God," Rania exclaimed.

"How the fuck do you know that?" I asked Asjad shocked.

Rania was looking at me in disbelief and I was doing the same to Asjad.

"Waleed just called, apparently his driver told him that he dropped you off here and he wanted me to contact Rania, to ask her to convince you not to get an abortion," Asjad replied.

"What the fuck, you are getting an abortion?" Rania went into another shock.

Ohh my God, I just wanted to kill Waleed, if only two people knew about my pregnancy now they had doubled. The more people found out about it, the more difficult the decision will be for me.

"I don't know, I am considering the option, he asked me who the father is, and if he doesn't want to accept his child, then why should I be obliged to keep it and raise it by myself. I have equal right to reject it as Waleed," I replied in a firm voice.

I don't know, how, convinced they were with my answer but they didn't tell me anything further and I was grateful to them for it.

"Mia, did you have dinner?"

Rania asked me when she heard my stomach growl, I had eaten in the afternoon and now I was starving, I was craving for something sweet right now.

"No, I haven't eaten anything since lunch, I was waiting for him, to have dinner together. I even cooked dinner for him, but that asshole had to ruin everything," I started sobbing again.

I couldn't forget how exhausted I was after cooking and had drifted to sleep on the couch, and he didn't even had the etiquette to let me eat after all the hard work and then ask his fucking questions.

I had missed him so much and was so excited to see him again, to touch him, to feel his arms wrapped around me, I was pregnant for God's sake and my hormones were driving me crazy. I was even having wet dreams in the past week and he didn't even kiss me or took me in his arms, I hate him so much.

"Here, Mia, I didn't cook tonight, we both had dinner out, this is what I have got," Rania brought a tray filled with cupcakes, donuts, and croissants.

"Are you pregnant, too?" I asked her surprised, why did she have all this sweet food at home if she was not pregnant.

"God, Mia. Asjad has a sweet tooth, so I keep all these because he has a craving anytime during the night," She replied.

I didn't say anything but started eating, everything I could, they tasted so good, I had forgotten to stop until I cleared all the plates and then sat satisfied.

Little Mia inside me was happy, first I was calling it little Waleed, but now I don't think I will ever refer to it with Waleed's name no matter what.

And why the hell he didn't want me to get an abortion? So that he could have a DNA test? To find out if I cheated on him or not. That was the only reason I was able to think about right now. I don't know whether I would abort it or not, but I am not letting Waleed around it.

Walked

The moment I saw the expression on her face I knew that I did a mistake, I wanted to take back my words, but it was an impossible thing. The first few lessons that I have learned in my life was that you couldn't take back the words you have spoken once.

She raised her hand and slapped me, the impact was hard that I saw white spots in my vision. I know I deserved that slap, there were a thousand and nine ways to have framed the question to not make it offensive to her, but the choice of my words was the worst.

When she told me about Jeena I was shocked, did Jeena, really do such a thing? I knew she liked me maybe her feelings were more than liking. And it was not a coincidence that she met a guy who had feelings for Mia, I should have been sensible enough to figure it out myself, but my judgment was clouded by my rage.

I hadn't recovered from the shock of Jeena and Mia dropped another bomb, that she was going to get an abortion. Ohh my Lord, how could I let her abort her pregnancy, what if it was my child?

"No, what if? You fucking idiot. The child is yours, that is why she won't want it because you have insulted her. You have doubted her character and you accused her of adultery and no woman with self-respect will ever forgive this," I cursed myself.

I tried to stop her, tell her how much I missed her, and how much I wanted her. I asked her to forgive me, but she did not budge and left.

I had gestured the driver to call me after he dropped her off, and as soon as he dropped her at Rania's place he called and told me that she was at Rania's apartment.

Without wasting any time I called Asjad and told him how I fucked up and what Mia intended to do. I asked him to request Rania to convince Mia not to abort her pregnancy.

Asjad told me that I should go fuck myself, because what I had done was unforgivable, and I knew that myself, he didn't need to point it out.

"Asjad please, for the sake of our friendship, ask Rania to convince her not to abort the baby," I pleaded to him.

Asjad couldn't have imagined me, Waleed Kamal would plead to anyone in life ever. Seriously, the things I do for love.

"Okay, I will speak with Rania, but I can't assure you anything. It will be Mia's decision," He replied.

"Thanks, bro, I owe you one," I replied sighing.

I need to think about how I was going to get back to Mia if I know her, she will not forgive me ever again. Or who knows she might, after all, we made a baby together.

Yes, I know I fucked up, but I will make it up to her, I just need to give her time and make sure she doesn't get an abortion.

And there is one more thing I need to take care of first and that's Jeena, she and I need to have a conversation. I don't want any dark shadows lingering in our life when my baby comes into this world.

I booked a ticket for the morning to Jeena's town, it's been a long time since I visited her and return her favor.

My aunt was quite happy with my visit, I had told her that I had a meeting there and had thought to drop by to meet them.

I sat there chatting with my uncle and aunt for an hour and inquired about Jeena. Aunt Sarah told me, Jeena was not taking the cancellation of the publication of her book well. She was even seeing a therapist, for her anxiety and depression.

I knew the exact cause of Jeena's depression but I didn't want to hurt my aunt. Jeena was the one, supposed to tell her how she had fucked up my marriage and had nearly destroyed my life.

I went to Jeena's room, she was sitting on the couch, with what I recognized as my sweater. What the fuck? When had she sneaked that sweater from my closet? This girl was fucked up in more ways than I could have ever thought. The thought that I had considered marrying her once, made me sick to my stomach.

"Waleed," Her lips moved and I barely heard her voice.

She sprang up from the couch and ran and wrapped her arms around me. I couldn't hug her back, I couldn't make myself do it. I know she was sick and I felt pity for her, but I didn't want to give her any hope.

"I knew that you will come back to me, I knew you never loved that bitch. She doesn't deserve you, she is not good enough for you. Now we can get married, and live happily, and I will make you happy, I will take care of you," She was mumbling, her face was buried in my chest, and I differentiated the words with difficulty.

"Jeena, look at me, you need to listen to me carefully," I pulled her away from me and said looking into her eyes.

Those eyes didn't belong to any normal person, all I could see in them was madness and restlessness.

"Jeena, Mia is my wife, and I love her. We are going to have a baby together, she is pregnant with my child," It was hard, but I had to tell her the truth.

"Baby?" she asked with disbelief in her eyes.

"But she doesn't love you, she loves Riyaan," she said with spite.

"She loves me Jeena, and I love her," I said cupping her face in my hands.

I could only hope that Mia loved me. After what I did last night, she could only hate me. Still, I was not ready to give her up. I couldn't even imagine my life without her.

"No Waleed, I know you love me, you have always loved me. Waleed, when will you admit it?" Jeena shrieked hysterically.   Maybe this was a mistake, I did. I never should have come here, Jeena is not in a state to understand anything, she needs help. She needs to be in a facility.

"Waleed, I will love you, I will always love you. You just need to leave Mia, she is not worthy of you. She doesn't take care of you, she fights with you, she is not good Waleed. She threatened to kill me, she said if I ever try to take you away from her she will kill me like I killed her Red, stupid cat. Can you believe she brought a cat into your house knowing you detest them," She said, tilting her head.

She had lost it, she had truly lost her mind, why can't my aunt and uncle see this, why don't they take her to a good psychiatrist.

I need to tell them, I have to, she was my friend and cousin and I couldn't let her waste like this.

"Jeena, Waleed, come lunch is served," Aunt said as she came in.

She looked at Jeena than at me, I saw her expressions change within a second. I couldn't believe it, she knew it and was hiding it from me?

"Waleed," Aunt Sarah tried to say.

I raised my hand and gestured her to stop, there was no possible explanation for this, she had known Jeena's obsession and still, she had allowed Jeena to stay in my house for so many months and put mine and my wife's life in danger. What if Jeena tried to harm Mia, instead of Red.

"I can't believe that you allowed this, how could you, Aunt Sara?" I asked heartbrokenly.

"Waleed I had no idea, till she returned from your home a month ago. She was broken and mentally sick, we took her to a psychiatrist and he is treating her. He is hopeful that she will be cured and would become normal again," My aunt said taking Jeena in her arms and rubbing her back.

"Mama, Waleed does not want me, he wants her, why Mama, Why doesn't he love me?" Jeena started crying in my aunt's arms.

Bile rose in my throat, I was still not able to sink this in my mind, looking at Jeena in this state must have been so difficult for her parents, how were they coping with it?

"I have to go," I said as I walked back towards the door.

"Stay at least for lunch Waleed," My aunt called after me.

I didn't stop to listen to what she said further. I just wanted to get out of that place and never get back ever again. I couldn't see Jeena in this condition, if I had not seen her in this condition with my own eyes, I could never have believed it.

I never knew when her liking for me turned into an obsession and now she was on a stage where she had lost her sanity. What would have happened if she had harmed Mia in my absence?

I had fucking left Mia alone in that house with her. I had known what had happened with Red, still, I hadn't thought of her for once in my jealousy and insecurity that the person that had harmed Red could try to harm Mia.

I could never have forgiven myself if something would have happened to Mia. My inner turmoil and guilt had only increased by this trip.

I returned home late at night and stayed late in bed the next morning for the first time in my life.

I was awakened by the ringing of my cell. I searched for my cell in sleep and found it on the bedside table. I took the cell in my hand and looked at the screen, it was the private investigator that I had hired.

Checking the time, it was showing 11:30 in the morning, I sat up with a jolt and received the call.

"Mr. Kamal, your wife, she is in a maternity clinic", The detective said.

Chapter 32

Rameen

I spent the next day in bed. Rania went to work after preparing breakfast for us. Asjad had left late last night. They both had not said anything to me regarding Waleed after the initial conversation.

My morning sickness was getting worse each passing day. I hadn't slept well last night. My dreams were haunted by Waleed and Jeena and I was mad at myself, for letting Waleed in my heart.

Love was a stupid emotion, it only gave heartbreak in the end. I had been wise enough to stay away from it for my whole life. If I would have married Imaad, I am sure I might never have fallen in love with him.

Look what love had brought me, heartbreak. Stupid, stupid love. Why, just why had I fallen in love with that arrogant asshole? I had told him that I would get an abortion today, but still, I was lying in bed unsure of what my future might behold for me.

I heard a knock on the door, I looked at the watch it was six in the evening. I hadn't realized the whole day had passed. I had just eaten

a little Poha (a dish prepared out of beaten rice) for breakfast that
Rania had prepared and had not bothered with lunch.

"Come in," I sat up in bed.

Rania peeped inside pushing the door open, "Hi, I brought your
favorite donuts."

My mouth watered at the name of donuts, and my empty stomach
growled in excitement. Rania walked to the bed and handed me the
box of donuts. I opened the box hungrily, eyeing the half dozen
donuts with different frosting.

"Marry me," I joked.

"I would love to. Let's ditch our husbands, they both are just pain
in the ass for us," she replied.

"Agreed," I laughed at her reply.

I picked up a donut and dug into it. The chocolate frosting melted
in my mouth. These donuts were heaven. I was having a foodgasm.

"These are the best donuts, I ever had," I told Rania.

"There is this small bakery near my office. They are perfect at
everything," she smiled.

We chatted about work, while I ate four out of the six donuts.
Rania refused to eat any, she said she was on a diet. Too bad for her,
I don't think I could ever give up donuts for anything.

I knew that she wanted to talk to me regarding Waleed but was
hesitating. I was in a good mood after the treat I just got and didn't
want to spoil my mood.

"So what have you thought?"

The cat was out of the bag. I knew I couldn't avoid the discussion for long. I will have to come up with a decision. Right now, I just didn't want to think about anything.

I was hit by a sudden wave of nausea before Rania could say anything further, I jumped out of the bed and ran to the bathroom. I emptied my stomach, while Rania held my hair. She rubbed my back as I rinsed my mouth with water and then mouth wash.

"I hate being pregnant," I exclaimed lying down on the bed again.

All the donuts that I had eaten must be floating in the sewage tank. What a waste of hard-earned money.

"You should see an obstetrician for your morning sickness," Rania advised.

I had been thinking about the same thing for the last two weeks since I had found out that I was pregnant. My nausea was getting worse day by day. If I kept throwing up food like this, it won't be good for the baby.

"I still have not decided, what I want to do with the baby," I told Rania honestly.

"Why do you want to punish an innocent soul, for someone else's mistake? It's not the baby's fault if Waleed is a douchebag," she said.

"I don't know Rania, I want to be a mother. I love kids, but I don't think I could raise my child singlehandedly without the father. I am sure my family, would stand with me in every decision I make. Still, I don't want to raise a child without its father," I broke down again.

Damn this pregnancy hormone, they were being a pain in the ass for me. I never had cried this much in my entire life. I hated Waleed for getting me pregnant and now chickening out of it. I wish I could go back in time and undo my pregnancy. I didn't like the idea of getting an abortion but I don't think I have any choice. I don't want a child if the father doesn't even want to acknowledge that it's his child.

"Relax Mia, you don't have to make a decision now. Think about it, you still have time. I think you and Waleed should sit and talk, getting an abortion is not the solution. You might only regret your decision in the future, trust me you will never forgive yourself if you abort your child, " Rania held my hand in her mad stroked it with her fingers.

I hugged her and my crying only increased. I was witnessing one of the most beautiful wonders of life. I was pregnant, another individual was growing inside me. I had been so excited about getting pregnant. I always had wished for more siblings, but unfortunately, my mother couldn't conceive after my birth.

I got mad again at Waleed, if not for that asshole I would have been so happy for getting pregnant. He had ruined all my happiness with his accusation. I hate him. I really hate him.

I didn't want to admit but it hurts. He is the only man that I had ever loved and had given power over me and look where it got me. He abused the power he had over me and had hurt me so badly, I don't think that I could heal ever again.

"I don't want to see his face ever again in my life," I declared.

"I know you are mad at him right now, but Mia, think about it from his point of view. Men are possessive and territorial, and Waleed of all people is an alpha male. They feel threatened even if anyone as much looks at their woman.

What happened at the beach house, have hurt him. He loves you Mia and seeing you with another man has hurt his alpha ego. You just can't blame only him for whatever happened. He is just a victim like you, he was played by Jeena.

I agree that Waleed should have given you a chance to explain. He shouldn't have accused you right away of cheating, but think about it. You always brag about how you don't believe in love, how is he supposed to know that he is the most important person for you?"

Rania's words were sinking in my mind, I know most of the things that she said were correct. Whatever happened was not entirely Waleed's fault, still, I expected that he trusted me. It was a blow for me, to know that my husband didn't find me trustworthy enough to give me a chance for an explanation before accusing me of cheating.

"I know a gynecologist, we can go and see her if you want, tomorrow. You will need to get some medication for your nausea," Rania said changing the topic.

I nodded in reply, still thinking about what she had said earlier. Maybe, I should not hurry with my decision of getting an abortion. First I need to decide what I wanted to do with my marriage, getting an abortion can come after that. The next morning after breakfast, I walked into the maternity clinic alone. Rania had insisted to come along with me but I had told her I would be fine. I didn't want to disturb her more than I wanted, she and Asjad had done already so much for me that I didn't want to bother them more.

The clinic was crowded, there were many ladies in the waiting area, consisting of all age groups. There were a few couples, I noticed that everyone was accompanied either by their husbands or by some lady relative or friend. I was the only one alone in the waiting area.

I felt a pang in my heart if only Waleed could have not acted like that and accepted it, he would have been here with me, or at least I would have asked my mom to come with me. I felt my eyes moisten again, I had been a mess in the last two days, I couldn't control my tears, I started crying without any reason, it surely had to do with my hormones, but Waleed's accusations were on top of the list.

I don't want to say it, but I was missing him, I wished he was by my side at this moment, motivating and assuring me that everything would be fine, but I don't know where he was, he hadn't even called me since I had left. Though I was waiting for a call or text from him. I was hoping he would at least try to ask me to forgive him.

But I don't think I mattered to him anymore, I think maybe he was happy that I was gone from his life, all his promises and declaration of love, have been just fake.

It was almost an hour since I had arrived at the clinic but still, I was not called by the doctor. I was getting impatient and I didn't like the way the other couples were going all lovey-dovey with each other like they were the first to ever expect a baby.

I stood up from my seat and approached the reception, the receptionist was busy talking to someone on her cell, from the smile on her face it was not difficult to know, who she was talking to, had the whole world been infected with the virus called love? I thought bitterly.

And why it had to be me, who never believed in love, to fall for someone so hard and then got hurt and maybe lose him.

"Excuse me, how much more time it will take for my appointment?" I asked her.

" Your name Mam?" She asked me.

"Mrs. Waleed Kamal," I replied

" Your turn is next mam, please it will just take a few more minutes, " She said, smiling at me.

I was about to turn when someone came and stood beside me, and inquired.

"Is there an appointment in the name of Mrs. Waleed Kamal?"

I could recognize his voice from a million others, without even looking at him. We both turned towards each other at the same moment. Our eyes met and I saw relief spread all over his face, I knew why he didn't recognize me in the first place because I was wearing a Hijab today.

I had worn a hijab in fear if I run into someone, they won't recognize me immediately. Little had I thought that I would run into none other than yours truly Waleed Kamal.

"Thank God," The words left his mouth.

" What the fuck are you doing here?" I asked through the clenched teeth.

"Can we go somewhere, to talk, " he asked me.

I looked at him with contempt, who the hell does he think he is? And how the hell did he know, I was here in the clinic? Does he have me followed? Is he stalking me now?

" I don't think we have anything to talk about," I snapped.

"You are my wife Mia," Waleed said through clenched teeth, I knew he was trying to suppress his anger.

" Not for long," I retorted.

He helplessly looked at me, trying to figure out how he could convince me to accompany him so that he could accuse me of more of adultery.

"Mia please."

I saw his feature soften, but I was not going to fall into the trap.

"I have an appointment with the doctor," I replied.

"I won't allow you to get an abortion," he said in his signature CEO voice.

"Like I need your permission, it's my baby and I would do as I wish with it," I said crossing my arms on my chest.

I know I wasn't here for an abortion, but it won't hurt, will it? If he thinks that I am here for one. I had enough of his tantrums in the past one month and it was payback time now.

"Mam, your turn," The receptionist told me.

I arched my brow and looked at him challenging him to stop me if he could. I saw him rub his fingers on his face in frustration, I was glad I hadn't lost my touch. I was still able to rattle his nerves.

I turned and went towards the doctor's cabin, but my confidence was baffled when I saw Waleed following me in my peripheral vision.

Fuck.

If he comes with me into the Doctor's cabin he will know I was not here for an abortion.

"Where do you think you are coming," I snarled at him when he was beside me.

And before I could confront him fully, he pushed the handle on the door and was inside, I had no choice but to follow him.

"Mr. Kamal, what a pleasant surprise," The lady doctor said as soon as she saw Waleed.

"Hello, Mrs. Rehman," he greeted smiling.

This was the last thing I wanted, the gynecologist to be someone of his acquaintance, I needed to find someone else if I ever decided to get an abortion.

"So, what do we have here?" She asked looking at me.

I greeted her smiling and sat on the chair, opposite to her, she was a middle-aged woman, with soft features and hazel eyes. She looked like a nice lady, too bad I can't visit her again.

"My beautiful wife is pregnant with our first child, and we just came here to make sure everything is fine," he replied smiling.

The doctor asked me some questions, she then referred, some blood tests and a sonogram, which were available in the clinic. She asked us to come back after the completion of those tests.

We walked out of her cabin and went to the lab, where they took my blood. A nurse directed me to the radiologist after that. I was called in for the sonogram after nearly an hour.

The radiologist called us both inside, she asked us if it was our first child, and when we replied with a yes, she looked more excited than we were.

Waleed stood beside the bed, which the radiologist had directed me to lie on. She spread some cool jelly-like substance on my belly and started moving the head of the object attached to the machine over it. She pointed towards the little image that beeped on the screen and told us that it was our baby.

I looked at Waleed, he was looking at the screen, despite the darkness in the room, I could see how overwhelmed he was with emotions. He looked at me at that moment and I think I saw moisture in his eyes, I pressed his hand which he had placed beside me on the bed.

I don't think I needed any words from him. The expression on his face was enough to depict his inner joy. It was a feeling I don't think I can ever describe. It felt truly amazing to see something that we had made, the most beautiful creation of God. At that moment, I had forgotten that I was mad at him.

We were going to have a baby, our baby. The mere thought of a little bundle of joy in my hand was enough to cloud my eyes with tears. I didn't realize that I was crying with joy, it felt so good to see my baby for the first, no matter if it was on a screen or if it was just an undistinguished mass of tissue right now with a heartbeat.

"Hey," Waleed said as he found me crying.

He leaned and placed his forehead on mine, and gently wiped my tears. It felt so good to be close to him again. All my anger towards him subsided at that moment.

We were connected by a very strong bond with each other now, a bond that we can't break even if we tried.

The radiologist handed me the sonogram images and report after a few minutes, while Waleed collected the blood test reports from the lab.

When we went back to see the doctor, she assured us that everything was fine with my pregnancy. She prescribed me some medication for morning sickness and some vitamins.

"I will hire a cab," I told Waleed after taking the medicines from the pharmacy.

"Mia, I am taking you home, you need to look after yourself," He said grabbing my arm.

" What gave you the impression, I was going to come with you?" I asked pulling my arm back from his grip.

He left my arm, in fear of me getting hurt, my heart softened on this little gesture of affection, while my body protested on the loss of his touch. Damn these hormones, they are going to kill me someday.

"Mia please, I know you are mad and you have every right to be, but please think about our child, all this stress is not good for it," he said gently.

"Excuse me, our child?" I asked with spite.

He closed his eyes and took a deep breath, I took advantage of it and walked to a taxi standing nearby, and slid into the backseat. I saw

Waleed standing on the same spot where I left him and looking at the moving taxi with regret.

I was not mad at him like before, but still, I was not ready to forgive him this easily. If Waleed Kamal wanted to earn my forgiveness, he will have to work for it. I was not in a mood to bestow it on him this easily.

Chapter 33

Waleed

I saw her walk away from me and climb into a taxi, I wanted to stop her and throw her over my shoulder and walk to my car, but I didn't do any of those things. She was mad at me, and I wanted to give her time to forgive me.

I was going to pursue her, till the moment she forgives me and accepts me back. I know I had fucked up, I know I was not worthy of her forgiveness. I loved her and I know she loved me, I agree we were caught up in a difficult situation and I had not acted like a sensible person should have in that situation.

No matter how much time or effort it took, I was not going to give up. I loved her and I won't let her walk away from my life.

I kept turning up on places where she went, at first she used to get surprised when she spotted me, but gradually she understood that I had her followed. We had a big argument about it, but I still had her followed, her safety was my utmost priority, now that she was carrying my child, that priority had doubled.

She had gone to her parent's house after a few days, and she had told our families about her pregnancy. I know this because Dada called and congratulated me, he sounded so ecstatic that I too was filled with joy.

At least the fear that she might get an abortion was no more, because I know her parents would never allow it. I would show up at her parent's place every evening, and Mia was obliged to give me company, I know how pissed she was at me to exploit her like that, but I couldn't help it.

It was nearly impossible for me to stay away from her anymore, she had given her parents, the excuse that because it was her first pregnancy and there was no one in our house to take care of her in this condition she had come to stay with them.

Well, I was glad that there were so many people in her house to take care of her and she needed her mother in this condition, my company would have been of no help because I was as inexperienced as she was in matters of pregnancy.

One thing that I had learned about her pregnancy was that she was craving for anything sweet during her pregnancy. And I made a note to take some desserts along with me when I visited her parent's place. Her mom was not allowing her to go to work. She had made her resign from the job, and I was grateful to her for that. No matter how much I would have insisted Mia would have never listened to me.

"Why do you come here every day? You know, I am not forgiving you anytime soon."

Mia hissed when we were alone in her bedroom one evening at her parent's place.

"You think, I will stop trying?"

I replied turning the pages of a magazine, while I was stretched out on her bed. Thankfully, both Ali and Umair were not home today.

"I don't care, what you do or don't. Just don't bother me with your presence," She said through clenched teeth.

"You don't want me to come?" I asked getting up from the bed and stalking towards her.

"Waleed, if you as much as come one step close, I am going to scream for help, " She threatened me.

I know she was capable of acting on her threat, and I didn't want to create any scene.

"Mia it's been months since we made love, it's killing me to be with you and not able to touch you," I said frustrated, she needs to give me a break.

"Right, you are the one high on hormones," She shot back.

For God's sake, why was she so stubborn? I hated her stubbornness at this moment. I was dying to touch her, to pull her in my arms, to kiss her till she was short of breath and make love to her till she screamed my name.

"Let me take care of your hormones then," I said taking a step towards her.

"You have no fucking idea, how much I want you, I want you so much it hurts Mia,"

I closed the gap between us, and thankfully she didn't protest, I slid my arm around her waist and pulled her to me, she looked like she was done fighting with herself.

"Let me show you, how much I love you," I whispered in her ear.

"Waleed, you need to go," She said through clenched teeth.

She was still fighting it, I know she won't let go easily, I had acted like an asshole and she had every right to be mad at me.

"Please Mia, it's killing me," I said kissing her just below the ear.

"I don't know, I am still not sure if I could trust you," She replied helplessly.

"Please forgive me, I would never do something like that again I promise if I ever did anything like that, you have every right to kick me out of your life," I said wrapping my arms around her and pressing her into me.

I have missed her so much, I have missed the feel of her body against mine, I have missed her scent, Ohh my God, I have missed everything about her.

"Mia, I know, I fucked up baby, but please forgive me. Jeena had planned everything so well, I just couldn't think straight. You know how possessive I am about you, and I just couldn't tolerate seeing you in someone else's arms. And the way that bastard held you, the way he kissed you, I just wanted to kill him.

I left because I didn't want to do anything stupid, that I might regret later, but at last, I ended up doing that. I hurt you, I know, and I am really sorry for that. Will you please let me make it up to you?"

I was whispering in her ear, while she just stood there in my arms, I wanted her to say something, to at least yell at me but she didn't utter a single word.

There was a knock on the door and we pulled back from each other, I sighed as I saw Ali enter the room.

"Everyone is waiting for you two, to have dinner," He said.

We walked out of the room together, I was cursing Ali, if only he had come after a few minutes, might be I would have convinced her to forgive me.

I was in a meeting a few days after my conversation with Mia when I got a call from the detective, I excused myself from the clients to receive his call, I had told him to call me the moment my wife set foot out of the house and inform where she was going.

"Mr. Kamal, your wife, she is in a Mall," He said as soon as I picked up the call.

He was a very professional man, he didn't lose any seconds in useless formalities.

I told the client we will hold the meeting some other time because I had an emergency.

I was trying to talk to Mia, somewhere alone, and in her parent's house, it was nearly impossible because someone would be present with us all the time and if not we would be interrupted, like the last time.

Hence I had told the detective to inform me if she was out of the house alone, and I was glad he was doing his job efficiently. I had asked him the name of the mall and I was there within half an hour.

I called him as soon as I entered the Mall to know her exact location, he told me that she was in the food court. I hurried to the escalator and by the time I reached the desired floor, I saw her standing in front of the elevator. She was far from me, and calling her was of no use.

The elevator door opened and when I saw the person which was standing in there I was shocked and so was Mia, I fastened my pace to reach her, but Riyaan had grabbed her wrist and had pulled her inside, and before I was even ten feet close to the elevator it's doors closed.

I ran towards it and hit the button, I saw the P sign on the flashboard above the door, which meant he had taken Mia to the parking, was that bastard trying to kidnap her?

I had even told that detective to go home because I didn't want him lingering around when I spoke with Mia.

Dammit.

He could have helped if I had not told him to leave, the elevator door opened and I jumped inside hitting the parking button. I was pacing in the elevator, dreading and worried to death what that bastard would be doing to Mia.

It felt like the time had stopped and the elevator was moving with the speed of an ant.

"Fuck Waleed," I cursed.

By the time the elevator reached the parking floor, I was anxious as hell, that what might I find there, was he able to take her with him.

As the door opened I ran straight in the front, but I didn't see anyone, then I heard a scream and some voices of someone, cursing, followed by a painful shriek.

I ran in the direction from where the voices were coming, I was imagining myself as a gallant knight who was going to save a damsel in distress. I know Mia will be proud of me and might even forgive me after I save her from that son of a bitch.

I took a turn in the parking towards the voices and what I saw was enough to shock me, the damsel in distress was lying on the floor his hands on his crotch and yelling in pain, while my wife was kicking him in his gut and butt.

To say that I was shocked, would be an understatement of the century. I was fucking turned on by the sight of my wife kicking the ass of that bastard. And believe me, I had never been turned on like this before.

Rameen

"If you as much try to put a finger on me ever again, I will rip your throat with my bare hands you mother fucker," I screamed as I kicked him again in his stomach.

I don't know what the problem was with men, why do they think women are weak and pathetic to submit to their will?

I was in a state of shock when Riyaan had grabbed me inside the elevator, I tried to loosen his grip on my hand.

"I just want to talk Mia, just give me a few minutes then I will drop you off," Riyaan said leaving my wrist.

"I don't want to listen to a single word you say," I snarled at him.

"Please Mia, just five minutes", he said.

I took a deep breath and tried to calm my uneven breathing, there were a lot of things I wanted to ask him too, especially about him and Jeena.

When the elevator door opened in the parking, I followed him to his car, but instead, he brought me to a secluded spot at the back of the parking.

"Riyaan, why did you bring me here?" I asked him furiously.

He didn't reply, instead, he pinned me to a pillar, and leaned to kiss me, before his lips could touch mine I kicked him in his groin with all my strength. The attack was unexpected for him, he stumbled back and held his groin with both of his hands, I was sure I had done some serious damage to his anatomy. Before he could retaliate I kicked him on his leg and he fell on the floor with a thud.

As soon as he fell on the floor, I started kicking him, without even bothering to look where I was hitting him. I would have kicked him more, but someone had pulled me away from him grabbing my shoulders, a fear engulfed inside me, did he have company? And how many were they?

Soon I found myself in someone's arms and pressed into a hard chest. I didn't need to see who it was, I had recognized him by the smell of his perfume and his cologne, only one man in this world used that combination, I heaved a sigh of relief, knowing it was Waleed and not some accomplice of Riyaan.

He flipped me in his arms and leaned and captured my lips in a passionate kiss, I was so high on adrenaline right now, and not to mention the high levels of estrogen and HCG, that I didn't even protest. I had my arms wrapped around his neck, my fingers tugging his silky hair.

His hands slid from my waist to my ass, he pressed me closer to him and squeezed one of my ass cheeks, I moaned in his mouth and he kissed me harder. I wanted him, I wanted him to be inside me, I have been waiting for so long, it had been two months since we made love.

I heard someone groaning in pain behind me, and I was out of the trance, I pushed Waleed away from me, he looked at me surprised and when I punched him on his face he was astonished.

"Okay, I deserve that, " He said holding his jaw with his hand and moving it to and fro to check if I had broken any bones.

"You asshole," I cursed and pulled him by his collar and met his lips with mine.

I kissed the breath out of him and pulled away. When my breathing was even, I punched him on the other side of his face.

"What was this for?" He asked in shock.

"For turning me celibate for the last two months," I yelled.

He kept looking at me in disbelief for a few seconds then closed the gap between us and kissed me again. This time his kiss was urgent and he didn't stop until he had taken everything he wanted from me. My lips stung when he pulled from me to breathe.

"I fucking want you so much, Mia, " He whispered.

"I want to take you right now, right here, but we need to take care of this fucker first," He said as he withdrew his cell from his pocket.

He dialed the police and within a few minutes, a police van was present in the parking. They lifted Riyaan on a stretcher and sent him to a hospital. The inspector asked Waleed if he had hit Riyaan, and when Waleed pointed towards me, I saw the expression of shock all over his face.

Men will be men. They will always underestimate women. I could never understand why they don't believe a woman was capable of defending herself. I know the condition in which Riyaan was, no one would believe that a girl had beaten him.

Waleed pulled me in his arms as the inspector walked to his car, it felt so good to be back in his embrace, I had missed the warmth of his body so much.

"Promise me, you will never leave me alone," I asked flattening my palm in front of him.

"I promise," He said as he placed his hand on mine and closed it with assurance.

"Am I forgiven now?" He asked.

I nodded in reply. I think it was high time I forgave him. There was no doubt he loved me and was sorry for how he treated me. It was difficult for me to forget everything, but still, I need to give him another chance. He had been a perfect husband before Jeena and Riyaan had come into our life.

I didn't believe in love, still, I had fallen for him. Our love was strong than any mind games of some bitch. Waleed walked me to his car, holding me in his arms.

I think this was a test of our love for each other and I was overjoyed that we didn't give up upon each other. Getting married to Waleed Kamal had been an accident, but I was sure that we were destined for each other.

Epilogue

F ive Years Later

Waleed held her hand and pulled her with him, she was surprised where he was taking her, it was their fifth wedding anniversary party.

Their son Ahad was going to be four years in a few months and they had celebrated their daughter's first birthday two months back. The last five years have been bliss for them both. Their love had only grown and their bond had gotten stronger with time.

Mia had joined Waleed's firm and they both were working together, Mia had taken over their construction firm, as Waleed was busy expanding his business, in other sectors as well.

Dada had come back to live with them, after the birth of their daughter at their insistence, he was getting weak with each passing day and Mia and Waleed didn't want him to stay alone in their native village.

Riyaan had been convicted for 7 years for sexual assault and an attempt at kidnapping and Jeena was in mental rehab. Her condition had worsened with time until she was admitted to rehab. Waleed's aunt had told him that she was doing better now and was recovering.

Mia didn't have any hard feelings for her, Jeena had been sick and she needed help. Unfortunately, no one realized Jeena needed help until it was too late.

Sheema and Saad had got married and were living a happily married life, blessed with a daughter. Asjad's parents had accepted Rania as their daughter-in-law and they were blessed with a twin boy and girl two years ago.

The twins were driving Rania crazy, each passing day and she had decided that she was not having any more children.

Ali had gotten married to his college sweetheart Huda and they were expecting their first child together.

"Waleed, will you just tell, where you are taking me?" She asked him again impatiently.

Waleed kept dragging her until they were in front of a broom closet, he opened the door and walked in and pulled Mia inside with him, and closed the door.

"Are you cra..." She couldn't complete her sentence because he had captured her lips.

Mia was taken by surprise but she kissed him back, his kiss was passionate and demanding and she was ready to give him all that he wanted to take.

Their tongues were fighting for dominance, and when he won, she nibbled at his lower lip, earning a groan from him.

"Fuck Mia, you still drive me crazy," He said as he broke the kiss and started kissing her jawline than her neck.

Mia started giggling because of the tickling by his stubble, he growled to warn her to stay silent.

This man still made butterflies flutter in her stomach, even after nearly 6 years of marriage, they both were still as insatiable as they were in the early days of marriage.It was nearly impossible for them to keep their hands off each other, but because of the birth of their children, they had become more cautious, still, they didn't let go of any chance to be in each other's arms.

"Waleed, everyone will be looking for us," Mia said as she noticed him lift the hem of her designer gown.

"I want you. I wanted you since the moment I saw you in this black gown.I can't tell you how good black color looks on you, just do me a favor and wear black every day", He said between sucking and kissing her neck.

"So that you can fuck me daily, No thanks," She replied annoyed.

Waleed didn't even listen to what she said, he was busy kissing her collar bones when he slipped lower towards her cleavage she pushed him away as much as she could in this cramped closet.

"What a killjoy Mia," He said with fake disappointment.

She laughed at him and opened the door and walked out, it was more than 10 minutes they had been gone from the hall and she was sure someone might have noticed their absence in the hall.

Waleed followed her to the hall, teasing her the whole time. She was trying hard to suppress her smile, but it was nearly impossible.

"Next time we could use the closet in the guest room," He whispered in her ear.

She just glared at him in response, because she knew if she will open her mouth to say something, she will start laughing.

As they entered the hall together, Rania and Sheema gave her a knowing smile, she blushed and ignored them, but they were not ready to give up.

They both came towards her and Waleed walked away seeing them walking towards Mia.

"So, where did you make out this time?" Rania asked with a smirk.

She looked at her surprised, Rania knew them very well, and it hadn't taken her any time to figure out, where they were.

"Broom closet," She replied with a shy smile.

She looked at Waleed who was standing a few feet away from them and was looking at her with amusement, as soon as their eyes met he gave her a wink.

"Charmer," She mouthed at him and he chuckled understanding what she said.

"Will you both stop eye-fucking each other," Sheema said disgustedly.

" He is my husband, and I will fuck him in any way I want," She snapped back at her, and when she realized what she had said her cheeks got heated up.

Sheema and Rania laughed loudly at her words, and everyone around them turned and looked at them. Mia felt more embarrassed than before, she hoped no one had heard her.

After some time when she was pouring herself water from a table in the corner, Waleed approached her and stood with his back to the table and looking at her carefully.

"So tell me," He said to her.

"Tell you what?" She asked confused.

"Tell me in which ways, you want to fuck me?" He asked with a teasing smile.

Mia blushed at his words and looked away from him, she hadn't expected he had heard her declaration.

"Tell me, Mia, I am waiting, " He said holding her face with his hand and turning her face to him.

"Waleed."

"Mia."

"You are impossible, " She said annoyed.

"How am I supposed to be impossible, when you have done me more than a thousand times," He teased her again.

Mia blushed harder this time, she was not expecting him to keep the count, "You counted?" she asked furiously.

He nodded in reply, Mia wanted to drown in embarrassment.

"One thousand, one hundred and nineteen to be precise," He chuckled at her embarrassment.

Mia punched his shoulder in embarrassment, she had no idea till today that he kept the count.

Bastard.

"You know what is my target?" He asked looking at her face in amusement, which had turned a shade of red.

She looked at him with a frown on her face.

"Five thousand," He said with a wink.

"Are you out of your mind?" She screamed.

"Yes, just when you are around," He replied with a smirk.

He pulled her to him and wrapped his arms around her waist, and leaned his face until their foreheads and nose were touching.

"Did I ever say, I love you?" He asked her.

"Yes, a million times," She replied smiling.

" Then let's make it a million and one, shall we?

"I love you, Mrs. Waleed Kamal", He said with his voice full of warmth and emotions.

"I love you too, Mr. Waleed Kamal", She replied with the same passion.

Lightning Source UK Ltd.
Milton Keynes UK
UKHW020927281122
412977UK00016B/994